Human Rights Journalism and its Nexus to Responsibility to Protect

Senthan Selvarajah

Human Rights Journalism and its Nexus to Responsibility to Protect

How and Why the International Press Failed in Sri Lanka's Humanitarian Crisis

palgrave
macmillan

Senthan Selvarajah
Centre for Media, Human Rights
and Peacebuilding
London, UK

ISBN 978-3-030-49074-4 ISBN 978-3-030-49072-0 (eBook)
https://doi.org/10.1007/978-3-030-49072-0

Cover image: oxygen/gettyimages
Cover design by eStudioCalamar

This Palgrave Macmillan imprint is published by the registered company Springer Nature Switzerland AG
The registered company address is: Gewerbestrasse 11, 6330 Cham, Switzerland

I dedicate this book to my late Mum Sambavi Selvarajah, who passed away when she was middle-aged, 14 years ago. Without her dedication and inspiration, I would never have made it to this stage, both in my academic path and my personal life.

Foreword

As the realities of Kosovo and Rwanda dawned upon the world in the face of an increasingly weak UN system, the International Commission on Intervention and State Sovereignty (ICISS), an independent panel made up of scholars and political leaders, and funded by the Canadian government came up with a ground breaking report called 'The Responsibility to Protect' (R2P), which was officially adopted at the 2005 World Summit.

Since its introduction, the R2P doctrine has importantly entered the international diplomatic agenda, and spearheaded the setting up of a 'Global Centre and network of regional affiliates committed to advocacy and research, and international coalition of non-governmental organizations (NGOs), a journal and book series, and a research fund sponsored by the Australian government' (Bellamy 2010, p. 143). What is more, it is now used by governments and humanitarian NGOs as a diplomatic language of emergencies to justify 'behavior, cajole compliance, and demand international action' (Ibid.). Yet, as Bellamy puts it, the Responsibility to protect doctrine remains contentious in many areas. Critics still point to it as being dangerous and imperialist poised to undermine the sovereignty of the weak nations with little consideration for the protection of the human rights of the most vulnerable populations. Another serious problem is that it is still being abused by the strong powers to control the weak states who fail to cooperate in the furtherance of their geo-strategic interests. For example, recently, the French, in Myanmar, and the Russians, in Georgia, used the doctrine to 'justify the actual or potential use of coercive force' when there was no clear evidence of the failure of those states to protect populations against acts of gross human rights violations, whereas they, nor other big powers, attempted any such action in Somalia, Afghanistan and Iraq despite the recording of ongoing gross human rights violations of populations in these countries (Bellamy 2010, p. 144). As Pattison (2010) notes, the problem of inconsistency in recent interventions has been the subject of one of the most frequent criticisms of humanitarian intervention. The NATO intervention in Kosovo but not in Sierra Leone, Somalia, Rwanda (Shaw 2012), or in the DR Congo (Damrosch 2000) easily comes to mind. This selectivity gives the impression, albeit problematically, that 'some are more worth protecting than others' (ICISS 2001, p. 150). This smacks of selective justice. 'If humanitarian intervention really is to be humanitarian, the objection continues, it has to be consistently applied whenever there is a serious humanitarian crisis' (Pattison 2010, p. 170).

A most recent case in point of this problematic R2P is the ongoing civil conflict in Yemen which has become the World's worst humanitarian crisis. Big Western powers such as the USA, Canada, UK and France continue to sell arms to parties to the conflict, especially Saudi Arabia, which backs the Yemeni government against the Houthi rebels. A panel of UN Experts on Yemen have found that there have been serious human rights violations mostly caused by indiscriminate air strikes by the Saudi-led coalition which also implicate the Western countries selling arms to them in war crimes. According to the 2019 Human Rights Watch Report, more than 17,500 civilians have been killed in Yemen since 2015, majority of them women and children killed by airstrikes, while 20 million face food insecurity.

My book *Human Rights Journalism* published in 2012, provided an insight into how journalists have the moral responsibility and duty to both inform and educate the public about their rights, as well as monitor, investigate and report on all human rights violations within the Kantian context of proactive humanitarian intervention and just peace. I referred to this type of journalism as human rights journalism and called the failure of journalists to practice this type of journalism as human wrongs journalism.

However, while my book identified some connections between human rights journalism and successful humanitarian interventions drawing on Western humanitarian intervention in Kurdistan led by US and Britain under George Bush senior and John Major, respectively, against the forces of Saddam Hussein, among few others as a case in point, on one hand, and between human wrongs journalism and the failure of humanitarian intervention drawing on Rwanda, Sierra Leone and Somalia, among few others, on the other hand, it failed to provide an explicit connection between human rights journalism and R2P. This scholarly deficit is succinctly addressed by this new book by Senthan Selvarajah, a journalist, media researcher and human rights activist. Senthan's book, which primarily draws on the rather problematic international press coverage of the last phases of the Sri Lankan war in 2009 and mass human rights violations that woefully failed to provide the much needed global compassion necessary for the international community to invoke R2P. It is a comprehensive microscopic study of how not only the Sri Lankan state, the International Community, but also most importantly the international journalists who covered the last phases of the Sri Lankan war in 2009 failed as duty bearers of R2P to diagnostically provide coverage that will expose the politics of the Sri Lankan state aggression scrupulously hiding behind the so-called War on Terror, expose the mass atrocities caused by this aggression, and in this way encourage the international community to intervene and save lives in the context of R2P.

Another massive contribution of this book to the fast growing scholarly and pragmatic conversation on human rights journalism is its emphatic provision of an innovative methodological framing matrix to analyse human rights journalism and human wrongs journalism models. This book is indeed very rich in both theoretical and empirical insights. It is a must-read for all students and scholars, as well as humanitarian activists and policy makers, who are interested in how the media can report and change the world, especially in times of conflicts and humanitarian crises.

Freetown, Sierra Leone
June 2020

Dr. Ibrahim Seaga Shaw
Chairman and Information Commissioner
Right to Access Information Commission

References

Bellamy, A. J. (2010, Summer). Responsibility to Protect: Five Years On. *Ethics and International Affairs, 24*(2), 143–169.

Damrosch, L. F. (2000). The Inevitability of Selective Response? Principles to Guide Urgent International Action. In A. Schnabel & R. Thakur (Eds.),

Kosovo and the Challenge of Humanitarian Intervention (pp. 405–419). New York: United Nations University.

ICISS (International Commission on Intervention and State Sovereignty). (2001). *The Responsibility to Protect: Report of the International Commission on Intervention and State Sovereignty*. Ottawa: The International Development Research Centre. Available at: http://responsibilitytoprotect.org/ICISS%20Report.pdf. Accessed 06 Oct 2020.

Pattison, J. (2010). *Humanitarian Intervention & The Responsibility to Protect: Who Should Intervene?* Oxford: Oxford University Press.

Shaw, I. S. (2012). *Human Rights Journalism: Advances in Reporting Distant Humanitarian Interventions*. Basingstoke: Palgrave Macmillan.

Preface

Research, professional practices and education are three mutually interdependent facets of life as insights from our professional practices reshape the education, and vice versa. Meanwhile, our experiences, learnings, and insights that we gather through our professional practices improve our research and vice versa. A similar reciprocal interaction exists between education and research. I have always believed in this idea and for the past 18 years I have also practiced it in my capacity as a journalist, researcher, and human rights and media educator-activist. *Understanding Human Rights Journalism and its Nexus to Responsibility to Protect: The Case of Sri Lanka's Humanitarian Crisis in 2009,* is such an outcome that resulted from the fusion of the knowledge that I have gathered through my research experience, professional practice and education and through their reciprocal interaction.

This book provides a platform for research, innovation and learning that empowers human rights-based journalism practice to work towards bringing social change. This book takes a balanced middle-ground between critical research and transformative research. Critical research emphasises on credibility and bringing change. This underlines the research importance of media's role in empowerment, human rights, justice, advocacy, peace building and conflict prevention. Conversely, transformative research focuses on what works and what people should do to change/transform inequitable/oppressive systems. This highlights the importance of media's human rights-based approach with regard to the conflicts, along with its roles of monitoring and accountability.

This book provides a holistic approach to establish the nexus between Human Rights Journalism (HRJ) and Responsibility to Protect (R2P), embracing various concepts of media such as agenda-setting and spectatorship of distant suffering, as well as various other disciplines such as human rights, conflict transformation and international relations.

This book captures various perspectives and viewpoints concerning the practice of HRJ, while particularly focusing on its application with respect to Sri Lanka's humanitarian crisis of 2009. It utilizes various research approaches, all of which corroborate the arguments with substantial evidences. Many of these approaches are evidently informed by my professional experience, and consequently, the book is successful in portraying several key factors which were obvious actors in the process and all these factors depict complementary perspectives. Throughout the discussion, a careful eye is kept on assessing foreign correspondents' first-hand experiences negotiating the relative affordances and constrains associated with practising HRJ. This paves way for some important questions concerning the ways in which R2P interventions can be devised, strategized and facilitated through a dynamic change in journalistic practices and forms.

In addition, it contributes uniquely towards the development of an epistemological grounding for the practice and research of HRJ within 'pragmatic objectivity', grounded in the critical constructivist epistemology as well as the development of Frame Analysis Matrix, and the Multimodal Discourse Analysis Matrix for scrutinising the practice of HRJ.

London, UK Senthan Selvarajah

Acknowledgments

This work would not have been possible without the enthusiasm, support and guidance of my colleague and my Ph.D. Supervisor Dr. Ibrahim Seaga Shaw; therefore I owe him a big 'thank you'. I'm also extremely grateful to him for writing the forward of this book as well. My sincere and special thanks to Professor Stuart Allan for writing the endorsement for this book. This book would not have been possible without the support of the foreign correspondents who narrated their experiences when I interviewed them. I owe them a huge 'thank you'. I shall not forget the support and help offered by Mrs. Anandhi Suriyaprakasam, Mr. Bhagwan Singh and Mr. Nirmanusan Balasundaram to conduct interviews with the foreign correspondents. I must thank Northumbria University, Newcastle for my Ph.D. studentship award and all the support during the course of my Ph.D. project. I would like to express my gratitude and appreciation to the entire team at Palgrave Macmillan for all their hard work, support and expertise. I am grateful to Lucy Batrouney and Mala Sanghera-Warren, Commissioning Editors (*Journalism Media and Communication*) and Bryony Burns, Editorial Assistant (*Journalism Media and Communication*) at Palgrave Macmillan, for their commitment, advice and constant support which helped me complete writing this book successfully. I am also very grateful to Ms. Karthika Purushothaman of Scientific Publishing Services (P) Ltd, India for her diligent work to facilitate the proofreading and production process. I wish to acknowledge the support given by Ms. Meghana Wunnava for her excellent proofreading and editing. I shall not forget to acknowledge the invaluable comments provided by Palgrave's anonymous reviewers, most of which I have taken on board. I take this opportunity to offer my special thanks to Professor Stig-Arne Nohrstedt, Professor Rune Ottosen, Professor Jake Lynch and Professor Kevin Williams, who were all my mentors and played an instrumental role in providing several opportunities and helped me in many ways in the past. A bouquet of thanks goes to all of my colleagues at the Centre for Media, Human Rights and Peacebuilding. And last but not least, I would also like to acknowledge the tremendous support and encouragement that I have received from my friends and family—particularly, I appreciate my wife Mrs. Premalatha Senthan for encouraging me and giving me the time to help make this book a reality.

Contents

Abbreviations

BBC	British Broadcasting Corporation
CDA	Critical Discourse Analysis
CEWARN	Conflict Early Warning and Response Network
CNN	Cable News Network
EWER	Early Warning and Early Response
FMMDAM	Framing Matrix and Multimodal Discourse Analysis Matrix
GT	Grounded Theory
HRJ	Human Rights Journalism
HWJ	Human Wrongs Journalism
ICISS	International Commission on Intervention and State Sovereignty
LTTE	Liberation Tigers of Tamil Eelam
PJ	Peace Journalism
R2P	Responsibility to Protect
R2R	Responsibility to Report
UDHR	Universal Declaration of Human Rights
UK	United Kingdom
US	United States

List of Figures

List of Tables

CHAPTER 1

Introduction: Human Rights Journalism and its Nexus to Responsibility to Protect

Responsibility to Protect (R2P) is a liberal and a holistic notion that aims to promote a sense of obligation among individual states as well as the international community, to engage in a manner that prevents violence, promotes peace-making and rebuilds societies during and after mass atrocities such as genocide, war crimes, crimes against humanity, and ethnic cleansing. This study's understanding of an 'International Community' aligns with the International Scholar Hendry Bull's (1977, p. 13) definition of the term. He states that an international society exists 'when a group of states, conscious of certain common interests and common values, form a society in the sense that they conceive themselves to be bound by a common set of rules in their relations with one another, and also whilst sharing amidst working of common institutions'. With this in mind, this book contextualises and streamlines the term 'international community' as the Member States of the UN. Furthermore, their activities within the United Nation's framework in reference to the Security Council, United Nations Human Rights Council and the General Assembly, entail maintaining peace, security and human rights.

The norm 'Responsibility to Protect' was first introduced in the International Commission, in the Intervention and State Sovereignty report published in 2001 (ICISS 2001). However, Francis Deng brought forth the assumption that sovereignty entails responsibility, much later, in the middle of the 1990s (Deng 2009a, b). This conception argued that the right of a country to protect itself from non-interference by an outsider

S. Selvarajah, *Human Rights Journalism and its Nexus to Responsibility to Protect*, https://doi.org/10.1007/978-3-030-49072-0_1

was conditional, which means that when a state is unable to protect its own population, it stands to lose this right. Deng stated that in those cases, the international community not only has a right, but also a duty to step in (ibid.). Therefore, this means that sovereignty is not absolute and it can be tackled, if human rights are not respected appropriately. The sources of responsibility for R2P interventions, as the ICISS report highlights, are 'universal human rights' and 'common humanity' (Welsh and Banda 2010, p. 283) and it is on this premise that the three pillars of R2P have been built: (1) The State carries the primary responsibility for protecting populations from genocide, war crimes, crimes against humanity and ethnic cleansing and their incitement. (2) The international community holds a responsibility to encourage and assist States in fulfilling this responsibility. (3) The international community has a responsibility to use appropriate diplomatic, humanitarian and other such means to protect populations from these crimes. If a State is manifestly failing to protect its populations, the international community must be prepared to take collective action to protect populations, in accordance with the Charter of the United Nations.

The protection and prevention of human rights is the core objective of R2P. The aspect of 'prevention' is a pro-active and pre-emptive process aimed at changing conditions that minimise the probability of violence and human rights violations. In contrast, 'protection' is a reaction to the (near-in-time) outbreak of such violations. According to the Office of the High Commissioner for Human Rights (n.d.), 'human rights are rights inherent to all human beings, whatever our nationality, place of residence, sex, national or ethnic origin, colour, religion, language, or any other status. We are all equally entitled to our human rights without discrimination. These rights are all interrelated, interdependent and indivisible'. In this book, I define human rights as those inalienable prerogatives established in international human rights instruments, conventions, declarations and legal instruments under international law.[1]

Therefore, these human rights and security norms, grounded in the cosmopolitan principle of humanitarianism, has evolved as a unique doctrine (R2P) primarily due to two specific reasons: (1) It was the first major organised initiative of the international community to draw global attention and create responses to address humanitarian crisis and causes. (2) It has redefined the concept of sovereignty by changing its role from 'sovereignty as an impunity of states' to 'sovereignty as a responsibility' to protect every individual in the society.

This concept has drawn considerable scholarly attention regarding how to implement this doctrine in a legitimate and a rightful manner, free from political manipulations and abuses, in times of extreme violence and crisis. Media as a witness, promoter and protector of human rights, seemingly has the ability to facilitate an R2P intervention, wherein it is necessary and appropriate. Nevertheless, conventional journalism has been accused of not fulfilling the duty of the protection of human rights and the prevention of genocide and mass atrocities in times of war.

1.1 Why Is Human Rights Journalism Important for R2P?

The coverage of the Crimean War (1853–1856) by William Howard Russell of *The Times*, is commonly seen as the marker of the beginning of organised efforts to report war to the population at home, using the services of a civilian reporter (Carruthers 2000, pp. 4–5). Since then, the profession of journalism has undergone dynamic changes due to the continuous advancement and development of newer communication technologies, massive growth and competition in the media industry, changes in global socio-political landscapes, and the constantly evolving international relations. This has, on the one hand, changed the way journalists gather and report information about wars, conflicts and other forms of human rights violations, and on the other hand, resulted in media being used as a tool for both peace and war. Nevertheless, conventional journalism has been accused of being either compliant or complicit with the systems that implant and perpetuate violence, injustice and suffering (Shaw 2012; Lynch and McGoldrick 2007; Shaw et al. 2011; Lynch 2008; Galtung 2002). This is because, as scholars argue, the ideology of objectivity inscribed in the principles of conventional journalism, which demand journalists to 'just report the facts as they see', has no meaning in the context of modern journalism, that has evolved and shifted far from its comfortable accommodation within the positivist framework in the early twentieth century, and was developed by Walter Lippman, a writer, reporter and political commentator. According to American Press Institute (n.d.), objectivity was proposed as a scientific approach to news reporting in response to yellow journalism which was practised in abundance back then, wherein exaggeration and sensationalism was used to sell papers by distorting 'truth'. Nevertheless, the modern-day conventional journalism, which operates within political manipulations, power struggles, lack of journalistic independence, economic constraints, rise of PR agents and organised propaganda ploys, is too restrained by its objectivity convention to search for the truth, expose the lies and the human rights violations, and promote human rights and peace. Additionally, in many instances, conventional journalism has been used as a tool for fuelling conflict and igniting genocides and mass atrocities (see Thompson 2007; McLaughlin 2002). This is the reason why journalism scholars and practitioners have called for 'pragmatic objectivity' (Ward 2008) and actively searched for a form and practice that is more responsive to the needs of journalists' societies. The 'journalism of attachment'", advocated by correspondents such as Martin Bell, Christine Amanpour and Michael Nicholson, is one such example (Bell 1998) and Peace Journalism (PJ), initially articulated by Johan Galtung (2002) in the mid-1990s, as a new field in the area of conflict resolution. Human Rights Journalism (HRJ), the theme of this book, is another good example.

In the aftermath of the war in Bosnia, Bell claimed that journalists could and should not remain neutral in 'the face of modern evils' but they must take the side of the victims and must actively demand attention and action towards the situation. He criticised what he calls 'bystander journalism'—the conventional journalistic tradition of keeping a distance and being detached from the news events. He argued that objective and dispassionate journalism does not have a place in the midst of war and human atrocities (McLaughlin 2002, pp. 152–154; Kempf 2003, p. 59, see Bell 1998). Bell also stated that journalists should act responsibly when reporting conflicts; he encouraged reporters to obey their *moral* responsibility (McLaughlin 2002, p. 178). Nonetheless, to question the validity of objectivity challenges the legitimacy of the profession, and the power it holds. Critics of the journalism of attachment say that drawing a line between the victim and the aggressor will expose and make journalism prone to propaganda. If there is a 'righteous' side to a conflict then the temptation to leave out information that does not best suit their 'truth' could go unchecked. According to Galtung, the philosophy of PJ is to prevent violence and war (Galtung 2002) by offering a form of critical reporting of the war and also a set of practical plans and options for journalists (Webel and Galtung 2007, p. 248). Lynch and McGoldrick, who are advocators of PJ, believe that PJ is reflected when editors and reporters make choices—of what stories to report, and how to report them—which create opportunities for society at large to value non-violent responses to conflict (Lynch 2008, p. 3). Journalists in many Western countries have generally been hostile to the notion of PJ, seeing it as a violation of the basic tenets of journalism, such as objectivity (Loyn 2007). Other reporters have attempted to put the concept into practice. *Reporting the World*, a network of almost 200 reporters has attempted to provide an alternative to traditional war reporting by embracing some of the basic components of Galtung's model (http://www.reportingtheworld.org).

The concept of Human Rights Journalism (HRJ) has attracted significant attention and has become popular over the last few years. HRJ, as introduced by Ibrahim Seaga Shaw (2012, p. 2), is based on the reporting of 'physical, structural and cultural violence within the context of humanitarian intervention' with the aims of promoting: (1) 'the understanding of the human-rights based approach to journalism', (2) the journalistic role that entails informing and connecting people all over the world, (3) 'public knowledge' of human rights and (4) the journalistic 'moral responsibility' and 'duty' to 'educate the public, increase awareness in its members of their rights and monitor, investigate and report all human rights violations'. HRJ finds its inspiration in the Universal Declaration of Human Rights (1948) and calls for a 'more pro-active role of journalism as an agency that knows no borders, no race, no age, no gender and no class – a journalism with a human face and for the human race' (ibid., p. 36). Downman and Ubayasiri (2017), term this contemplation as 'journalism for social change', which is:

> Journalism that should not be pinned to a model or type. It is a brand of journalism that provides pragmatically objective truths and realities that can be relied upon to inform, educate and challenge. Journalism that includes advocacy is required to report complex issues like human rights. It is the kind of journalism that has the capacity to change the world.

Although Shaw's (2012) book provided the conceptual framework for the theory of HRJ, for the construction of social reality as a means of protecting and promoting human rights, it fell short of providing the epistemological foundation to understand its feasibility, exercise and power. Therefore, this book aims to address this scholarly deficit by proposing Stephen Ward's (2008, p. 77) idea of 'pragmatic objectivity.' This concept in this book is argued as a pragmatic means to the goals of truth, fair judgment and ethical action, and as the philosophical framework for the practice of HRJ within the critical constructivist epistemology. It argues that if 'truth' is the highest goal for a journalist, the practice of HRJ, as a 'rights-based' approach is viable and effective within the critical constructivist epistemology, which allows a journalist's intellect to guide them in understanding the issues and uncovering the truth through a diagnostic process. This book enlightens that the construction of the reality of human rights violations, through the practice of HRJ within the critical constructivist epistemology, can help establish a *prima facie* case. This will enable the international community (responsibility holders) to invoke appropriate responses, including the R2P intervention, to prevent mass atrocities and build peace in a constructive and legitimate manner.

While the scholarly interest in media's impact on politics is not new, there has been no in-depth discussion to critically explore the role of that the media plays in humanitarian interventions in the context of R2P doctrine, since it was adopted at the 2005 UN World Summit. Moreover, the R2P doctrine placed the responsibility to protect human rights only on the state and the international community, and was thus silent on the responsibility of other important players such as the media. The primary aim of this book is to address these deficits by proposing a nexus between R2P and HRJ as a functional theoretical framework determining the role of media in humanitarian interventions. I argue that human rights journalists, as truth seekers and watchdogs, can play a vital role in establishing a *prima facie* case and mobilising support for humanitarian interventions within the R2P framework. Drawing on HRJ's epistemological theories, this book explores the key elements that define the nexus between HRJ and R2P, and show how they justify the indispensable 'Responsibility to Report' (R2R) role of the media as proposed by Allan Thompson (2007).

Although Thomson (ibid.) stressed on the journalists' responsibility to promote R2P and expose the human rights violations perpetrated by the warring parties, and consequently mitigate and prevent the violence by addressing its causes, he fell short of explaining how the media can act as the facilitators in the implementation of R2P in an appropriate manner. In addition, Sampaio-Dias (2016) underlines journalists' accountability to perform R2R in line with the international human rights regimes, in which media are obligated to exercise R2P legitimately. However, she fails to propose the functional relationship between the media and R2P. Highlighting the role of the media in facilitating the R2P doctrine, Simon Cottle (2019) elucidates how the local and international media can play a critical role in its implementation through the pillar approach. Within this premise, this book fills the knowledge gap by proposing five parameters which define the HRJ–R2P nexus, which in turn illustrate R2R.

In addition, this book inter-disciplinarily explores the themes of media, human rights and conflict transformation, and proposes the 'HRJ– R2P nexus conceptual model' to explain the how HRJ can be used within the agenda-setting mechanism to construct human rights-focused discourse and thereby prevent human rights violations and mass atrocities, and invoke policy responses. Under the HRJ–R2P conceptual model, this book examines the nature and the gravity of practice of HRJ in the international newspapers, during the humanitarian crisis in Sri Lanka, amidst the overrunning of the Liberation Tigers of Tamil Eelam (LTTE) by government forces in May 2009. This book provides a scientific explanation for those in search of the answer to why one of the worst humanitarian crises in the world, which took place in Sri Lanka in the twenty-first century, did not create any global compassion or garner attention, as well as the reasons that led to the failure of coverage of the crisis by the international media. This book uses various methodological approaches such as content analysis, frame analysis, multimodal discourse analysis, interviews, and surveys in a holistic assessment approach to answer the primary research inquiry, which focuses on the extent to which the international press practised HRJ in reporting the Sri Lankan humanitarian crisis, to invoke R2P interventions. The analysis is performed with supplementary research inquiries using the above research methods, which have been illustrated in individual chapters.

This book remarkably contributes to the research methodology in two major ways: Firstly, in an innovative manner, this book proposes a Framing Matrix, for the analysis of HRJ and HWJ. Although Shaw, in his theory of 'Human Rights Journalism', uses a number of case studies to identify the frames of HRJ and HWJ, he fails to provide a methodology to distinguish between HRJ and HWJ scientifically. Therefore, this book makes an original methodological contribution for assessing the practice of HRJ.

Secondly, in order to identify the typology of news stories, this book adopts a Multimodal Discourse Analysis Matrix by re-contextualising Chouliaraki's (2006, 2008) qualitative analytical framework in a quantitative manner. Furthermore, this book explains how to use Chouliaraki's 'Multimodal Discourse Analysis', which was originally designed to analyse television news coverage and examine the newspaper coverage of distant sufferings. The application of Chouliaraki's theory of 'Spectatorship of Suffering' and the 'multimodal analysis' is extremely useful in understanding the practice of HRJ and scrutinising its R2R role within the HRJ–R2P conceptual model.

The primary advantage of using the Framing Matrix as well as the Multimodal Discourse Analysis Matrix in the content analysis framework, is their ability to analyse a large number of news stories of a particular event over a period and thereby examine the media's role in a holistic and comparative manner. Also, it enables us to use multiple variables such as the type of news sources, type of articles, mode of news coverage, the section of newspaper etc., which is impossible in a qualitative analysis framework.

This operationalisation of the analytics of mediation and the framework of pity, within a quantitative research project, has potential to expand further and work in other empirical contexts too, and thus can greatly assist students and researchers in their research of media and conflict.

1.2 Structure of the Book

The book chapters are organised in a logical, coherent manner to explain the need of HRJ, how HRJ gets its power, how it operates to pursue a human rights-focused agenda, and what functional elements form the HRJ–R2P nexus and how. Chapter 2 helps us understand the complexities associated with the 'failures' of conventional journalism in reporting conflicts, wars and human rights violations. The ethos of journalism including ethics such as objectivity are defined and discussed. This chapter also briefly conceptualises PJ and war reporting. Chapter 3 discusses the role media plays in fostering human rights. The theory of HRJ is enunciated and positioned within 'pragmatic objectivity' that is grounded in the critical constructivist epistemology. This chapter draws insights from related theories such as, agenda setting and the spectatorship of suffering, to highlight HRJ's capacity of pursuing a human rights-focused agenda setting to fostering human rights and preventing the infringements of such rights. Chapter 4 introduces and discusses the theoretical foundations of cosmopolitanism and just peace frameworks and their relevance to HRJ and R2P. This chapter explores some important theoretical frameworks using which it identifies the five key elements that define the HRJ–R2P nexus. Chapter 5 proposes a research framework (FMMDAM) that innovatively creates a matrix for the analysis of

HRJ frames (Frame Analysis Matrix) and the typology of news stories (Multimodal Discourse Analysis Matrix), which were integrated into the coding manual of the content analysis to scrutinise the practice of HRJ. This framework articulates the philosophy and the sociology of distant suffering, framing theories, and the construction of humanitarian crises by the media. Chapters 6–8 provide, discuss and analyse the international newspapers' content from their reporting of the Sri Lankan humanitarian crisis in 2009, and answer the aforementioned research inquiry using content analysis, the Frame Analysis Matrix, and the Multimodal Discourse Analysis Matrix (FMMDAM). Chapter 9 uses results from the interviews with foreign correspondents who were in Sri Lanka before, during, and after the humanitarian crisis in 2009 with an aim to report on the situation. Furthermore, data from a survey conducted among human rights activists who were involved in the Sri Lankan humanitarian crisis are also integrated in this chapter, to supplement the research inquiry. Finally, Chapter 10 aims to summarise the entire discussion and effectively conclude about the findings in the book.

Note

1. According to the Office of the High Commissioner for Human Rights (OHCHR), there area 9 core international human rights instruments. Each of these instruments has established a committee of experts to monitor implementation of the treaty provisions by its States parties: International Convention on the Elimination of All Forms of Racial Discrimination (ICERD), International Covenant on Civil and Political Rights (ICCPR), International Covenant on Economic, Social and Cultural Rights (ICESCR), Convention on the Elimination of All Forms of Discrimination against Women (CEDAW), Convention against Torture and Other Cruel, Inhuman or Degrading Treatment or Punishment (CAT), Convention on the Rights of the Child (CRE), International Convention on the Protection of the Rights of All Migrant Workers and Members of Their Families (ICMW), International Convention for the Protection of All Persons from Enforced Disappearance (CPED), Convention on the Rights of Persons with Disabilities (CRPD), Optional Protocol to the Covenant on Economic, Social and Cultural Rights (ICESCR—OP), Optional Protocol to the International Covenant on Civil and Political Rights (ICCPR-OP1), Second Optional Protocol to the International Covenant on Civil and Political Rights, aiming at the abolition of the death penalty (ICCPR-OP2),

Optional Protocol to the Convention on the Elimination of Discrimination against Women (OP-CEDAW), Optional protocol to the Convention on the Rights of the Child on the involvement of children in armed conflict (OP-CRC-AC), Optional protocol to the Convention on the Rights of the Child on the sale of children, child prostitution and child pornography (OP-CRC-SC), Optional Protocol to the Convention on the Rights of the Child on a communications procedure (OP-CRC-IC), Optional Protocol to the Convention against Torture and Other Cruel, Inhuman or Degrading Treatment or Punishment (OP-CAT), Optional Protocol to the Convention on the Rights of Persons with Disabilities (OP-CRPD) (see https://www.ohchr.org/EN/ProfessionalInterest/Pages/CoreInstruments.aspx).

Bibliography

American Press Institute. (n.d.). The Lost Meaning of 'Objectivity' [Online]. https://www.americanpressinstitute.org/journalism-essentials/bias-objectivity/lost-meaning-objectivity/. Accessed 13 Apr 2020.

Bell, M. (1998). The Journalism of Attachment. In M. Kiernan (Ed.), *Media Ethics* (pp. 16–22). London: Routledge.

Bull, H. (1977). *The Anarchical Society: A Study of Order in World Politics*. London: Macmillan.

Carruthers, S. L. (2000). *The Media at War: Communication and Conflict in the Twentieth Century*. Basingstoke: Macmillan.

Chouliaraki, L. (2006). *The Spectatorship of Suffering*. London: Sage.

Chouliaraki, L. (2008). The Mediation of Suffering and the Vision of a Cosmopolitan Public. *Television and New Media, 9*(5), 371–391.

Cottle, S. (2019). Humanitarianism, human insecurity, and communications: What's changing in a globalised world? In S. Cottle & G. Cooper (Eds.), *Humanitarianism, communications and change*. Peter Lang Publishing Inc.

Deng, F. M. (2009a). The Evolution of the Idea of "Sovereignty as Responsibility. In A. Adebajo. (ed.), *From Global Apartheid to Global Village: Africa and the United Nations* (pp. 191–213). Scottsville: University of KwaZulu-Natal Press.

Deng, F. M. (2009b). Frontiers of Sovereignty a Framework of Protection, Assistance, and Development for the Internally Displaced. *Leiden Journal of International Law, 8*(2), 249–286.

Downman, S., & Ubayasiri, K. (2017). *Journalism for Social Change in Asia: Reporting Human Rights*. Basingstoke: Palgrave Macmillan.

Galtung, J. (2002). Peace Journalism: A Challenge. In W. Kempf and H. Luostarinen (Eds.), *Journalism and the New World Order, Studying War and the Media* (pp. 269–272). Nordicom: Göteborg.

ICISS (International Commission on Intervention and State Sovereignty). (2001). *The Responsibility to Protect: Report of the International Commission on Intervention and State Sovereignty.* Ottawa: The International Development Research Centre. Available at: http://responsibilitytoprotect.org/ICISS%20Report.pdf. Accessed 20 Dec 2019.

Kempf, W. (2002). Conflict Coverage and Conflict Escalation. In W. Kempf & H. Luostarinen (Eds.), *Journalism and New World Order: Volume II. Studying War and Media.* Gothenburg: Nordicom.

Kempf, W. (2003). Constructive Conflict Coverage: A Social Psychological Approach. *Konstaner Online-Publikations-System* (KOPS). Available at: https://kops.uni-konstanz.de/bitstream/handle/123456789/10220/2003_Constructive_Conflict_Coverage.pdf;sequence=1. Accessed on 06 Oct 2020.

Loyn, D. (2007). Good Journalism or Peace Journalism. *Conflict & Communication Online, 6*(2), 1–10.

Lynch, J. (2008). *Debates in Peace Journalism.* Sydney: Sydney University Press.

Lynch, J., & McGoldrick, A. (2007). Peace Journalism. In C. Webel & J. Galtung (Eds.), *Handbook of peace and studies conflict* (pp. 248–264). New York, NY: Routledge.

McLaughlin, G. (2002). *The War Correspondent.* London: Pluto Press.

Shaw, I. S. (2012). *Human Rights Journalism: Advances in Reporting Distant Humanitarian Interventions.* London: Palgrave Macmillan.

Shaw, I., Lynch, J., & Hackett, R. (2011). *Expanding Peace Journalism: Comparative and Critical Approaches.* Sydney: Sydney University Press.

Thompson, A. (Ed.). (2007). *The Media and the Rwanda Genocide.* London: Pluto Press.

Ward, S. J. A. (2008). Truth and Objectivity. In L. Wilkins & C. G. Christians (Eds.), *The Handbook of Mass Media Ethics* (pp. 71–83). New York: Routledge.

Webel, C., & Galtung, J. (2007). *Handbook of Peace and Conflict Studies.* London: Routledge.

Welsh, J. M., & Banda, M. (2010). International Law and the Responsibility to Protect: Clarifying or Expanding States' Responsibilities? *Global Responsibility to Protect, 2*(2), 213–231.

Wheeler, N. J., & Egerton, F. (2008). The Responsibility to Protect: "Precious Commitment" or a Promise Unfulfilled? *Global Responsibility to Protect, 1*(1), 114–132.

CHAPTER 2

The Failings of Conventional War Journalism

2.1 Introduction

This book aims to elucidate the role media plays in fostering and safeguarding human rights in times of crisis and also emphasises on its 'responsibility to report' role. However, before embarking on this discussion it is important to analyse the role of conventional journalism in the reporting of conflicts and wars, and identify if there are any shortcomings or defects with the conventional war journalism to play the expected role.

With this premise as the basis, this chapter is devoted to exploring the failings of conventional war reporting, particularly as identified by advocates of Peace Journalism (PJ) and Human Rights Journalism (HRJ). However, these problems have their roots further back in history, as highlighted by authors such as Knightley and McLaughlin. With an aim to understand the shortcomings of the profession of war correspondent in a broader context, this chapter will also dissect history to deliberate the situations that have led to the evolution of this specialisation. This chapter will set the foundation for the next chapter which will elaborately discuss the approaches to reshaping journalism practices within the context of human rights principles. These approaches will identify alternatives to the failings of the conventional war journalism and will prepare the fraternity to better respond to the humanitarian crisis in times of conflicts.

S. Selvarajah, *Human Rights Journalism and its Nexus to Responsibility to Protect*, https://doi.org/10.1007/978-3-030-49072-0_2

This chapter is divided into four sections. The first provides an overview of the development of the war correspondent and media–military relations. The second describes the restrictive nature of 'objectivity' and discusses how the current work conventions [the reliance on official sources, the favouring of events over processes and the focus on 'dualism' (Zero-Sum game) in reporting conflicts] mean that conventional war journalisms reinforce war and conflict by magnifying the 'us' and 'them' binaries, the effects of violence, and the activities and operations of the military. The third section looks at patterns of conventional war reporting. Despite the persistent tensions between war reporters and the military-government, the former often played the role of a mouthpiece for the propaganda of the military, with their narrative often focusing on violence, the progress to victory and the views and opinions of the elite, instead of the efforts to find peace. It emphasises on mechanisms and practices of journalism which play a role in promoting war, while also simultaneously stressing on the consequences not necessarily being the result of a conscious action. The last section analyses the causes for this form of journalism and the form of reporting which stems from the concept of Peace Journalism (PJ) by describing the features formulated by its principal founder John Galtung and the exponents, Jake Lynch and Annabel McGoldrick.

2.1.1 The Emergence of the War Correspondent

Before the introduction of formal modern journalism, histories of wars were written when the wars were over and by mostly by those who were not there. What happened was not witnessed but put together from the accounts of others. Herodotus is known to be the initiator of such writings with his account of the Persian Wars (499–449 BC). He was not a participant but commented on the events afterwards (Breisach 1997, p. 15). Following him, many other accounts were recorded of wars and conflict in the form of writings, accounts, sketches and paintings. They were based on the observations, accounts and stories of those who were there, but, as with Thucydides' celebrated history of the Peloponnesian war, they were second-hand reports (Menake 2004, p. 166).

One of the first eye-witness observations of war was produced by the Dutch painter Willem van de Velde. In 1653 he voyaged to witness a naval battle between the Dutch and the English. He drew several sketches of what he witnessed in a report he wrote about the wars. For many historians, he was the 'first, and far away the greatest, of all the war correspondent artists' (Papadopoulos and Pantti 2011, p. 44). More crucially, he was the first to witness, and then report, what happened in battle.

Technological advances have facilitated the direct observation of war and the emergence of the war correspondent. The advent of photography in 1833 created a difference in the presentation of war news by making the nature of war clearer to the audience (Roth 1997, p. xi). Roger Fenton became the first war photographer when he photographed the Crimean War in the mid-1850s (Knightley 2005). Fenton's images were not particularly accurate as he did not photograph the suffering of warfare. More significant was the invention of the telegraph in 1844, which enabled reporters to send stories home much faster. Telegraph use enabled news reporters to travel to the scene of war and file their reports soon after the events that they referred to had happened. The telegraph enabled newspapers to respond to the public demand for war news, which in turn increased the circulation of the newspapers, creating a pattern that remains unchanged today (Roth 1997, p. x). This technological advance saw a change in the nature of how accounts of war were constructed. It facilitated the development of the war reporter. Prior to the telegraph, the military in the nineteenth century dominated the reporting of war. Military commanders and officers supplied their own accounts of their victories to the press. The telegraph meant the press could send their own men to the battlefield and not depend on the military for explanations and descriptions of what had happened.

2.1.2 *The First Modern War Correspondent*

William Howard Russell reported for *The Times* on several wars, including the Crimean War in the 1850s, and is considered to be the first modern war correspondent. The coverage of *The Times* of the Crimean War (1853–1856) by Russell is seen as marking the start of organised efforts to report war to the population at home using the services of a civilian reporter (Carruthers 2000, pp. 4–5). Other claims of 'being first' have been made. *The Times* correspondent Henry Crabb Robinson covered Napoleon's campaigns in Spain and Germany in the early 1800s (Carruthers 2000, pp. 4–5). But he was, unlike Russell, not present at the events, reporting on them from places nearer the conflict and using clippings from local newspapers (Hohenberg 1995). Russell, as with his colleagues in the nineteenth century, reported anonymously; there were no by-lines. Instead, correspondents used to write under pseudonyms or initials and therefore they were not identifiable to the public (Dyas 2004). However, during the latter part of the nineteenth century, the so-called 'Golden Age of War Reporting', the war correspondent became a celebrated figure in Victorian society. Russell, Archibald Forbes and others became household names, mainly through their own personal accounts of war published either at the end of their careers or after the campaign they were reporting on was over.

The American Civil War (1861–1865) was the first war that received full documentation by the media facilitated by the telegraph. The struggle between the Union and Confederacy created tremendous demand for news. At one point during the war around 500 journalists were reporting on the struggle from the Union side. Only a few correspondents were supportive of the Confederacy (Knightley 2005). There was no mechanism to report a war of such geographic magnitude at the beginning, but the press found ways of organising their news-gathering on an extensive scale. Most newspapers had at least one reporter in the field, while larger newspapers such as New York dailies, *The Herald* and *The Times*, spent large amount of money on their own war departments (Sloan 1991). There were changes in the dynamics of the media industry; these put an end to the personal journalism in which individual reporters were more important than the newspaper. Newspapers from the 1860s began to deploy their own correspondents on a large scale as part of a concerted and organised effort to cover wars. This was motivated by commercial concerns and the professional desire to be first with the news as a result of the telegraph. They were ready to invest heavily in this competition and thereby paved the way for 'breaking stories' (Carruthers 2000, pp. 20–21).

Despite the technological improvement and the engagement of large number of journalists, the quality of the news coverage of the American civil war was deemed to be unsatisfactory. The journalists who covered the war were young and inexperienced. The prime duty of the correspondents was to stay close to military headquarters and gather reports from the officers in command or one of their staff. Many papers were still connected ideologically, if not financially, to political parties. Very few correspondents accompanied the Confederate armies in the field and Confederate officials bribed journalists to write stories in favour of them. British correspondents especially received bribes to write and publish Southern propaganda (Roth 1997, p. 5).

2.1.3 Organised System of War Reporting

The organised system of war reporting was established by the Franco-Prussian War of 1870–1871, which initiated the public interest in the war correspondent. From this conflict onwards the position of the war correspondent developed. Each war brought advances in the work of the war reporter and new media technology can be seen as advancing the profession of war correspondent. The 1898 Spanish-American War was brought to the public by the telegraph. The Second Boer War (1899–1902) was the first war that was covered by moving images and photography. Audiences worldwide for the first time followed a conflict by radio during the Second World War. Vietnam was the first television war. The first Gulf War was brought to the public by satellite and on a 24-hour basis as round-the-clock coverage established the reputation of Cable News Network (CNN) as an international broadcaster. The attack by the United States (US) on Afghanistan in 2001 was covered live with videophones while the 2003 invasion of Iraq was seen as the first war reported via the internet. Further, in 2003 an alternative player in the media, the Qatari satellite company *Al Jazeera*, broadcast coverage of the US occupation of Iraq (McLaughlin 2002, pp. 202–203). *Al Jazeera* is perhaps an example of the media's increasingly interconnectedness in a world where conflicts are closer to 'home', and where we ought to take the neighbour's point of view more seriously.

2.1.4 New Media Technologies and the Rise of Data Journalism

New media technologies have driven the development of the war correspondent but in the process, it has also shifted the reporting of war from the professional correspondent to alternative communicators and different voices. Activists, as well as ordinary citizens, can be involved in the reporting of war, as the grainy mobile phone images of the fighting in Syria today show. A range of people besides journalists have access to new media tools, such as mobile phones, streaming technologies, wireless networks, and the high-quality publishing and information sharing capacities of the internet. This enables them to report on war and conflict and heralded the growth of citizen journalism (Allan 2013). Recently, social media, such as Facebook and Twitter, have played their part in the political upheavals in the Arab World—the Arab Spring has been dubbed by some the 'Twitter revolution' as a result of the importance of this technology in mobilising demonstrations against the regimes. This new generation of media technology is used to communicate conflict to the world regardless of the boundaries of geography and culture (Bennett 2003). Lance Bennett (ibid., p. 13) states that global activists have developed models for empowering uses of digital communication media. The ordinary citizen can communicate his or her view of war and conflict, empowering them in the process of communication by enabling links that connect people across time, space and issues.

The rapid advancement of digital technology in the recent period has enabled a flow of data that is profoundly fashioning the news reporting. This connected and digitally facilitated method of gathering and disseminating information of data journalism complemented by the fields of design, computer science and statistics has revolutionised journalism. It has added a dimension to journalism by providing a platform for analysis, investigation and evaluation in the news reporting to contextualise the news. Data journalism, as Simon Rogers (2008) defines is 'a field combining spreadsheets, graphics data analysis and the biggest news stories' (para. 110). According to Mirko Lorenz (2010), it is a process that involves analysing, filtering and visualising data in a form that is linked to a narrative and is useful to the public. As explained by journalist Catherine Gicheru (2016), this means that there is a shift in how journalists report. They are no longer reliant on the 'he-said she-said' format. The Guardian Datablog is considered to be the 'world's most popular data journalism website' due to its systematic and informative approach in news reporting (Lewis 2018).

Data journalism has redesigned the way media report issues ranging from health to wars. Moreover, it has demonstrated its potential to facilitate and enable justice and accountability for the war crimes and crimes against humanity committed during war. Data journalism has the capacity to document human rights violations and expose them globally through data, statistics, charts, infographics, maps and other visualisations. It greatly assists traditional journalism to make its content rich and informative, and thus gives people actionable information. Information is knowledge, and therefore data helps journalists to reveal truth. This is the power of data journalism. Recently, the most popular news concerning data journalism has been the leakage of massive amounts of files related to the government that were very sensitive in nature, which has facilitated large-scale cooperation and collaboration between various competing media houses. According to Wired magazine as well as several other news agencies, in recent times, the most complicated, major, and controversial 'Big Data' plans which the journalists partook in, which subsequently led to leaking of secrets, in chronological order are as follows (1) 'Cablegate' on Wikileaks spearheaded by Julian Assange leaked a 1.73 gigabyte worth of US State Department documents. (2) Edward Snowden who was a contractor for National Security Agency (NSA) released close to 1.7 million internal documents. (3) a leak by an anonymous source which brought the 'Panama Papers (Lewis 2018) to light. WikiLeaks played a pivotal role in bringing to light multiple brutal abuses by the United States, including but not limited to torture, extrajudicial executions, and war crimes. For the purpose of exposing these heinous crimes committed against Afghans by NATO troops in the Afghan war, a database (Afghan War Diaries) with adequate documentation was created by the *New York Times*, *The Guardian*, and Der Spiegel in 2010, as they worked in collaboration (Kayser-Bril 2018). WikiLeaks was also instrumental in initiating the Tunisian and Egyptian revolutions in 2011. It is also given credit for bringing to light unlawful activities of various governments in the world.

Crowdsourcing is another form of data journalism through which journalists and media institutions obtain information. It uses public to gather and share data and information about their problems. Crowdsourcing platforms enable the public to take part and contribute towards the gathering of information pertaining to the issues that affect their life. Consequently, they become partners of the problem-solving process by proving useful data and insights. The combination of mapping and crowdsourcing information led to the development of a collective form of data journalism. Alaveteli.org enables the public to seek and access information under freedom of information legislation and also enables the replies to be visible to every individual. Since all the requests and further communication unfold online, it is extremely useful for both citizens as well as for those who campaign for right to information. Across the globe, different websites for freedom of information have been established under Alaveteli, such as Whatdotheyknow.com in the UK. Some example of certain others setups are Afrileaks, Securedrop, and websites for monitoring and charting corrupt practices and violence such as Ushahidi.com in Kenya (Clements 2018).

In the recent past, there has been an exponential use of crowdsourcing for mapping ISIS and other Middle East conflicts. For instance, an image of a munitions truck blowing up in Syria has been shared by Thomas van Linge, a 19-year-old high school student in Amsterdam. The truck was probably blown up by the First Coastal Division, which is a faction of rebels associated with the Free Syrian Army. Linge shared a link to a YouTube video which showcases the explosion, wherein he tagged the location as 'near Joureen, Ghab plain'. Moreover, he cross-referenced this particular location with a map to ensure that he could keep track of the activities of the Syrian rebels. There are several other citizen cartographers on the internet who are constantly charting the situation in the Middle East. These are useful for journalists, and also human rights practitioners and security analysts in the region (Bajak 2015).

2.2 Media–Military Relations

The evolution of war journalism has brought the media into conflict with the military. In response to the growth of war reporting, the military have attempted to control what the media reports. The emergence of the war correspondent has been accompanied by increased tension between the media and the military. War propaganda and censorship have developed hand in hand with war reporting. The advance of war reporting has changed the interaction between the media and the military. Belknap (2002, p. 101) notes the duty of the media are to 'ensure equilibrium among the people, its elected officials, and its subordinate military', to report events fully and fairly. War reporting is committed to covering actual events without bias. It is committed to full disclosure while the military places the emphasis on secrecy, seen as essential to the prosecution of war. Several accounts of war histories quote the MoD leaflet instructions issued to British correspondents with the Task Force: 'the essence of successful warfare is secrecy; the essence of successful journalism is publicity' (McNair 2011, p. 193). These dual interests are contradictory and bring the military and the media into conflict with each other. This tension has increased with the rise of the war correspondent and is manifest in the development of censorship and propaganda.

Indeed, the military started imposing censorship following the Crimean War, in the 1850s, when William Howard Russell, reporting for *The Times*, brashly criticised the military's actions. Whether or not the fault was completely Russell's, the military's experience of a new critical breed of journalism led to the introduction of a formal military censorship that has been commonplace in most wars ever since (McLaughlin 2002, pp. 50–51). In the history of journalism, the war correspondents first experienced the introduction of systematic and organised censorship during the Russo-Japanese War of 1905 (Sweeney 1998). The military bureaucracy kept journalists from the front and under strict censorship. A few reporters managed to dodge these restrictions and produce some high-quality reporting, but in general the Japanese military succeeded in limiting the flow of information. The military began to learn that information was best controlled not only by limiting journalists' freedom of movement but simply by denying them any facts about the war itself (ibid.). Severe censorship was brought into force during World War One. The introduction of the Espionage Act of 1911 in the US was directly concerned with spying and the protection of military secrets. This law had provisions affecting the journalists in the production of news items. The press censorship provision banned the publication of any material the US President deemed 'useful to the enemy'. The provision outlawed any dissemination of information that could hinder military activities or operations. Following this, the implementation of the Sedition Act of 1918, aimed at silencing criticism of the United States during World War I, restricted freedom of speech in the interests of national security (Katherine 2015, p. 117; Riley 1998). Meanwhile, in Britain, Parliament passed the Defence of the Realm Act in 1914. It gave the government vast powers to regulate the media, especially to impose severe censorship. Those who accepted this control and cooperated with the military in disseminating the war news received rewards of social rank and political power (Purseigle 2013).

The implementation of the law brought more obstacles to the reporters in dispatching true reports about what was actually happening in the fighting. In most cases, the correspondents had to win accreditation from the military and wear a military uniform to report from the front. The journalists who were accompanied at all times by military officers, who determined where they could travel, censored their reports and even read their private letters (Knightley 2005). In order to witness war and conflict, the war correspondents had to compromise their integrity and reach an accommodation with the military, something that has characterised the development of war reporting since the World War One.

The capacity to witness war was challenged by several factors in the inter-war years—the rise of dictatorships in Europe, the simultaneous growth of public relations agencies and the establishment of information and propaganda ministries in several countries (McLaughlin 2002).

The legacy of the World War One as also meant that journalists' susceptibilities to propaganda and manipulation were carried over into the 1920s and 1930s; during this war journalists tended to stick with one side or the other for the duration of the fighting, thus becoming 'fully immersed in the propaganda war' (ibid., p. 57). This influenced their relations with the military, making them more willing to cooperate with the authorities. The same situation continued during the Russian Revolution (1917), where war correspondents, to gain access to cover the events, had to agree with the conditions set down by the Russian or Allied forces. Journalists were barred from covering the events if it was found their reporting was unfavourable to the Allies, and only a few correspondents refused to adhere to censorship rules. Walter Lippmann has emphasised that 'at a time when objective reporting was vital, and could even have influenced the course of history, their contribution to public knowledge on this matter of world importance was about as useful as that of an astrologer or an alchemist' (cited in Carruthers 2000, p. 139).

As during the First World War, the US government came up with a comprehensive plan for filtering the information about the fighting during World War Two. The government started its plan with a crackdown on all domestic radio traffic within the United States immediately after the attack on Pearl Harbour (Knightley 2005). The censorship authorities suppressed such information for many years, even after the end of war. Bureaucrats justified the censorship of information on the grounds they were essential to stop enemy espionage and sabotage and maintain public acceptance of war.

By 1944, 150 war correspondents from the United Kingdom (UK) and the United States were filing stories to over 278 million readers worldwide. These reporters wore army uniforms with the letter 'C', indicating their independent status as correspondents. Radio, newspapers, magazines, and newsreels were the major sources of war news and besides providing information were also used to sell the war to the American public. They acted as propaganda tool of the American government for mobilising American support for the war effort in Europe. The news presentation of Germany, particularly at the start of World War Two, left no room for a negotiated settlement; the message was simple—Germany had to be stopped in order for democracy and freedom to be preserved (McLaughlin 2002, pp. 64–65). This was not controversial as both media and military shared this view and journalism was 'on team' for most of the conflict, accepting the restrictions as part of the war effort. This situation did not translate comfortably to the post-war world in spite of the efforts of the military to continue to impose restrictions.

Whatever the content, whatever the version, whatever the source and whatever the purpose, the demand for war news has increased in the post-war world. Massive audiences worldwide now follow conflicts and wars around the world. World War Two had been followed over the radio but in the years after the war it was the advent of television that opened conflict to public scrutiny television as a medium came to dominate the reporting of war but every medium increased its audience when war broke out (Knightley 1975, p. 30). The 25 biggest selling newspapers of the United States gained in circulation, while Cable News Network (CNN) experienced a ten-fold increase in its audience (Rai 2000).

In the post-war atmosphere, two other features of conflict were noteworthy: the greater notion of public transparency and the changing nature of post-war conflicts. The early stages of the Korean War, 1950–1953, was unique in that journalists were free to portray the war in its full horrors, without any censorship regulations (McLaughlin 2002, pp. 68–69). However, as the war escalated, censorship was reintroduced (Luostarinen and Ottosen 2002), but the intervention in Vietnam in the 1960s was also characterised by an openness and lack of censorship which endured throughout the war. Wars and conflicts in the post-war period were not full scale total wars but often internal conflicts in countries in far-off places. The absence of attacks on the American soil is the major characteristic difference between World War Two and the American wars in the second half of the twentieth century. Such wars were not targeted directly at America but rather precipitated American involvement. The regulation of news and information had to be coordinated with host countries and the regulation of the war information required re-thinking as troop movements and operational security had to be seen in a broader political context. It was crucial in wars such as Korea, Vietnam, Panama and the Gulf to ensure a consensus of the electorate in favour of the prosecution of war. Politics became a central feature of the conduct of war, which was one of the key lessons learned from Vietnam War (Smyth 2013; Riley 1998; Knightley 1975).

The history draws attention to a dilemma which many see being at the heart of war reporting and journalism since Russell's day. The correspondent's duty as a citizen is to support the government's decision to go to war; as a journalist, the duty is to provide truthful information to fellow citizens. Balancing these claims when your country is at war is not easy and journalism tends to follow the flag. The claims of citizenship are more compelling than the claims of professionalism. Furthermore, some of practices of the profession of journalism are infused with practice of giving the benefit of the doubt to government or accepting government interpretations and explanations. The institutional realities, professional routines and ideologies that shape the practice of journalism have been laid out by Herman and Chomsky (1988) in their propaganda model. These influences are obscured by the professional ideology of political neutrality but any claim to neutrality is false: there is no neutral ground on which to stand. Choices about which stories to cover from which angle and which sources to use undermine the claim to neutrality (Jensen 2005, p. 81). The war correspondent is never neutral and struggles to be independent from the authorities and powerful political forces. These limitations to war reporting are examined in the next section.

2.3 The Challenges of War Reporting

In recent years, human rights issues have become integral in public policy and also a part of the larger public discourse as the issues of contention of global civil society rapidly changed. Media, as an integral component of global civil society and a 'Fourth Estate,' has a moral responsibility to focus on the issues of human rights and act as an educative medium to protect and promote human rights in times of conflicts by exposing abuses and their underlying causes wherever they occur. This role necessitates media to analyse news while covering conflicts, wherein it can deconstruct the situation in its actuality thereby aiding human rights advocates and conflict resolution practitioners in tackling the situation.

Information dissemination about oppression and injustice can serve both as a means and as an end to the promotion and protection of human rights and peace. By acting as an information-provider and catalysing formation of opinions, media can become a key contributor of peace, which is imperative for human rights promotion and protection (Shaw 2012, p. 12). According to Shaw (ibid., p. 2), apart from the basic functions of information dissemination and promotion of public knowledge, journalists hold the moral responsibility of educating their audience, informing the members of their rights, and monitoring, reporting, and investigating all human rights violations.

Aligning with this expectation, human rights reporting has improved dramatically over the past few years. All over the world we have witnessed aggressive media campaigns advocating for the rights of persons with disabilities and gender equality. In particular, the ethical and professional standards have advanced to a certain degree (Theofilopoulos 2019; GLAAD 2016). As a result, there has been an improvement in the standards in reporting disability, indigenous people, LGBTQ+ communities people (lesbian, gay, bisexual, transgender, queer and intersex related communities) (van Eeden-Moorefield 2017). According to a report released by Glaad (2020), an organisation that tracks representation of lesbian, gay, bisexual and transgender people in the media, LGBTQ Representation on TV has improved gradually in the United States over the past few years (Aridi 2018). However, things are not perfect and the media reporting of the indigenous and gender issues is not yet satisfactory. Studies continue to show that there are serious deficits in the first nations people representation in the media. Thomas, Jakubowicz and Norman (2020) analysed 45 years of print media reports of Aboriginal initiatives for self-determination and found that media have systematically and substantially failed—if not undermined and denied—Aboriginal aspirations for self-determination and for enduring political settlements. Anderson and Robertson (2011), reveal in their research consistent use of recurring stereotypes and misrepresentation of Indigenous people by media. Similarly, McInroy and Craig (2015), in their study of LGBTQ people, found that traditional media continue to represent LGBTQ people as one-dimensional and stereotypical, ignore many LGBTQ sub-groups, limit LGBTQ young people's perceptions of their future trajectories, and offer no opportunities for criticism .

Thus, it is not wrong to say that the human rights responsibilities of the media are not being fulfilled adequately. Consequently, the audiences are put in a vulnerable position wherein their access to human rights discourse regarding the violations of rights, actions, policies of governments and other authorities is impeded and restricted. The coverage of human rights issues by media is selective, inaccurate and subjective, often focusing only on political and civil rights, and thereby ignoring the economic, social and cultural rights (ICHRP 2002). This failure in fulfilling the obligations of media, to protect and promote human rights is a function of socio-economic, cultural and political aspects. This is particularly true in the case of conflict and war situations (Williams 1992; Kempf and Reimann 2002; Luostarinen 2002 and Kempf 2003), and as a result fails to create opportunities for stakeholders to address the problems in a holistic and rightful manner.

Conventional journalistic practices followed by diverse media, as highlighted by Shaw (2011) interpret the human rights violations as caused by individuals and not due to system/structure that constructs and sustains long-term relations in conflicts. This reporting style does not identify root causes of human rights violations and how it functions as causes of violent conflicts.

Proponents of alternative forms of journalism hold conventional journalism practices partially accountable for the realisation of negative peace and positive peace as well as negative rights and positive rights (Shaw 2012).

Lynch and McGoldrick, describe conventional war reporting as an exercise in framing, though it may not actively aim to construct positive public opinion with respect to wars (Lynch and McGoldrick 2007, p. 258). There have been considerable concerns about the role conventional war journalism plays in providing support for wars. Practising war correspondents hold the concept of 'objectivity', while human rights activists believe there are various aspects of conventional journalism which promote war: their orientation towards violence, propaganda, support for the interpretations of elites, and victory. These concerns are discussed in the next section. Initially, journalists' perception of the concept of 'objectivity' in their practices during conflict, is discussed. Secondly, the section explores the prevailing conventions (such as the biases in favour of official sources, event over processes, and dualism in reporting conflicts, that make conventional war journalism supportive of war (Lynch 2008, p. 25).

2.3.1 Debate Around Objectivity

There has been substantial deliberation about objectivity among scholars, who have found it to be a problematic concept, as they believe journalism is a tool to safeguard human rights. John Merrill (1989), a journalism scholar and professor, defines the term 'objectivity' as 'detached, unprejudiced, un-opinionated, uninvolved, unbiased, omniscient and infallible' (quoted in Friedman 2004, p. 164). The journalistic ethics, require journalists to be emotionally distant from their work, to ensure an unbiased approach.

As explained by McNair, objectivity is a method of gathering and processing news, which requires the organisation to profess its resources which must be independent of ideology so as to ensure reliability and trust in the reported stories (2013, p. 84).

The gap between objectivity and practicality of employing objectivity in everyday activities of journalism has been questioned and commended by many scholars (Tuchman 1972; Altschull 1984; McLaughlin 2002). The difficulty of maintaining objectivity in journalism has been expressed by some, though it is seen to be the key principle of practicing journalism.

According to Tuchman (1972), objectivity is a tool which protects the reporter from mistakes and criticism. Meanwhile, Altschull (1984, p. 128) views objectivity as a 'code' which helps maintain the power balance in a capitalistic setup and safeguards the structure from any pressures for deviation or change.

According to McGoldrick (2006), though many journalists claim to be objective, a close examination of their pattern of reporting reveals that their narrative is often pro-war. As objectivity is often defined within a socio-economic context, these journalists cannot be said to have strayed from objectivity.

Journalist and Editor Brucker (1969) has suggested seven ingredients that he believes guide journalists along the path of objectivity: (1) correspondence to reality, (2) accuracy, (3) lack of bias, (4) honesty, (5) fairness, (6) completeness and (7) dispassion. Bearing these principles in mind, according to Brucker (Ibid.), there is a common notion among audiences and journalists that objectivity is the key to good journalism. Majority of the journalists have been at the receiving end of criticism for not being objective over a certain issue. Despite this demand for objectivity, this mode of journalism may sometimes be detrimental to truth. A popular British reporter James Cameron expressed that objectivity is of less importance than truth, and maintaining objectivity in situations involving ethical conflict is both meaningless and impossible (cited in Brucker Ibid.; see McGoldrick 2006).

Maggie O'Kane of *The Guardian* says that objectivity and truth do not always intertwine. Though the truth is not always objective, it has to be the topmost priority for a journalist. Talking of her experience in Bosnia, she states that ethnic cleansing is a one-sided event with no space for objectivity (Kane 2002). Remaining unbiased in a situation of violent crisis, disregarding the perpetrator and victim is certainly a distortion of reality (McNair 2013). Contrastingly, Kurspahic, a journalist who covered the war in Bosnia argues, that is possible to remain objective without being neutral (2003, p. 80; see Nieman Reports 2003, pp. 79–80). Veteran ITN reporter Michael Nicholson is of the opinion that facts and emotional anguish need not be contradictory (quoted in McLaughlin 2002, p. 154).

Such concerns have led to what British Broadcasting Corporation (BBC) correspondent Martin Bell has called the 'Journalism of Attachment'" (Bell 1998). According to Bell, there is no place for objective and dispassionate journalism amidst war and human atrocities (McLaughlin 2002, pp. 152–154; Kempf 2003, p. 59).

Philip Hammond believes that journalism of attachment invariably leads to inaccurate reporting due to the inherent need to side with the 'victims' of war (Hammond 2000, p. 378). As an example, he notes the lack of evidence to support the claims of systematic rape as a weapon of warfare in Bosnia and Kosovo. Many journalists reported about these 'rape camps' despite insufficient information (ibid., p. 379). Kempf blames the journalism of attachment for this deviation from professional rules and standards of truth 'in the name of a moral enterprise' (Kempf 2002, p. 59).

Conversely, several scholars point out the bias conventional journalism carries which may accentuate violence. For example, Lynch and McGoldrick (2007, p. 258) have identified three conventions of objective reporting that predispose traditional war journalism to violence. They are: (1) A pre-disposition in favour of official sources (2) A focus on events over process (3) An emphasis on 'dualism in reporting conflicts'.

Obtaining information from official sources saves time, money and resources and is also considered 'newsworthy'. At the same time, it excludes voices of all the other stakeholders involved voices and in particular the 'voices of peace' and negotiation. Those advocating peace and human rights in face of an official stance that war is necessary are often neglected (Lynch 2008, p. 63; Hackett 2011, p. 6).

Secondly, the 'emergency'" of an event that disturbs the normality comes first in the process of reporting. News often sidesteps the context and the underlying causes of conflicts and violence. Instead, their main focus becomes to 'break the news' due to their economic interests (Lynch and McGoldrick 2007, p. 258). According to McGoldrick (2006), journalists are expected to ask six basic questions when producing a news story: *who, what, when, where, why* and *how.* Most stories only touch upon the 'why' on a superficial level or even entirely disregard it, sometimes owing to the stories becoming too long to contain the readers' interest.

The failure of conventional war reporting in answering the six basic questions in its conflict reporting, makes peacemakers and human rights practitioners unaware of curbing of a group's human rights by the system of governance. Consequently, nothing is done to address the conditions of inequality, inequity, injustice and insecurity, stagnating the power imbalance of a society.

Thirdly, dualism is an important element of objectivity. Dualism is a concept in which conflict is looked at as a win-lose situation, that is, a zero-sum game of two parties (Webel and Galtung 2007, p. 258). The paradigm of dualism 'frames out multi-party initiatives, complex causes and win-win situations' (McGoldrick 2006, p. 4). Therefore, these three orientations of conventional journalism produces news that predisposed towards war journalism.

2.3.2 *Characteristics of Conventional War Reporting*

Researchers have identified a particular pattern that emerges from aforementioned reporting type. Galtung claims that war news is war/violence-oriented, elite-oriented, propaganda-oriented and victory-oriented. Stories with these orientations shift the news agenda towards an emphasis on war over the protection and promotion of human rights and peace (Galtung 2002), and thus prevents journalists from exposing the human rights violations committed by all parties in a war.

War journalism is inherently *war/violence-oriented* as the profession awaits war violence to break out before reporting it. As the occupation only functions during a war, it becomes a driver of escalating the violence, rather than looking for solutions to end the conflict. Galtung and other media scholars have identified a number of orientations of war journalism which emphasise war and violence. Firstly, it focuses only on the visible effects of war and primarily its impact on the 'other side'. For Lynch (2005, 2008), war journalism waits until the violence occurs to report its physical outcomes, such as the coverage of the killed, injured, destruction of buildings and other possible consequences of violence.

According to Lynch and McGoldrick (2005, p. 6), the conventional war reporting concentrates on the 'conflict stadium', and like a football match, there are two sides and one goal. Only one can emerge victorious and the narrative is built around it. Instead of understanding the underlying causes, the game of war is reported in the context of the effects on those who are involved in it. For Nohrstedt, the framing of war journalism describes the actual conflict in a radically polarised way by creating a division of 'good guys' and 'bad guys' or 'black' and 'white' (Nohrstedt

2009; Nohrstedt and Ottosen 2001). As Howard makes it clear, terms like 'terrorist', 'fanatic' and 'extremist' are emotional and such strong words are impossible to negotiate with (Howard 2004, p. 16). These labels not only cause sensationalism, but also lead to fear among the public. This framing of conflict makes conventional war reporting one-sided, and this applies to both intrastate and interstate wars. The influence of nationalist sentiments is so strong that it overwhelms the meaning of 'truth' and feeling of 'compassion'. Falk elaborates that nationalisation of truth is divisive in nature, wherein only 'our' tragedy evokes emotions (Falk 2008, p. vi).

The result of the 'zero-sum' journalism described above is that much of the reporting focuses on victory. Peace is proposed to be achieved only through a ceasefire, which must be preceded by winning a war (Peace=Victory+ Ceasefire). Thus, peace endeavours are rendered pointless until victory is achieved (Galtung 2002). Conventional War reporting is *victory-oriented*; it often functions like a sports game demonstrating a zero-sum orientation where the winner is the one and only gainer (Shinar 2009, p. 10). Reporting is often reduced to a commentary on who is winning, while ignoring the violations of human rights and suffering of the people. Since victory is seen as the end goal, it overlooks promotion and protection of peace and human rights. As a result, conventional war reporting with its objectivity conventions, does not fully address human rights violations committed to the other side and their causes, in order to create peace (Lynch 1998).

Galtung and Ruge (1965) have speculate that journalism is elite-oriented, which specifically applies to Conventional War reporting. It focuses on problems and concerns of elite people and elite nations. There is a news hierarchy as to what is newsworthy. McLaughlin (2002, pp. 185–187) noted the arbitrary, short-lived reporting Western media carries out when there is a conflict in a foreign country. While McLaughlin clarifies that there is no single factor which garners media attention towards a conflict, but the significance major powers' involvement has on this decision-making process, cannot be ignored. The main focus is on the political leaders of each side, with the opposition being labelled the wrongdoer and their leader is blamed for being a perpetrator of the conflict. The elite-orientation is also materialised through journalists' dependence on official sources, which are deemed to be more newsworthy and reliable. The official sources are prioritised while a general citizen caught up in the conflict is either ignored or seen as a statistic. Though victims of war are beginning to find voices through media (Lynch 2008; Hackett 2011; Nohrstedt 2009), their opinions are still overpowered by media's preference for the views of their leaders.

Lastly, conventional war journalism is also propaganda-oriented. Propaganda is the process of influencing an individual's opinions, sentiments, and beliefs to match them with those of the propagandist to meet certain aims (Zerrouki 2012). For Carruthers, propaganda is disseminating information which has been manipulated, distorted, wrongly emphasised on, or partly omitted with an end goal of influencing certain opinions of the general public (Carruthers 2000, p. 81). Propaganda is a failing of conventional war reporting as the authorities have exploited this orientation to include media in their war effort. Before and during the war, media are important to the war aims of the warring parties. Journalists come under the influence of the propaganda strategies (Höijer et al. 2002, pp. 4–11; Nohrstedt and Ottosen 2014).

2.4 The Genesis and Consequences of Conventional War Reporting

This section explores how and why conventional journalism has become instrumental in fuelling war, and is failing to protect human rights and peace, as outlined above. The reasons for the same can be pointed out towards the nature of news values, the relationship between journalists and power, the influence of news sources and the use of language, which are discussed below.

2.4.1 News Values

War journalists follow what Wilhelm Kempf refers to as three 'turning points' in their reporting which actively contribute to the process of escalating the conflict beyond its actual level (Kempf 2003, p. 70). This is discussed in detail in chapter nine. The first turning point is *mis-coverage*, which is the tradition of only covering conflicts that have already turned violent. The second point is the habit of interpreting *conflicts as lose-win situations*. The final turning point is journalists' *use of elites as sources*. The turning points, according to Kempf (ibid.), make journalists especially vulnerable to official propaganda. Kempf's three turning points, which have seeped into become a part of the traditional news values, affect what and how the media cover war and conflict. According to Galtung and Ruge (1965), in news value theory, priority is often given to negative, elite-oriented, personal, and conflict-related content. According to this hierarchy, conflict news involves a negative event like violence, happening in a known country. Peace stories find place while only covering the victims and involve costly interventions by elite individuals and nations (Galtung 2002). Galtung and Ruge's news values model makes an attempt to describe media practices across cultures, and this is extensively discussed and examined in Chapters 6, 7 and 8.

For journalists to gain access to the battlefield, close cooperation with the military is vital. Embedding has been a feature of war journalism since the World War One. Due to their continuous interactions with the military, journalists often cover war from the military's perspective using their terminology. In the contemporary world, news is telecasted 24-hours, which has created tremendous pressure and demand over journalists, who no longer find time to dissect the situation and understand the underlying causes of conflict.

2.4.2 News, Journalists and Power

The societal influence on media is significant, as journalists themselves are a part of a society. When their society is involved in a conflict, there is an increased pressure on the journalists to take their side. Journalists are citizens as well as members of a profession which inadvertently creates an internal conflict between professional duties and the responsibility of citizenship (see Williams 1992). Appeals to reporters' 'patriotic duty' evokes emotional tension, which makes them more susceptible to propaganda and manipulation (Kempf and Reimann 2002).

Journalists' collaboration with political and military elites is not due to a conspiracy between policy-makers and the media, but comes from a point of being members of society. They are equally vulnerable to processes of social identification and hence take sides with one's own elites, soldiers and victims (Kempf 2003, p. 69). They feel the same patriotic instincts and commitments as other members of their society, and are equally susceptible to dehumanising those on the opposite side of the conflict. Due to their membership in the society, journalists are inclined to humanise their own political and military leaders and are more proactive in featuring victims of their own side (ibid., p. 70). Embedding plays an integral role in the reporting narrative, as when a journalist lives together with a soldiers' unit, the journalist depends on the unit for their life and well-being, thereby forming a bond. This bond restricts the soldiers from weaving a critical commentary on their compatriots (Tumber and Prentouis 2003).

2.4.3 News Sources and Their Effects

The military is a powerful institution in any society, particularly when compared to peace organisations. There are multiple resources at play to keep the war culture and military machine going, including propaganda, public relations, war movies, war games and military museums. Conflict-based propaganda not only increases the power imbalance of a society, but acts as a constraint for peace and human rights practitioners to implement programmes successfully. Because, they cannot compete with the propaganda efforts of the military, which are carefully designed to influence human beings to agree with their ideologies. Budgetary constraints also decrease the visibility of human rights and peace organisations' in the media and they are not used regularly as sources and 'experts' (Luostarinen and Ottosen 2002). However, journalists often just use sources with authoritative or military titles and 'expert' labels to emphasise their statements as they believe such sources offer more credibility.

The power official sources hold on news agenda has increased with the decline in foreign bureaus and specialist correspondents. Therefore, when an internal conflict arises, international media are solely reliant on elite sources and government officers for their news reporting. Also, there has been an increase in inexperienced and freelance journalists (McLaughlin 2002, p. 187; Hawkins 2015). Since covering wars is still an expensive business, foreign news bureaus have often been shut down. Parachute journalism has consequently seen a rise, which involves flying down teams of journalists into a war zone when a war begins and flying them out as soon as the violence is over. This is an inexpensive option as opposed to employed staff (for whom the insurance policies are excessively expensive) and they take more risks (paid as they are by the story). Thus, their coverage is often superficial and does not touch upon the latent conflicts and factors involved such as the issues of justice, accountability, and redressal. Parachute journalism is also a consequence of budgetary restrictions and does not aim to address editorial concerns, directly affecting what is covered in a foreign conflict. These inexperienced journalists are not well-equipped to ask key questions of their sources and analyse the situation well, and are more likely to be dependent on experts (ibid.; Riegert 2003). Another trend is that media outlets increasingly rely on both news and pictures from news agencies.

2.4.4 *Military Terminology*

The dependence on official news sources has directly affected the language of the coverage, which often mimics the language of the sources. Military PR machines focus special attention on constructing the words and phrases they use to describe what they do. For example, the usage of 'collateral damage' to describe civilian casualties, is constructed to neutralise the negative consequences of the conflict. They seek to sanitise the process of warfare and embedding is the tool used to transfer these terms into media's reporting. As Luostarinen points out, manipulating the journalists to use the military's vocabulary and terminology, is practically making the journalists work for them (2002, p. 276). In this way, journalists lose their moral responsibility to expose human rights violations and sufferings and fail to protect people from the same. Instead, war is constructed as a 'good war' and as the only option for creating peace.

The 9/11 also contributed to the polarity in the media language, creating an 'us versus them' divide that was largely prevalent in Cold War rhetoric. War has been described as 'a peace initiative', military invasions are described as 'regime changes', and occupations have been called 'humanitarian interventions'. Media buying the phrases such as 'war for peace' and 'Humanitarian war' significantly diminish the prospect of protecting the victims of human rights violations.

These described failings of traditional war reporting have led to a different way of reporting wars and conflict. Much of this has been articulated in the context of Western liberal democracies and focused on the concept of Peace Journalism (PJ) and Human Rights Journalism (HRJ). The next section briefly discusses how the theory and practice of PJ have evolved as an alternative counter-hegemonic model as well as how HRJ serves as a complementary strand of PJ.

2.5 The Emergence of Alternative Form of Journalism

2.5.1 *Peace Journalism (PJ)*

Norwegian Scholar Johan Galtung first proposed the PJ as a normative theory in the 1970s. He suggested that conflict analysis and transformation could be used to update the concept of balance, fairness, and accuracy in reporting conflicts and war. According to Galtung, PJ is a journalistic movement with conflict transformation as one of its main areas of attention. PJ's main focus is journalism following a proactive, peace/solution-oriented approach, instead of solely reporting the statistics of the war. This is done by finding peace or conflict resolution opportunities by understanding the problem and finding a solution, before escalating into violence (Galtung 2002, p. 260). This requires the journalists to be experts in peacekeeping and conflict resolutions, as the model expects journalists to be 'enablers' instead of mere 'watchdogs' (Lynch and McGoldrick 2000, p. 46). According to Galtung, the first victim in war is not truth, but peace. Truth is only the second victim. He claims that the third and fourth victims are 'the people and the solution' (Galtung 1998). In summary, PJ focuses on all four of these 'victims'.

This concept was further developed and articulated by Lynch and McGoldrick. According to Lynch and McGoldrick (2005, p. 5), 'when editors and reporters make choices – of what stories to report, and how to report them – is what create opportunities for society at large to consider and to value non-violent responses to conflict'. Kempf (2003, p. 2) further defines PJs views as a normative journalistic approach to covering war and conflict. As Falk (2008, p. VII) remarks, PJ necessitates the journalists' exploring the reasons for conflict instead of just reporting the surface-level consequences. Lynch and McGoldrick identify four basic components of PJ, which counter the shortcomings of war journalism: solution-oriented, peace-oriented, truth-oriented and people-oriented.

PJ is critical of objectivity, at least if objectivity means that journalists 'just report the facts', and hold no accountability for the possible consequences of their reporting. In a way, PJ resonates with the journalism of attachment: it is impossible for a journalist to be neutral, uninvolved and unfeeling to the mirror in which reality is reflected (McGoldrick and Lynch 2000, p. 10).

For some journalists PJ is 'too critical' and 'too involved'. Many disapprove the critical self-awareness of journalistic structure inscribed in the PJ approach. They argue that objectivity should not be compromised at any cost as it is a sign of good journalism and must be the basis for all forms of journalism (see Lynch 2008, p. 6). British journalist David Loyn is a proponent of this idea and is therefore, a high profile critic of the concept of PJ. Loyn (2007, p. 1) categorically rejects Lynch and McGoldrick's emphasis on 'critical self-awareness' and states that 'the opposite of PJ is good journalism'. According to Loyn, PJ's demand for critical coverage and active involvement in a conflict is detrimental to the concept of 'objectivity' and antithetical to the practice of journalism, and is hence a fundamental deviation from the journalistic function.

Loyn rejects 'peace journalism' as he believes that fairness, objectivity and balance should govern the practice of war reporting. War news must cover what is happening and can sometimes, if relevant, be reported with imagination and scepticism. He stresses that journalists should and can limit their role to being 'witnesses' and must refrain from actively participating in any conflict (Loyn 2003, 2007, p. 4). According to Loyn (2003), PJ would hinder the practice of good journalism by making reporting subjective or partial.

Lynch rebukes Loyn for failing to note issues pertaining to objective journalism. Rather than focusing on the principles of objectivity, he argues that Loyn should analyse the contents and consequences of conventional war reporting. He cites Galtung and Ruge's (1965) explanation of what event becomes news coverage and the reasons for the same. News is a systematic process in which gatekeeping decisions on specific news stories follow discernible patterns. They explain why certain events become 'news'. He also emphasises on the connection between conflict reporting and propaganda (Lynch 2008, p. 8), arguing that Loyn does not adequately examine the influence of propaganda on reporting.

Loyn expresses concerns over 'active' involvement of journalists in the conflict to contribute to the peace-making process, as they become 'players' in the conflict, not 'observers'. Such a role, as Loyn (2003) notes, may jeopardise the integrity of journalists as they cease to be impartial disseminators. According to Loyn, PJ is a 'theoretical construct' which does not deep-dive into the practical problems of the profession. He believes that any such endeavour to attempt to alter journalism will possibly be used to create a 'distorting effect on the news agenda' (para. 10).

Loyn (2007) does not say that journalists should not influence the events of a conflict, only that they should not get directly involved. For him, the role of a journalist is to bear witness to the truth. Though his reporting can influence events, one must avoid doing it consciously. Loyn admits there are 'imperfections' in conventional war reporting, and that though 'absolute objectivity is impossible', one must constantly aim to pursue it. He argues that objectivity is the 'journalist's goal' (quoted in Berry 2008, pp. 135–136; Lynch 2008, p. 7). However, this appears to be an ideological assertion completely ignoring the problematic nature of the end result.

2.5.2 PJ's Epistemological Vacuum

Several media scholars are also critical of PJ and have pointed out several problems with the concept. Thomas Hanitzsch is among the academics who supports Loyn's reservations as he believes that ignoring objectivity goes against the philosophical foundation of journalism, thereby raising the question of PJ's epistemological vacuum. The proponents of PJ believe that conventional war journalism produces news that distorts reality, necessitating to take a closer look at the reality of news reporting. This is what PJ attempts to do, which according to Hanitzsch is erroneous. Referring to Schudson, who argues that news cannot be a 'mirror' of reality, he says that news is a representation of the world although all representations are selective (Hanitzsch 2007a; b).

Responding to Hanitzsch's claim, proponents of PJ defend the model saying it does honour fairness and accuracy in its practice. There are appropriate standards to report the views of all the sides of the conflict. Peleg believes that peace journalism's standards for journalism are fairness and accuracy. With that orientation, he asserts, taking a stance is allowed, if both sides are given voices and are presented accurately. This is a good replacement of objectivity, as it is balanced and fair.

According to Lynch and McGoldrick, 'the external goal of peace is added instrumentally, to deliver more successfully on internal goals of fairness and accuracy' (Lynch and McGoldrick 2010, p. 92). In other words, the journalistic concepts of balance, fairness and accuracy are updated using conflict analysis and transformation in the PJ approach (Lynch and McGoldrick 2005, p. 5).

For Hanitzsch (2004, p. 33), PJ is not sufficiently critical to reflect the reality of events using conflict analysis and transformation. PJ's assumption of the power of journalists and media to influence political decisions is also contested. He believes PJ is naïve to expect the audience to remain passive consumers and be enlightened by peace reporting. They actively hold views that need to be challenged or addressed. Hanistzsch sees PJ as 'not critical enough' to pursue its aims, while Loyn finds it 'over critical', so much so that it jeopardises the canons of objective journalism (Lynch 2008, p. 15). The question then is how critical can or should PJ be and does criticism transform reporters from 'observers' into 'participants'?

Responding to the criticism on the critical capacity of PJ, Lynch (2014) draws attention to the value of 'critical realism' as an epistemological approach, stating that the practice of PJ is grounded. Lynch argues that critical realism balances objectivity and engagement and that the source of distortion of news production is the disregard for the background and underlying causes of conflict.

Apart from the controversies over PJ, another weakness of this theory is its lack of focus on the nexus between human rights and peace. As Shaw points outs, 'there is a little scholarly work focusing, firstly, on the journalism–peace–human rights nexus and, secondly, on the critical discussion of the failure of mainstream journalism to foreground positive peace and positive rights issues' (2011, p. 98). PJ's lack of agency role, in its approach to address the underlying forms of causes, is its primary weakness. Instead it tries to address misconduct of the elite by deliberating over their attitudes and behaviours. This doesn't enable PJ to perform a proactive (preventive) role; instead it demonstrates a dramatic, reactive (prescriptive) role, and thereby fails to balance the imbalances of communities (*ibid.*, p. 108).

In this context, the concept of Human Rights Journalism (HRJ) anchored in Lisa Schirch's (2002, 2008) 'just peace' framework, draws insights from Frank's (2007) ethic and the logic of just peace, and Kant's philosophical framework of the peace and human rights nexus. Kant's position aims to address the violations of human rights due to violent conflicts. Shaw argues that this can be considered 'as a new complementary strand of peace journalism that can contribute meaningfully to the promotion and protection of peace and human rights' (2012, p. 98). Just Peace approach enables HRJ to explore solutions in a win-win-win manner, with the third party being the 'Community' (The Third Side).

This 'Third Side' essential to work for a global, triple-win is absent in PJ (ibid., p. 107).

What follows in the next chapter is a more theoretical insight of HRJ corresponding with the theories of news production such as agenda setting and spectatorship of suffering.

2.6 Summary

This chapter has described the problems of doing conventional war reporting and identified the factors which have oriented war journalism towards propagating war and violence. To explain why conventional war journalism has gravitated towards war, a number of factors have been identified, including the nature of news values, the relationship of journalism to power, the dependence on news sources and the language used to describe war. This chapter also examined the theory of PJ. The theory has been outlined and its particular orientations have been described. It is solution-, truth-, people- and peace-oriented and addresses the identified failings of conventional war reporting. The problems with PJ, as outlined by the practitioners and academics, were also discussed. Particularly, PJ's weakness in terms of its lack of agency role to address the underlying forms of causes was emphasised. Against this backdrop, the concept of HRJ was introduced and how it can be considered "as a new complementary strand of peace journalism" was highlighted.

Bibliography

Allan, S. (2013). *Citizen Witnessing: Revisioning Journalism in Times of Crisis Key Concepts in Journalism*. Malden, MA: Polity Press.

Altschull, H. (1984). *Agents of Power: The Role of News Media in Human Affairs*. New York: Longman.

Anderson, M. C., & Robertson, C. L. (2011). *Seeing Red: A History of Natives in Canadian Newspapers*. Winnipeg: University of Manitoba Press.

Aridi, S. (2018, October 25). L.G.B.T.Q. Representation on TV Improves, Glaad Finds. *The New York Times*. [Online]. https://www.nytimes.com/2018/10/25/arts/television/lgbtq-tv-characters.html. Accessed 14/06/2020.

Bajak. A. (2015, July 30). *Crowdsourcing Maps of ISIS and Other Middle East Conflicts*. Northeastren University. [Online]. https://www.storybench.org/crowdsourcing-maps-isis-middle-east-conflicts/. Accessed 13/06/2020.

Belknap, M. H. (2002). *The CNN Effect: Strategic Enabler or Operational Risk?* Parameters 32 (Autumn 2002): 100–114.

Bell, M. (1998). The Journalism of Attachment. In M. Kiernan (Ed.), *Media Ethics* (pp. 16–22). London: Routledge.
Bennett,W. L (2003). *New Media Power: The Internet and Global Activism*. [Online] http://depts.washington.edu/ccce/assets/documents/pdf/newmediapower.pdf. Last Accessed on 17 March 2020.
Berry, D. (2008). *Journalism Ethics and Society*. Burlington, VT: Ashgate Publishing Company.
Breisach, E. (1997). *Historiography: Ancient, Medieval, and Modern*. Chicago, IL: The University of Chicago Press.
Brucker, H. (1962). *Eyewitness to History: Journalist*. New York: The Macmillan Company.
Brucker, H. (1969, October 11). What's Wrong with Objectivity? *Saturday Review*, P. 77.
Carruthers, S. L. (2000). *The Media at War: Communication and Conflict in the Twentieth Century*. Basingstoke: MacMillan.
Clements, J. (2018). Collaborative Journalism and the Law in the UK. In R. Sambrook (Ed.), *Global Teamwork: The Rise of Collaboration in Investigative Journalism*. Oxford: Reuters Institute for the Study of Journalism, Department of Politics and International Relations, University of Oxford.
Dyas, E. (2004, October 19). William Howard Russell and the Crimean War. *Times Online*, UK.
Falk, R. (2008). Foreword. In J. Lynch (Ed.), *Debates in Peace Journalism* (pp. v–x). Sydney: Sydney University Press.
Frank, T. (2007). *Idealist and Realist Aspirations for Just Peace: An Analysis of Ethics of Military Force and the Discursive Construction of an Ethic of International Policing within the Framework of Just Peace and the Contemporary Hegemony of International Law*. Århus: Det Teologiske Fakultet.
Friedman, B. G. (2004). *Web Search Savvy: Strategies and Shortcuts for Online Research* (p. 164). Lawrence Erlbaum Publishers.
Galtung, J. (1998). *Peace Journalism: What, Why, Who, How, When, Where? What are Journalists For?* Taplow Court: Transcend.
Galtung, J. (2002). Peace Journalism: A Challenge. In W. Kempf & H. Luostarinen (Eds.), *Journalism and the New World Order, Studying War and the Media* (pp. 269–272). Nordicom: Göteborg.
Galtung, J., & Ruge, M. H. (1965). The Structure of Foreign News. *Journal of Peace Research, 2*(1), 64–91.
Gicheru. C. (2016). *8 Reasons Why Journalists Should Use Data to Improve Their Stories*. International Journalists Network. [Online]. https://ijnet.org/en/story/using-data-journalism-to-tell-better-stories. Accessed 12/06/2020.
GLAAD. (2016). *GLAAD Media Reference Guide*. [Online]. https://www.glaad.org/sites/default/files/GLAAD-Media-Reference-Guide-Tenth-Edition.pdf. Accessed 7/10/2020.

GLAAD. (2020). *LGBTQ Inclusion in Advertising & Media*. [Online]. https://www.glaad.org/sites/default/files/P%26G_AdvertisingResearch.pdf. Accessed 7/10/2020.

Hackett, R. A. (2011). New Vistas for Peace Journalism. In Lynch, J. et al (Eds.), *Expanding Peace Journalism: Comparative and Critical Approaches*. Sydney: Sydney University Press.

Hammond, P. (2000). Reporting Humanitarian Warfare: Propaganda, Moralism and NATO's Kosovo War. *Journalism Studies, 1*(3), 365–386.

Hanitzsch, T. (2004). Journalists as a Peacekeeping Force? Peace Journalism and Mass Communication Theory. *Journalism Studies, 5*(4), 483–495.

Hanitzsch, T. (2007a). It Should Be Fair to Criticize Even Noble Ideas: A Response to Jake Lynch and Samuel Peleg. *Conflict and Communication Online, 6*(2), 1–4.

Hanitzsch, T. (2007b). Situating Peace Journalism in Journalism Studies: A Critical Appraisal. *Conflict and Communication, 6*(2), 1–9.

Hawkins, V. (2015). Peace and the Absence of Journalism. In J. Hoffmann & V. Hawkins (Eds.), *Communication and Peace: Mapping an Emerging Field* (pp. 51–56). London: Routledge.

Herman, E., & Chomsky, N. (1988). *Manufacturing Consent*. New York: Pantheon Books.

Hoffmann, J., & Hawkins, V. (2015). *Communication and Peace: Mapping an Emerging Field*. London and New York: Routledge.

Hohenberg, J. (1995). *Foreign Correspondents: The Great Reporters and Their Times*.

Hoijer, B. (2004). The Discourse Of Global Compassion: The Audience And Media Reporting Of Human Suffering. *Media, Culture and Society, 26*(4), 513–531.

Höijer, B., Nohrstedt, S. A., & R. Ottosen. (2002). The Kosovo War in the Media—Analysis of a Global Discursive Order. *Conflict & Communication Online, 1*(2), 1–18.

Howard, R. (2004). *Conflict Sensitive Journalism*. Denmark: International Media Support and Institute for Media, Policy and Civil Society.

ICHRP (The International Council on Human Rights Policy). (2002*). Journalism, Media and the Challenge of Human Rights Reporting*. Available at http://www.ichrp.org/files/reports/14/106_report_en.pdf. Accessed 17 January 2020.

Jensen, R. (2005). The Problem with Patriotism: Steps Toward the Redemption of American Journalism and Democracy. In L. Artz & Y. R. Kamalipour (Eds.), *Bring 'Em On: Media and Politics in the Iraq War*. Lanham: Rowman & Littlefield.

Kane, M. O. (2002, December 5). This Time I'm Scared: US Propaganda Fuelled the First Gulf War. It Will Fuel This One Too—and the Risks are Even Greater. *The Guardian*. Available at http://www.guardian.co.uk/world/2002/dec/05/iraq.comment. Accessed 3 March 2020.

Katherine, F. (2015). *Protecting Government Secrets: A Comparison of the Espionage Act and the Official Secrets Act*, 38 B.C. Int'l & Comp. L. Rev. 91. [Online]. http://lawdigitalcommons.bc.edu/iclr/vol38/iss1/4. Accessed 12/04/2020.

Kayser-Bril, N. (2018). Collaboration—One Tool Among Many. In R. Sambrook (Ed.), *Global Teamwork: The Rise of Collaboration in Investigative Journalism*. Oxford: Reuters Institute for the Study of Journalism, Department of Politics and International Relations, University of Oxford.

Kempf, W. (2002). Conflict Coverage and Conflict Escalation. In W. Kempf & H. Luostarinen (Eds.), *Journalism and New World Order: Volume II. Studying War and Media*. Gothenburg: Nordicom.

Kempf, W. (2003). *Constructive Conflict Coverage: A Social Psychological Approach*. Konstaner Online-Publikations-System (KOPS). Available at https://kops.uni-konstanz.de/bitstream/handle/123456789/10220/2003_Constructive_Conflict_Coverage.pdf;sequence=1. Accessed 6 May 2019.

Kempf, W., & Reimann, M. (2002). The Presentation of Alternative Ways of Settling the Gulf Conflict in German, Norweigian and Finnish Media. In Kempf, W & Luostarinen, H (Eds.), *Journalism and the New World Order: Vol.II: Studying War and the Media* (pp. 59–72). Göteborg: Nordicom.

Knightley, P. (1975). *The First Casualty: From the Crimea to Vietnam: The War Correspondent as Hero, Propagandist, and Myth Maker*. New York: Harcourt Brace Jovanovich.

Knightley, P. (2002). *The First Casualty: The War Correspondent as Hero and Myth-Maker from the Crimea to Kosovo*. Baltimore: Johns Hopkins University Press.

Knightley, P. (2005). *The First Causality: From the Crimea to Vietnam: The War Correspondent as Hero, Propagandist and Myth Maker*. New York: Harcourt Brace Jovanovich.

Kurspahic, K. (2003). *Prime Time Crime. Balkan Media in War and Peace*. Washington DC: United States Institute of Peace.

Lewis, C. (2018). Tear Down These Walls: Innovations in Collaborative Accountability Research and Reporting. In R. Sambrook (Ed.), *Global Teamwork: The Rise of Collaboration in Investigative Journalism*. Oxford: Reuters Institute for the Study of Journalism, Department of Politics and International Relations, University of Oxford.

Lorenz, M. (2010, June). *Data Driven Journalism: What Is There to Learn?* Paper presented at the IJ-7 Innovation Journalism Conference, Stanford, CA.

Loyn, D. (2003). *Witnessing the Truth*. Open Democracy. [Online]. https://www.opendemocracy.net/en/article_993jsp/. Accessed 0218/04/2017.

Loyn, D. (2007). Good Journalism or Peace Journalism. *Conflict & Communication Online, 6*(2), 1–10.

Luostarinen, H. (2002). Journalism and Cultural Preconditions of War. In W. Kempf & H. Luostarinen (Eds.), *Journalism and the New World Order, Studying War and the Media* (pp. 273–283). Nordicom: Göteborg.

Luostarinen, H., & Ottosen, R. (2002). Propaganda and War Reporting after the Vietnam War. In W. Kempf & H. Luostarinen (Eds.), *Journalism and the New World Order, Studying War and the Media*. Gothenburg: Nordicom.

Lynch. J. (1998). The Peace Journalism Option. *Conflict and Peace Forums*. Available at http://www.globalissues.org/article/534/the-peace-journalism-option. Accessed 20 July 2019.

Lynch, J. (2005). War and Peace Journalism in the Holy Land. *Social Alternatives, 24*(1), 11–15.

Lynch, J. (2008). *Debates in Peace Journalism*. Sydney: Sydney University Press.

Lynch, J. (2014). Critical Realism, Peace Journalism and Democracy. *Ethical Space: The International Journal of Communication Ethics, 11*(1/2), 29–36.

Lynch, J., & McGoldrick, A. (2000). Peace Journalism: What It Is? How To Do It? *Transcend International: A Peace Development Environment Network*. Available at http://www.transcend.org. Accessed 5 March 2015.

Lynch, J., & McGoldrick, A. (2005). Peace Journalism: A Global Dialog for Democracy and Democratic Media. In R. A. Hackett & Y. Zhao (Eds.), *Democratizing Global Media* (pp. 269–288). Lanham: Rowman and Littlefield.

Lynch, J., & McGoldrick, A. (2007). Peace Journalism. In C. Webel & J. Galtung (Eds.), *Handbook of Peace and Conflict Studies* (pp. 248–264). London: Routledge.

Lynch, J., & McGoldrick, A. (2010). A Global Standard for Reporting Conflict and Peace. In R. L. Keeble, J. Tulloch, & F. Zollmann (Eds.), *Peace Journalism, War and Conflict Resolution* (pp. 87–104). New York: Peter Lang.

McGoldrick, A. (2006). War Journalism and "Objectivity". *Conflict and Communication, 5*(2), 1–7.

McGoldrick, A., & Lynch, J. (2000). *Peace Journalism: What Is It? How To Do It?* Available at http://www.transcend.org/tri/downloads/McGoldrick_Lynch_Peace-Journalism.pdf. Accessed 08/10/2020.

McInroy, L. B., & Craig, S. L. (2015). Transgender Representation in Offline and Online Media: LGBTQ Youth Perspectives. *Journal of Human Behavior in the Social Environment, 25*(6), 606–617.

McLaughlin, G. (2002). *The War Correspondent*. London: Pluto Press.

McNair, B. (2011). *An Introduction to Political Communication*. London: Routledge.

McNair, B. (2013). Trust, Truth and Objectivity: Sustaining Quality Journalism in the Era of the Content Generating User. In P. Chris & M. J. Broersma (Eds.), *Rethinking Journalism: Trust and Participation in a Transformed News Landscape* (pp. 75–88). London: Routledge.

Menake, G. T. (2004). *Three Traditions of Greek Political Thought: Plato in Dialogue*. Maryland: University Press of America.

Merrill, J. C. (1989) T*he Dialectic in Journalism: Towards a Responsible Use of Press Freedom*. London: Louisiana State University Press, Baton Rouge.

Nieman Reports. (2003). "Reporting on Health". VOL.57 NO.1 SPRING 2003. *The Nieman Foundation for Journalism at Harvard University* [Online]. Available at http://nieman.harvard.edu/wp-content/uploads/pod-assets/pdf/Nieman%20Reports/backissues/03spring.pdf. Accessed on 18/11/2019.

Nohrstedt, S. A. (2009). New War Journalism: Trends and Challenges. *Nordicom Review, 30*(1), 95–112.

Nohrstedt, S. A., & Ottosen, R. (Eds.). (2001). 'Journalism and the New World Order'. *Vol. I. Gulf War, National News Discourses and Globalization*. Göteborg: Nordicom.

Nohrstedt, S. A., & Ottosen, R. (2014). *New Wars, New Media and New War Journalism: Professional and Legal Challenges in Conflict Reporting*. Göteborg: Nordicom.

Papadopoulos, K. A., & Pantti, N. (2011). *Amateur Images and Global News*. Bristol: Intellect and Chicago, IL: The University of Chicago Press.

Purseigle. P. (2013). First World War Propaganda and the Tragedy of Consent. *Telegraph*, UK. 01 Nov. [Online]. https://www.telegraph.co.uk/history/world-war-one/inside-first-world-war/part-three/10417056/world-war-one-propaganda.html. Accessed 11/04/2020.

Rai, A. J. (2000). *Media at War: Issues and Limitations, Strategic Analysis*. IDSA. pp. 1681–1694. [Online]. Available from http://www.idsa-india.org/an-dec-00-6.html. Accessed on 18 March 2020.

Riegert, K. (2003). *The Image of War: Nato's Battle for Kosovo in the British Media*. Orebro: Orebro University Press.

Riley, G. B. (1998). *Censorship*. New York: Facts on File.

Rogers, S. (2008, December 18). *Turning Official Figures into Understandable Graphics, at the Press of a Button*. Inside the Guardian Blog. [Online]. https://www.theguardian.com/help/insideguardian/2008/dec/18/unemploymentdata. Accessed 12/06/2020.

Roth, M. P. (1997). *Historical Dictionary of War Journalism* (pp. XI–X). Westport, CT: Greenwood Press.

Schirch, L. (2002, March). *Human Rights and Peacebuilding: Towards Just-peace*. Paper presented to 43rd Annual International Studies Association Convention, New Orleans, Louisiana.

Schirch, L. (2008). Strategic Peacebuilding: State of the Field Peace Prints. *South Asian Journal of Peacebuilding, 1*(1), 1–17.

Schirch, L. (2013). *Conflict Assessment and Peacebuilding Planning: Toward a Participatory Approach to Human Security*. Boulder: Kumarian Press.

Shaw, I. S. (2011). 'Human Rights Journalism': A Critical Conceptual Framework of a Complementary Strand of Peace Journalism. In I. S. Shaw, J. Lynch, & R. Hackett (Eds.), *Expanding Peace Journalism: Comparative and Critical Approaches* (pp. 96–121). Sydney, NSW: Sydney University Press.

Shaw, I. S. (2012). *Human Rights Journalism: Advances in Reporting Distant Humanitarian Interventions*. New York: Palgrave Macmillan.

Shinar, D. (2009). Can Peace Journalism Make Progress? *The International Communication Gazette, 71*(6), 451–471.

Sloan, W. M. (1991). *Perspectives on Mass Communication History*. Lawrence Erlbaum Publishers.

Smyth, D. (2013). Avoiding Bloodshed? US Journalists and Censorship in Wartime. *War & Society, 32*(1), 64–94. https://doi.org/10.1179/0729247312Z.00000000017.

Sweeney, M. S. (1998). "Delays and Vexation": Jack London and the Russo-Japanese War. *Journalism & Mass Communication Quarterly, 75*(3), 548–559.

Theofilopoulos, T. (2019). *Media Reporting and Reference Guide on LGBT Issues. KMOP Social Action and Innovation Center & Colour Youth Athens LGBTQ Youth Community*. [Online]. https://www.ethos-project.eu/wp-content/uploads/2019/06/Media-reporting-and-reference-guide-on-LGBT-issues.pdf. Accessed 7/10/2020.

Thomas, A., Jakubowicz, A., & Norman, H. (2020, March 15). Condescending and Disempowering, Australia's Media Have Systematically Thwarted Aboriginal Aspirations. *The Guardian*. [Online]. https://www.theguardian.com/commentisfree/2020/mar/16/how-the-media-fails-aboriginal-aspirations. Accessed 14/06/2020.

Tuchman, G. (1972). Objectivity As Strategic Ritual: An Examination of Newsmen's Notions of Objectivity. *The American Journal of Sociology, 77*(4), 660–679.

Tumber, H., & Prentoulis, M. (2003). Journalists Under Fire: Subcultures, Objectivity and Emotional Literacy. In D. K. Thussu & D. Freedman (Eds.), *War and the Media* (pp. 216–29). London: Sage.

van Eeden-Moorefield, B., Few-Demo, A. L., Benson, K., Bible, J., & Lummer, S. A. (2017). Content analysis of LGBT research in top family journals 2000–2015. *Journal of Family Issues, 2018*(39), 1374–1395. https://doi.org/10.1177/0192513X17710284.

Webel, C., & Galtung, J. (2007). *Handbook of Peace and Conflict Studies*. London: Routledge.

Williams, K. (1992). Something More Important Than Truth: Ethical Issues in War Reporting. In A. Besley & R. Chadwick (Eds.), *Ethical Issues in Journalism and the Media* (pp. 159–162). London: Routhledge.

Zerrouki, Y. (2012, January 29). The Illusionist Hegemony of Political Propaganda. *Morocco World News*. Available at http://moroccoworldnews.com/2012/01/24874/the-illusionist-hegemony-of-politicalpropaganda/. Accessed 10 June 2018.

CHAPTER 3

Human Rights Journalism: Tracing Its Epistemological Foundation

3.1 Introduction

Media, as an entity, holds the extreme power of influencing the issues that plague people. But with this power, comes the massive responsibility of utilising their role in a constructive manner for the societal good, instead of becoming a part of the problem. Media practices centred around the concept of 'Committed Journalism', which is based on democracy, free choice, openness, morality, and working towards common good, is a way to materialise accountability and responsibility (Lusgarten and Debrix 2005, p. 365). This is the construct which emphasises the media's responsibility to promote and protect human rights. The media's role of uncovering and exposing misconducts like human rights violations or corruptions, is also connoted through its 'watchdog' and 'investigative' roles (De Burgh 2000). Mass media holds the means and the power to bring to light issues of human rights infringements, and its failure to achieve that may adversely impact public perceptions (Heinze and Freedman 2010).

A part of this chapter is a revised and expanded version of the chapter 'Human Rights Journalism: Towards a Critical Constructivist Epistemological Approach', which I co-authored with Ibrahim Seaga Shaw and included in our edited volume 'Reporting Human Rights, Conflicts, and Peacebuilding: Critical and Global Perspectives', published by Palgrave Macmillan.

S. Selvarajah, *Human Rights Journalism and its Nexus to Responsibility to Protect*, https://doi.org/10.1007/978-3-030-49072-0_3

Despite thorough theoretical understanding, a large part of the media fails to perform its expected responsible role optimally. Media covers human rights issues abysmally and selectively, often only subjectively covering human rights violations in a conflict situation. When they do cover these issues, the focus is largely on political and civil rights, while they ignore problems concerning economic, social and cultural rights for most part (Pollock 2014). Media are capable of educating its audience about such rights and continually keep aware of such violations, while also alerting the international community about these violations. Instead, media does not try to delve into the issues when they do occur, but reports them in a superficial manner. As Downman and Ubayasiri (2017, p. 2) underline, in order to advocate human rights and social change, media has to involve a combination of advocacy and objectivity, but these 'two concepts are not mutually exclusive'. While the former requires a proactive style of reporting, the latter demands the complete absence of subjectivity.

Therefore, media does not proactively contribute in crisis situations. This was evident from the previous chapter, where we discussed how the conventional war journalism fails in covering events in a human rights oriented approach to bring about a positive social change. We have also noted the constraints that this fraternity holds with respect to fulfilling its responsibilities which include promoting and protecting human rights and peace; yet there is increasing research suggesting the contrary—that this role is biased, violence-oriented, propaganda-oriented, elite-oriented and victory-oriented (Lynch and McGoldrick 2005). Journalists do not give context or adequate information, and do not conduct regular follow-ups, leaving the audiences practically uninformed about an event. Their ignorance towards their moral responsibilities is blatant, as they are failing to increase awareness about the rights of the individuals, while monitoring, investigating and reporting such violations. Media's responsibility of promoting and protecting was put forth in the 1990s and 2000s and was conceptualised around the philosophical foundations of free speech and exposing human rights abuses. This concept developed with time, and when coupled with Human Rights Journalism (HRJ) approach is a powerful tool to promote and protect human rights and peace in times of crisis. This mechanism can also help empower the groups that have been marginalised, when brought under the 'just peace' framework. HRJ, theorised by Shaw (2012), tries to find a holistic approach, thereby including both the First Generation of the civil and political rights and the Second

Generation of social, economic and cultural rights, which are the twin covenants of the UN Universal Declaration of Human Rights.

The conceptualisation of HRJ is on the basis of the reporting of 'physical, structural and cultural violence within the context of humanitarian intervention'. It aims to promote four aspects: (1) 'the understanding of the human rights-based approach to journalism', (2) the responsibility of journalists to connect people across borders; (3) public knowledge of human rights, and (4) the journalistic 'moral responsibility' and 'duty' which encompasses educating the public about their rights and monitoring, investigating and reporting all human rights violations' (ibid., p. 2). Therefore, HRJ aims to push journalists to undertake a more proactive role for the human race, and to not be restricted by borders, race, age, gender and class.

Though Shaw's (2012) book defined the conceptual framework for the theory of HRJ, it could not fill the epistemological gap concerning its feasibility, exercise and power. This chapter, therefore, aims to address these shortcoming and also provide ways in which the theory can be developed. Since journalists pursue 'truth' as their ultimate goal, this chapter argues HRJ is a viable journalistic practice within the critical constructivist epistemology, as it relies on the journalist's intellect being their source of understanding the issues and uncovering the truth.

This chapter is divided into four parts: The first part pertains to media and human rights, including media's power and ability to protect and promote human rights and prevent mass atrocities. The second part shines the spotlight on the agenda setting theory to understand the mechanism in which the media can pursue a human rights agenda in time of crisis situations. The third part explains the concept of HRJ highlighted its proactive role of HRJ as a watchdog of human rights violations and the nexus between HRJ and the theory of spectatorship of suffering to understand these theories in each others' lights. The fourth part justifies the epistemological grounding of HRJ within the critical constructivist framework.

3.2 Human Rights and Media

Although the Second World War resulted in formally establishing the Universal Declaration of Human Rights (hereafter UDHR) in 1948, the history of human rights goes back to many centuries ago. We can see utterances of human rights in the religious teachings and literature such as Manu Dharma Shastra of Hindu religion (emphasises justice), Buddhist philosophy dhamma/dharma (recognises equality), Old Testament of Judaism (underlines responsibility towards others), New Testament of Jesus Christ (stresses the duty towards marginalised) and Quran of Islamic religion (emphasises equality). All of them highlight the notions of people's duties, rights, and responsibilities, which became intrinsic to the modern human rights framework.

As Sampaio-Dias (2016) remarks, religions have remarkably contributed to the evolution and development of international human rights framework. They have helped determine the standards and ideals of human dignity and have inspired and empowered the human rights movement around the world. They have also played a greater role in shaping the concept of responsibility towards humanity by developing moral obligation and normative beliefs towards all.

Naturally, all societies have had systems of propriety and justice and ways of tending to the health and welfare of their members, even if some did not have it in writing. According to philosophers, human rights existed in a state of nature. Natural law suggests that individuals have intrinsic rights based on their humankind as opposed to it being a divine gift. Hobbes recognised that all human beings have natural liberty as well as equality, on the basis of which they are licensed to undertake whatever actions might be necessary to preserve themselves from their fellow creatures. To prevent a war of all against all in the 'state of nature', Hobbes argued that there should be a system of coercion—'the creation of a strong state with untrammelled authority' to provide 'sanctions against the abuse of trust, and create a climate for mutually beneficial co-operation' (cited in Dunleavy and O'Leary 1987, p. 84). John Locke conceptualised human rights as natural and inalienable and believed in a natural right to life, liberty, and property (Savirimuthu 2013).

Within the current international world system, as Baehr (1999) describes, human rights are a set of rules, values and standards agreed upon internationally in order to regulate the use of the states' power, concerning both their citizens and non-citizens. This concept also holds the government responsible for protecting their citizens from all kinds of violations and restricts them from misusing their power to infringe on peoples' rights. The 1948 Universal Declaration on human rights (UDHR) is a broadly accepted definition of human rights, and holistically includes civil and political on the one hand and economic, social, and cultural on the other. This declaration (Preamble 1948) begins with the recognition of 'the inherent dignity and of the equal and inalienable rights of all members of the human family is the foundation of freedom, justice and peace in the world'. The principles of universality, inalienability, indivisibility, and equality are the cornerstones of international human rights law. These principles have been emphasised in various international human rights conventions, declarations, and resolutions since the declaration of UDHR.

Within the context of UDHR, Donnelly (1998, p. 18) defines human rights as those 'held by all human beings, irrespective of any rights or duties individuals may (or may not) have as citizens, members of families, workers, or parts of any public or private organisation or association. They are universal rights'. This definition highlights that human rights apply to all people in all states.

Article 1 of the UDHR embraces the freedom and equality of all human beings, in terms of dignity and rights. Article 2 targets discrimination by stating that everyone is entitled to the aforementioned rights and freedoms without any distinction on the basis of race, colour, sex, language, religion, political or other opinion, national or social origin, property, birth or other status (United Nations 1948). The civil and political rights, which aim to protect individuals from the interference or abuse by a third party, are called the first generation of rights—these rights are based on liberty. It also promotes a society where its members can exercise their full potential without any restrictions. It includes, for example, the right to life, freedom from torture and ill-treatment, freedom from slavery, the right to liberty, a fair trial, respect for privacy and freedom of religion, expression, and assembly and association (Weston 1992; Claude and Weston 2006).

Social, economic and cultural rights are called second generation of rights, focusing on the welfare of the people, as individuals and communities—these are based on equality. They mainly focus on aspects such as right to social security, right to work and protection against unemployment, right to rest and leisure including periodic holidays with pay, right to standard of living adequate for good health and well-being of self and family, right to education, right to protection of one's scientific, literary and artistic production, right to free choice of employment, right to form and join trade unions, right to freely participate in the cultural life of the community and right to food (ibid.; Cismas 2004).

Globalisation facilitated by developments in technology and communication in the recent decades, led to the addition of the third generation of human rights. This is also called collective rights based on solidarity, such as right to political, economic, social and cultural self-determination, right to economic and social development, right to participate in and benefit from the common heritage of mankind, right to peace, right to healthy and balanced environment and right to humanitarian disaster relief (ibid.; Wellman 2000). Nevertheless, there is some debate as to whether this categorisation is conceptually appropriate. As Donelly (1989) underlines, the third generation of human rights are inconsistent with the idea of human rights, as they are based on solidarity rather than human dignity, which serves as the basis for the first two generations of human rights. Emerging post-colonial states support this new generation of human rights alleging that Western values mostly embrace individual civil and political rights, whereas the cultural and religious traditions of the third world countries favour the welfare of groups (Sampaio-Dias 2016). These rights are mostly found in agreements classified as 'soft law'. An example is the 1992 Rio Declaration on Environment and Development.

While the scholarly debate on the evolution of human rights continues, new international laws, covenants and declarations continue to be enacted and policies are adopted to strengthen the human rights framework and their implementation. Thus, both in public policy and public opinion, the human rights issues have become more important today, pushing the media to become a responsible social institution, enhancing the human rights regimes and looking more carefully into the issues while reporting.

Media's role is not limited to preserving human rights, but also involves finding out the causes of violations and conceiving ways and means to prevent abuses. The media's watchdog role comes into play here, as it could safeguard the people against human rights violations by exposing infringements and also by creating awareness on the subject human rights issues among the general public. Media must analyse incidents and issues relating to human rights, and disseminate information including both violations and their causes to create discourse of human rights education. In this way, media can help set up an acceptable standard of human rights practices within which the society has to operate (ICHRP 2002; Shaw and Selvarajah 2019a, b).

According to studies, although media's attention to human rights issues has increased tremendously over the years, their reporting has been largely descriptive, and thus fails to analyse and mitigate the underlying causes leading to the human rights violations. Instead, as some scholars claim, this dysfunctional coverage of the media often becomes a part of the problem (Cole 2010; Ron et al. 2005). According to Cole (ibid., p. 306), in a repressive country where there is a lack of accurate and verifiable information about atrocities being committed, media reporting tends to create a negative impact on the situation by enabling repressive countries to garner the most attention. This situation is regarded as 'information paradox'. To quote Cole, 'Lack of information regarding a country's practices can distort its human rights record, producing a more anodyne perception than is warranted. As the availability and accuracy of information increases, abuses that were once concealed come to light; consequently, evaluations of a country's human rights practices can worsen even if actual levels of repression and abuse remain constant'. A study by Ron, Ramos, and Rodgers also sheds light on the tendency of the human rights organisations such as Amnesty International to focus their attention in countries where there is already an increased media attention on the human rights violations. This highlights the fact that impact is most noticeable in places where abuses are moderate but not severe, in smaller countries, and in places where the press already have interest (Ron et al. 2005; Ramos et al. 2007).

Selvarajah (2016), in his study of the local media coverage of the civil war in Sri Lanka, finds a similar 'information paradox effect' given the highly oppressive nature of the regime. However, his findings expose other local factors that cause the media to play such a problematic role: ethnic interest, interest of ownership, political party affiliations, language and lack of professionalism. He stressed on the fact that restricted media freedom was never the primary reason for journalists' underplaying their role of increasing awareness of the people regarding their rights and monitoring, investigating and reporting all human rights violations without any bias. The functional connection of the communicative process of the Sri Lankan media in the construction of threat image has been dysfunctional, particularly caused by the superseding influence of *ethnic factor* and contributing to create crisis tendencies, and thereby playing a negative role in the ethnic conflict. However, Selvarajah's (2019, p. 16) recent comparative study of the local media coverage of the conflicts in Sri Lanka and Nepal, differentiates the behaviour of the media's reporting of the human rights issues in terms of the shared and unshared media culture of these countries. In Sri Lanka, it is an ethnic conflict, whereas in Nepal, it is a political conflict.

> Due to the nature of this identity-based "ethnic conflict", the Sri Lankan media operation has built-in a mutually influencing exclusive "media-audience" relationship bonded by ethnicity and language, creating an unshared media culture. This unshared media culture negatively impacts on the conflict in Sri Lanka. In contrast, in Nepal, the political conflict is based on inequalities in living standards and access to resources among various groups of people with a common political understanding among them. There are no divisions in the media in terms of ethnicity and language, which thereby builds a shared media culture, which in turn plays a constructive role in the conflict.

In the case of industrial journalism, profit becomes the driver of all media ventures instead of any particular set of moral values. Profitability requires a good market position, which is influenced by targeting a particular set of audiences/segmented audiences. Therefore, Economic factors weigh heavily on many media organisation nowadays. Hanitzsch (2007a, b) sees the 'marketplace of attention' as central to the operation of the mainstream media. In addition to this, to explain why conventional war journalism has gravitated towards war and sensationalism rather than focus on protecting and promoting human rights and peace, a number of factors were identified in the pervious chapter, including the nature of news values, the relationship of journalism to power, the dependence on news sources and the language used to describe war.

What is considered as important in the news production today is the 'News Value', and how quickly it gets connected to the reader. As Balabanova described 'Pressures to attract reader/viewer interest and to respond to the most topical and controversial issues are powerful considerations. Today's media has a clear preference for stories that are relatively simple, graphically compelling and easily photographable' (2015, p. 32). This justifies Galtung and Ruge's claims, in their groundbreaking study 'The Structure of Foreign News' (1965), that news reporting is no longer an organic process, but is dependent on cultural factors. They believe that, even if news selection varies based on news value, there is not much difference as news selection is based on the 'Human Culture'. Galtung and Ruge (ibid.) identified twelve news values which prioritises a news story over others: frequency, threshold, unambiguity, meaningfulness, consonance, unexpectedness, continuity, composition, reference to the elite nations, and reference to the elite people, personalisation and negativity. Many scholars have added on to that list with time (McGregor 2002; Harcup and O' Neill 2001): Cultural Proximity; Relevance; Rarity;

Continuity; Elite References; Negativity; Composition; Personalisation. Galtung later announced infotainment as the 13th news value, apart from those mentioned by him and Ruge.

Despite these constraints, underperformance and deficiencies, media scholars emphasise on media's capacity to pursue a human rights approach on various aspects like education, protection and promotion of human rights, foreign policy changes (Berry and McChesney 1988) along with its ability to influence public opinion who can in turn impact the decisions of the policymakers and Members of the Parliament to consider human rights in their foreign policymaking (Gilboa 2005; Cottle 2017, 2019; Wolfsfeld 1997; Robinson 2013; Pollock 2014). Studies throw light upon media's ability to go beyond the interests of elites to empower the interests of the most 'vulnerable' people (Pollock 2014). Downman and Ubayasiri (2017) stress on the idea that journalism should focus on creating social change, and if the media focuses its attention on people within the human rights framework, it may instigate positive social change. This emphasises on the principle that profitability must not be considered while reporting news when human lives are at stake, and the focus must instead be on protecting public interest. This will enable information and knowledge to serve as instruments of human rights.

Downman and Ubayasiri (Ibid.) have proposed the concept of 'human-focussed' news values to create an opportunity to rethink the way the stories are told, as opposed to Galtung and Rug's events-based news values theory such as consonance, meaningfulness and unambiguity. Human-focused news values place the subject of the stories at the forefront of the news production process. As Downman and Ubayasiri (ibid., pp. 26–27) remark, it 'relates directly to the way the person, or people, telling the story are represented and framed within the storytelling process. This is a significant change, given that news attracts and captures an audience because people are interested in the lives of other people'.

Human Rights reporting provides an opportunity to rewrite the way journalism works. This change is not just focused on the way in which the stories are written and produced, but centres around the journalist, their motivation to join this field, and the method they use to acquire information which becomes the foundation of their news reporting (ibid.). Human rights journalism does not include merely reporting facts about human rights violation, protection, and promotion. Instead, it is an analysis developed by a journalist who willingly understands and addressing the visible and underlying narratives which have shaped the event.

The protection and promotion of human rights through the media are embedded in two international human rights documents: Article 19 of the UDHR 2 and Article 19 (2) of the ICCPR. These articles form the basis of expectations from media such as uncovering human rights violations, uniting human rights organisations, and exposing the activities of the government, among others (Balabanova 2015, p. 35).

The only way human rights can be respected, is if all the stakeholders are aware of them. This increases the spectrum of responsibilities of the journalists, as they are obligated to educate people about human rights matters so informed decisions are taken in relation to these issues. Anderson (2007, p. 43) therefore proposed that free media with quality journalists is essential enlighten citizens with accurate and thorough information, so they can actively participate in the social and political happenings.

The mere knowledge of human rights violations can enlighten and consequently empower the policymakers. Conversely, media are able to fulfil its responsibility by setting an agenda that begins deliberations over human rights violations. The method of reporting influences the frequency of thinking by the public over that issue dictating what they believe is important. This coverage is often done selectively, thereby shaping the public opinion and setting agenda (McCombs 2003; Pan and Kosicki 1993; Scheufele 1999; Manheim and Albriton 1984; Love 2008). This is heavily dependent on the extent of quantitative and qualitative news coverage. An important point to remember is that, it is not just the reporting of human rights issues that sets the agenda, but also the way in which the issue is covered (Balabanova 2015, pp. 36–37).

This is where the nexus between framing a news event and agenda setting is demonstrated. Framing is not the only factor affecting the agenda, as the frequency of coverage of an issue also determines its importance. For example, in newspapers, there is ample difference in the attention a front page headline news with photographs garners, in comparison to a story published in the inside pages. Therefore, media decides the importance of a news taking into consideration the worth of a news story based on various contexts and factors. Keck and Sikkink

(1998) in their study of 'Networked Advocacy' describe this as 'Information Politics', where networks gather credible and politically acceptable information quickly.

With the rise in information technology, 'Information Politics' has become an integral part of the world, wherein when media exposes human rights violations of any country, it will create problems for the country in question. When the information garners attention from the international community, the country is subjected to pressures by human rights organisations and diplomatic interventions. Informed civil society organisations and human rights organisations also begin to create unfavourable situations for the government or to those who engage in human rights violations (Balabanova 2015, p. 38).

Ovsiovitch (1993), further emphasised on its importance, as documentation of human rights violations by the media, can also be used by human rights organisation to seek help from the international community and create a global movement. News reports, as Ovsiovitch, emphasises can be used as an informal means of documenting abuses, and they have the power to shape public opinion and influence the development of foreign policy.

Mutua (2007) and Dhir (2007) further add to this idea, stating that the broadcasting of information about human rights violations, by human rights organisations and non-government organisations such as, such as Amnesty International and Human Rights Watch can even draw the attention of media, thereby implicitly becoming a part of the agenda-setting process. According to Mutua (ibid.), media's focus of a specific event may be a determinant of its prioritisation within the UN circles. One striking example which he provides is the media coverage of the Yugoslav and Rwanda genocides in the first half of the 1990s. This media focus resulted in powerful countries forming war crimes tribunals. These instances also led to the establishment of certain standards related to international criminal law, universal jurisdiction, war crimes, genocide, rape and crimes against humanity.

Against this backdrop, a key concept emerging from the discussion is the concept of 'CNN effect', which according to Robinson 'encapsulated the idea that real-time communications technology could provoke major responses from domestic audiences and political elites to global events' (Robinson 1999, p. 301). The media coverage of Kurdish crisis in Northern Iraq in 1991, enabled humanitarian intervention which was legitimated by UN, creating 'safe havens' to protect Kurds. In 1992, the media coverage of famine conditions in Somalia during the civil war which threatened one-fourth of its population, and whose distribution of humanitarian aid was prevented by rival warlords, prompted President George Bush (Snr) to send a military mission to save Somali people (Robinson 2013). Media, therefore, holds the power to influence foreign policy decision-making during mass atrocities. The 'CNN effect' underlines this power that the media has in setting people's agenda.

According to Livingston and Eachus the CNN effect, 'is about a presumed shift in power away from the foreign policy machinery of government to a more diffuse array of nongovernmental actors, primarily news media organisations' (1995, p. 415). The validity of the CNN effect theory has been actively debated among scholars. Edward Herman and Noam Chomsky, in 'Manufacturing Consent: The Political Economy of the Mass Media', explain the influence tactics the ruling elite use on media to keep the mass public in conformity with their policies through propaganda, due to the common circles, values, and interests of the ruling elite and decision-makers (Herman and Chomsky 1988). In their propaganda model, they have laid out the institutional realities, professional routines and ideologies shaping journalism practices. This model explains the systematic process of propaganda in the media, which shapes the minds of people, their sentiments, feelings and behaviours to gain their support in favour of the aims promoted by propagandists. Yet, some scholars such as Dan Hallin and Michael Schudson rejected the arguments of Herman and Chomsky, saying that their reasoning to political economic approach is of limited value (Hallin 1994; Schudson 1995).

However, ITN News Service's Diplomatic Editor Nik Gowing (1994), in his study, found cosmetic effect of media power in setting agenda with regard to foreign policy during crisis situations, particularly creating tactical decisions such as safe areas. A Study of Livingston and Eachus (1995) underlines the media's behaviour of reflecting the views of policymakers, as opposed to CNN effect.

Meanwhile, Robinson's Policy-Media Interaction model depicts media's potential influence in times when the policy remains uncertain during humanitarian crises, through its coverage of human sufferings and critical reporting (Robinson 2000). Hitherto, his theory doesn't reject the power of media to influence policy response even when a policy is certain.

In general, studies conducted with regard to the CNN effect argue that the influence of media over foreign policy during crisis situations is uncertain and is dependent on the political circumstances within which the media functions. As Robinson (2013) explains, realpolitik calculations and boomerang effects such as the concerns of the so-called 'body bag effect' primarily determine these political conditions.

Livingston (1997) found that the policies not concerning military dimension, come with lower political risks and costs, and are therefore more likely to be influenced by media pressure. Van Belle (2009) also underline the potential media power of conditioning non-coercive interventions and aiding distribution as opposed to coercive interventions to fix humanitarian crisis.

Wolfsfeld (1997) developed 'Political contest model' of the media, in which he argued that though the news media typically reflects and garners support for dominant views in the society, at times it does fulfil the needs of the marginalised communities. For him, the interaction between media and polity is a cycle, in which changes in the political environment lead to changes in media performance, which further influence the political environment.

Martin Shaw in his theoretical construct of 'global society' in 1999, identified media's capacity to actively represent the victims of violence and being part of the 'global voice'. He further argued that such a representation with potential leverage of shaping the policymaking seldom happens (Shaw 1999). Hoijer in her study of 'Global compassion' identified similar effects of media in its representation of distance sufferings. Her study, though highlighted media's capacity to create global compassion for mass atrocity crimes, also underlined the impotence of such compassion in making the audience active with strong moral commitment. Thus, her research highlights the effect of 'fathomless distance' in media's representation of victims to influence policy decisions (Höijer, 2004).

Chouliaraki, through her study of hierarchical typology, sheds light on the potential media power to create 'cosmopolitan spectatorship' in which, coverage of distance suffering invites audiences to proactively act on conditions of human existence, beyond their own communities of belonging (Chouliaraki 2008). Her study of hierarchical typology of news stories consists of adventure (news that blocks feelings of pity), emergency (news that produces a demand for action) and ecstatic news (news that manages to bring the globe together), based on two broad ethical norms: communitarianism and cosmopolitanism. The process of communitarianism influences the spectator to respond to the suffering that is relevant and proximate to the community to which the spectator imagines themselves to belong. Conversely, cosmopolitanism influences the spectator to respond to the suffering on behalf of 'others', who are not seemingly a part of their own community (Chouliaraki 2006, 2008). Boltanski (1999) is also of the view that mediated distance suffering can go beyond the role of passive voyeur and enter the realm of creating actual political action.

Chouliaraki (2013, p. 2) later found changes in the communication of unity with vulnerable others and exposes the West's transformation into an 'ironic spectator', understood as 'an impure or ambivalent figure that stands, at once, as sceptical towards any moral appeal of solidary action and, yet, open to doing something about those who suffer'. She also argues that there has been a shift from objective representation of suffering, which views that the suffering is distinct from us and requires our contemplation regarding the condition of distant others. The shift has been towards a more subjective representation, which views suffering as inseparable from our own 'truths' and therefore requires contemplation of our own conditions. Therefore, the ethics of pity changed to an ethics of irony (Chouliaraki 2013, p. 3). Thus, Chouliaraki determines the rise of a novel solidarity and rationality, which is separate from the 'other-oriented morality', but is instead a 'self-oriented morality', where doing good to others is centred on how it makes us feel.

This highlights some scholars' pessimism regarding the effectiveness of the mediated distance sufferings, such as Moeller's (1999) warning of 'Compassion Fatigue', which can be caused by the increased exposure to images of suffering of human rights violations and Höijer's (2004), 'distantiation from compassion', instead of feelings of empathy.

As Tester defines (2001, p. 13), compassion fatigue is 'becoming so used to the spectacle of dreadful events, misery or suffering that we stop noticing them ... We are bored', and can lead 'to the conclusion that this is just the way things are and nothing can be done that will make a difference'. In other words, over-exposure to distance suffering through media affects audience's ability to be empathetic.

In other words, various scholars' research findings with regard to the coverage of distance suffering, denote variation in both nature and the consequences of the agenda-setting mechanism of the news media. This aids us in understanding the relationship between the factors associated with the agenda setting process, and the nature of the media coverage of the distant suffering.

It is important to discuss the agenda-setting mechanism that will be instrumental in understanding the case study examples presented in the later chapters which revolve around the practice of HRJ in the Sri Lankan humanitarian crisis reporting in the international media and its agenda-setting effect with the R2P framework.

3.3 Media's Agenda-Setting Role

The concept of agenda setting was first coined by Walter Lippmann in 1922 in his book titled 'Public Opinion' (Lippmann 1922, pp. 9–16). Lippman believed media has the power to create pictures of world issues in peoples' mind, and therefore people react not to the actual issues but to the pictures of the issues created by the media. His concept was later developed and elaborated by McCombs and Shaw in their ground-breaking study of agenda setting (McCombs and Shaw 1972). Their study on the US presidential campaign of 1968 found media's ability to influence the views of the voters who significantly relied on media for information, to form their opinions.

Dearing and Rogers in their (1996) 'Agenda-Setting' identified three phases of agenda setting: media agenda, public agenda and policy agenda. Media agenda refers to the issues and topics that are reported in the media. In the media agenda setting, journalists act as the agenda setters directly or indirectly with their power of deciding what to report and at what level. Public agenda is about the issues discussed in the media and their interaction with the pre-existing ideas of the public, to further influence their thinking. The policy agenda is about the issues that are important to the policymakers, where a 'persuasive communication effect' is produced out of the interaction between the media and public enabling the public to have an impact on policymakers (Littlejohn 2002).

Coleman et al. (2009, p. 147), define agenda-setting as 'the process of the mass media presenting certain issues frequently and prominently with the result that large segments of the public come to perceive those issues as more important than others. The more coverage an issue receives, the more important it is to people'. This definition shows that the frequency of the coverage of an issue or event by the news media, will influence the audiences' cognisance of the importance of that issue or event (Weaver et al. 2004). This means, in the case of a humanitarian crisis, media agenda setting initiates a process where distant suffering of mass atrocities is transferred from the phase of the media agenda to the public agenda, and eventually the public agenda effects the policy agenda.

3.3.1 First Level and Second Level Agenda Setting

The transfer of salience of issues or events is an important concept in the process of setting media agenda and public agenda. Kiousis (2004) identifies two characteristics that make media prominent: external (visibility) and internal (valence). Visibility of a news story is measured by the number of news stories published and their prominence. Therefore, while analysing the role of visibility, one should take into account the number of news stories published on that issue, as well as the prominence of that news, such as the positioning of the story, size of the headline, and length of the news content in the newspaper/television/radio. Meanwhile, valence is about analysing the difference of opinion regarding a news story in terms of its overall positive or negative attribution. For example, attributes related to a non-state actor in a civil war in a news story can be either good or evil in terms of stereotyping of terrorism. These two kinds of 'transfer of salience' are also known as first level (visibility) agenda setting and second level (valence) agenda setting, respectively.

The 'transfer of salience' through the two levels of agenda setting enables the prominent features of the media agenda, to become a permanent part of the public agenda gradually, where media not only conditions its audiences regarding what to think about, but also influences the audiences' thoughts and opinions about the issues. This highlights media's ability to activate audience's knowledge and enable them to process the agenda-setting effect. This knowledge activation of the audience in response to media information serves as the key for the agenda setting effect. In other words, this is a cognitive process in which the media's ability, which stems from its information and opinion-forming function, changes audiences' thinking this is called 'agenda-setting effect' (McCombs and Shaw 1972).

Media's transfer of salience can influence an individual's conscious decisions concerning exerting effort to engage in a particular behaviour. This operates on the persuasive theory of 'Planned Behaviour' (Ajzen 2002; Ajzen et al. 2004), which emphasises on the importance individuals place on evaluating information within their reach, before making logical decisions which are reflected on their behaviour. An individual's effort in engaging in such behaviour and their control over it (behavioural control) dictates if they actually engage in such behaviour (Ajzen 2002). Media plays an influential role in guiding the behaviour of an individual.

Ajzen (ibid.) further explains that various factors like an individual's attitude towards a behaviour, subjective norm, and their view over their control over such behaviour, directly impacts their intention to produce such behaviour. Behavioural control is influenced by an individual's impression regarding the difficulty of engaging in a behaviour, and therefore runs parallel to self-efficacy. A person's behavioural intention will be stronger if there is greater perceived control over that action, and a person's attitude towards such behaviour and subjective norms are favourable. Further, if an opportunity to produce a behaviour arises, and the actual control of people over such behaviour is adequate, they will be expected to perform it. Therefore, media's ability to be convincing along with its ubiquity can alter an individual's perception of control, consequently influencing their behaviour with regarding to an event or issue. This significantly underlines the principle of media's agenda setting through the transfer of salience.

The transfer of salience from media's agenda to the general public, significantly shaping their perceived reality of an event or issue (public agenda), is explained and distinguished by two concepts: accessibility and applicability (Price and Tewksbury 1997).

3.3.2 *Accessibility and Applicability*

Agenda setting is built on the concept of accessibility (ibid.). Accessibility is related to a process called 'priming', in which media draws attention of the audiences to certain issues while ignoring others (agenda-setting component). In this way, media makes audiences' tendency to recognise the prominence of an issue or an event as a representation of a theme or issue (McCombs 2005). This falls under the first level (visibility) agenda-setting process, because it conditions the audiences about 'what to think about', in terms of the salience of issues or events reported in the media.

Agenda-setting effect does not occur as a result of occasional media coverage of an issue, but it occurs due to sustained and widespread media coverage. Media, through its agenda-setting ability, greatly impacts peoples' opinions and thinking regarding an issue as well as their perception about what other people are thinking, and thus makes them focus their attention towards an issue that is covered more frequently and predominantly (Iyengar 1990). Accessibility level of an issue is determined based on the way in which the news sources are handled, which in turn dictates the 'agenda setting effect' (Price and Tewksbury 1997). In other words, accessibility is the extent of information provided to an individual about an issue or an event through the news sources. For example, the power of official sources to influence the news agenda has increased substantially with the decline in foreign bureaus and specialist correspondents. That is because, in situations of internal conflicts, international media tend to rely on elite sources and government officers for their news reporting (McLaughlin 2002, p. 187). The military is a powerful institution in any society, particularly when compared to peace organisations. Huge resources keep the war culture and military machinery active (such as through propaganda and public relations, as well as through war movies, war games, and military museums). This shows the power of the news sources in establishing the accessibility effect in the agenda setting.

According to Higgins (1996), people tend to make social judgements based on the information available and accessible at that time instead of engaging with a cognitive form of knowledge. This highlights the power that news media holds in influencing both thinking and the judgement of the people regarding an issue, because media are a highly prevalent and hence an accessible source of information. Thus, the frequency of an issue that is covered by media to activate one's cognitive capabilities, is central to creating this accessibility effect of agenda setting (Kim et al. 2002, p. 9). This means that the consumers of media make decisions and judgements on issues, not only on the basis of the information which is easily available, but also from the interrelated information stored in their memory (Iyengar 1990).

In contrast, the concept of applicability explains the nexus between the attributes of a reported issue and an audience's stored ideas or knowledge (Price and Tewksbury 1997). It refers to the perceptive interrelation an individual makes between concepts. For example, if an individual perceives that a global challenge (i.e. Islamophobia) is a result of a particular concept (i.e. threat image construction), then that individual believes that the concept of threat image construction about Muslims in the media is related to the concept of Islamophobia. This is referred to as 'framing effect'. Therefore, framing is built on the concept of applicability and regarded as an extension of the agenda setting process. On the other hand, this falls under the second level (valence) of agenda setting as the second level agenda-setting focuses on media's function of effecting the audiences to influence 'how to think about' an issue or event. This is primarily a cognitive process, in which the attributes ascribed in the media content become more salient in the minds of the audiences to influence their opinion-making and perceptions. Framing refers to the application of an individual's precursory information to associate with the attributes present in the news content to judge an issue or event (Kim et al. 2002).

As Gamson (1989) describes, facts sustain their neutrality until framed. He argues that facts have no intrinsic meaning until they are set within a frame or a narrative. Certain facts are organised by the frames in a conscious or an unconscious manner, and as a result they attain a sense of coherence and get highlighted over other facts. This shows how framing of an issue in media reporting highlights certain aspects of an issue or an event to draw the attention of the people, by evoking thoughts and feelings consistent with the pre-existing information retained in an individual's memory. This draws a parallel to how certain attributes in media content are accentuated to have an effect among the public in the second level agenda setting (Kim et al. 2011, 2012). In this context, framing and the second level of agenda setting are two sides of the same coin, and thus both models could be integrated (McCombs et al. 1997).

3.4 Human Rights Journalism (HRJ)

In the sections above, the influence and the power of the media to protect and promote human rights and pursue a human rights agenda have been highlighted. Yet, there have been many instances, wherein the media failed to play an active role in preventing mass atrocities and human rights abuses, the causes of which, have been stated above. The primary reason is the journalists' need to attain objectivity in their practices, which often leads to them remaining impartial in situations which require individuals to take a stand. It is to combat this issue that alternative models such as 'Human Rights journalism (HRJ)' have attracted the attention of the media industry.

Shaw (2012), in his book, argues that journalists have the moral obligation to educate the public monitor, investigate, and report all human rights violations. He further states that a journalist's duty is not just to report about the issues, but also connect people from across borders and improve public knowledge. The importance of HRJ is its holistic approach which is centred on both negative peace (the absence of direct violence) and positive peace (peace brought about by peaceful means, sustainability and justice, eliminating the underlying causes of violence). It also focuses on positive rights and negative rights, informed by Article 1 of the Universal Declaration of Human Rights (1948), which declares: 'all human beings are born free and equal in dignity and rights. As highlighted already, this is what Downman and Ubayasiri (2017) call journalism for social change. They stress on the importance of positioning this journalism as a framework for human rights reporting.

In this premise, to introduce the definition (Shaw 2012, p. 46), HRJ is

> A diagnostic style of reporting, which gives a critical reflection on the experiences and needs of the victims and perpetrators of human rights violations of all types – physical as well as cultural and structural – in order to stimulate understanding of the reasons for these violations and to prevent or solve them in ways that would not produce more human rights imbalances or violations in the future. Moreover, it is a journalism that challenges, not reinforces, the status quo of the powerful dominant voices of society against the weak and marginalised ones in the promotion and protection of human rights and peace.

In terms of 'diagnostic style', this is supported by Galtung's (1996) Diagnosis-Prognosis-Therapy triangle. Galtung (1996) argues that violence in any conflict, must be dealt with in a manner similar to health studies, and should first be diagnosed before any action is taken. As Shaw (2012) elaborates, diagnostic style of reporting demands journalists to critically diagnose the type of violence and the causes for its occurrence, before reporting the news of any conflict. That is, a journalist must clearly highlight in their news stories, if the violence is a result of structural (such as political repression and economic exploitation) or cultural (such as cultural discriminations) notions. Referring to Galtung's conflict theory, Shaw (2012) thus argues that 'if the indirect forms of structural and cultural violence are managed pro-actively by human rights journalism, the direct forms of physical violence would be minimised or altogether prevented'.

Clearly, Shaw's explanation of HRJ embraces Downman and Ubayasiri's (2017, pp. 39–49) idea of human rights as a news value for its effective function for social change. Their human-focused news values puts people at the forefront of the news production and is comprised of six key elements: (1) Human rights (2) Human condition (3) Humanity (4) Humanitarian issues (5) Human interest, and (6) Human response. Human rights as a news value is not a restrictive term, but includes a range of issues such as justice, legislation, crime, law and politics. Human Condition places importance where people live from a local, national and global perspective. Humanity emphasises on the importance of understanding the diversity, culture, ethnicity and religion in the construction of news. Humanitarian issues such as disasters, accidents, sufferings and war are important news value in the narrative as they can empower the marginalised by balancing the power imbalance in such crisis situations. Human Interest relates to entertainment, music, sports and arts particularly in the construction of soft news and features. Human Response such as interactivity, sharing, comments have a news value, as the audiences are no longer passive recipients of news, given the changed media landscape facilitated by Social Media and internet.

As we can see, it is in parallel to this new human-focused news value that HRJ calls for the 'more pro-active role of journalism as an agency that knows no borders, no race, no age, no gender and no class – a journalism with a human face and for the human race' (Shaw 2012, p. 1). Shaw believes that this preventive and proactive role that HRJ goes hand in hand with the theories of mass communication, human rights and peace. In other words, it resonates with the 'just peace framework' advocated by the peacebuilding scholar Schirch (2002). Shaw brings out the mutual dependency of human rights and peace, as one cannot exist without the other (Shaw 2012, p. 18).

Therefore, HRJ is a normative journalistic practice which is based on human rights in an all-inclusive manner (ibid., p. 1), and is inspired by Kant's ideals of enlightenment and cosmopolitanism. This is where HRJ becomes more important in comparison to the conventional journalism. Conventional journalism does not take into consideration the power imbalance in the society and thereby propagates status quo, indirectly contributing to the human rights violations. Shaw terms conventional journalism as 'Human Wrongs Journalism (HWJ)', identifying five factors of this practice which justify his claims: Distance frame, Evocative reporting, Reactive, Non-interventionist and War journalism (ibid., p. 96).

HWJ, as defined by Shaw (p. 47), is a journalism that 'reinforces instead of challenging the problematic representational imbalances in society…the concentration of power in the hands of the few resourceful people and political communities in global society'. Contrastingly, HRJ is a more proactive practice, which is based on critical, diagnostic, and intervention-centric methods, built around five frames: empathy/critical frame; diagnostic reporting; proactive; interventionist and peace journalism. This approach challenges the status quo of power politics against the marginalised minorities, to promote and protect human rights and peace (ibid., p. 46). HRJ practices revolve around empathy critical frames, which consequently promote pro-active and interventionist attitudes to combat human rights violations by addressing both direct and indirect violence with aim to abolish society's power imbalance.

Explicitly, the overall intention of HRJ is to be proactive and not prescriptive, with an underlying agenda of influencing journalists' actions to align with the protection and promotion of human rights and prevention of violations pertaining to the same. Conversely, the concept of HRJ depends on the agenda-setting feature to not just influence journalistic behaviour to act in line with its five frames at anatomical level, but to also influence the audiences' behaviour in a manner which protects and promotes human rights and prevent mass atrocities at functional level. This runs parallel to the 'Theory of Planned Behaviour' which we had discussed above, which aims to predict a person's intention to perform a behaviour at a certain time and place. HRJ wants journalists to craft news stories along the lines of the five frames which are interconnected across various dimensions of human rights and conflict transformation, to encourage the public to care for and act to end the suffering. For example, the empathy critical frames go a long way in creating 'global compassion' (Höijer 2004) or 'cosmopolitan spectatorship' (Chouliaraki 2006, 2008), by throwing light upon the problems of the victims in a conflict. The two models increase the audience engagement and proactivity, and instil in them the dedication to contribute to the interventionism framework, which is necessary to influence the policy response to curb direct and indirect forms of violence.

The nexus between Chouliaraki's study of mediation of suffering and Shaw's approach to HRJ is symbiotic in nature. Understanding the concept of mediation of distant suffering will help us better understand the function of HRJ in fashioning humanistic behaviour among the audiences to care for and empower all the concerned parties [both victims and offenders], and end the sufferings of those who are vulnerable.

The conceptual framework of HRJ enlightens Chouliaraki's (2006) theory of construction of spectatorship of suffering. Meanwhile, Chouliaraki's analytical approach of hierarchical typology of news stories of human sufferings, sheds light on understanding how the practice of HRJ creates a sense of obligation among distance audiences by influencing their behaviour to build compassion for the victims and influence policymakers towards peace and human rights interventions.

Chouliaraki's study of hierarchical typology depicts the power media holds through its ability to create 'cosmopolitan spectatorship', in which coverage of distance suffering invites audiences to care for and act on conditions of human existence that go beyond their own communities of belonging (Chouliaraki 2006, 2008). As highlighted already, the typology of news stories identified by Chouliaraki (2006, 2008) such as *adventure, emergency*, and *ecstatic*, shape the 'regimes of pity' to create a sense of obligation among the spectators towards victims.

As Chouliaraki (2006, pp. 10–11) explains, adventure news does not evoke a sense of pity towards suffering, as such reports are characterised by brief, factual reports represented by zero agency due to the absence of any human actors from the story. Thus, 'there is no possibility of human contact between the other and the spectator'. Meanwhile, emergency news evoked sympathy towards suffering, which depicts victims as individuals who can be helped by the action of distant others. Finally, ecstatic news, brings the sufferers as close to the spectators as possible, opening up and widening the space for identification.

The concept of the typology of news stories helps us understand Höijer's 'Distance Suffering' in which she identifies four types of compassion created by media's representation of human sufferings: 'tender-hearted', 'shame-filled', 'blame filled' and 'powerlessness filled' (Höijer 2004, pp. 522–524). *Tender-hearted* compassion is the response elicited in the audience, which are typically feelings of sorrow and empathy towards the victims. *Blame-filled* compassion is the audiences' indignation or anger towards those who are in power and are responsible for the sufferings of the people. *Shame-filled* compassion is a response of feeling shameful, as a result of the realisation that stems from the knowledge that they have dishonoured their responsibility of protecting and preventing the suffering of the people. Meanwhile, *powerlessness-filled compassion* involves self-awareness among the audience that their power to halt the suffering of the victims is limited. It signifies their powerlessness to act upon the sufferings towards a positive change.

This discussion leads to the understanding of the relevance of Chouliaraki's 'Typology of news stories' and Höijer's 'Distance Suffering', and also their interrelation with HRJ. Within this context, the typology of news stories enable us to examine the extent to which the practice of HRJ constructs '(global) compassion' and 'cosmopolitan spectatorship' by constructing the reality of distant suffering through its five frames mentioned earlier, so that interventions can be considered and designed in an appropriate and rightful manner to address both direct and indirect violence.

The analysis of the typology of the news stories in media can assist us in examining the role of the five frames of HRJ in media's coverage of distant suffering, and thus assessing the 'agenda setting effect'. These five frames of HRJ are interconnected and mutually reinforcing across the various aspects of human rights protection. For example, the empathy/critical frames, through exposure of sufferings of victims in a conflict, reinforce the diagnostic frames to construct a social reality which in turn helps to construct '(global) compassion' explained by Höijer et al. (2002) or 'cosmopolitan spectatorship' elucidated by Chouliaraki (2006, 2008). This, subsequently, would activate audiences' strong moral commitment to facilitate interventionism which can further influence policy response, and pro-activism framing to mitigate direct and indirect violence.

Although, the discussion until now has highlighted HRJ's as a proactive form of journalism with an inbuilt human rights agenda, instead of being dramatic, reactive or prescriptive in nature, it has not disclosed its epistemological foundations to underline its feasibility and success. The following section aims to introduce the epistemological foundation for the theory and practice of HRJ.

3.5 A Constructivist Epistemological Grounding of HRJ

The basis of all the frames of HRJ is to reflect social reality through information and knowledge of direct and indirect causes of violence, to safeguard and foster human rights. This is achieved by evoking compassion, creating public pressure, or balancing the power dynamics.

In conventional journalism, news values, journalism-power dynamics, dependence on news sources, and the terminologies describing war, play a role in maintaining status quo and propagating war ideologies, through distortion of reality. In this regard, Sonwalker points out that this practice goes a long way in reinforcing the power imbalance, by presenting selective information in a loop (cited in Shaw 2012, p. 99).

Shaw points out that HRJ follows a diagnostic approach, aiming to analyse various factors influencing a conflict, at various levels of a society, within a socio-cultural and political context (Shaw 2012, p. 99), thereby reflecting social reality and endorsing a change in human rights and peace-building strategies. In other words, for human rights and peace building strategies to be successful, actors should understand the true nature of events and their effects. HRJ, which focuses on holistic human rights, can play a pivotal role in achieving this by establishing *prima facie* case within a critical constructivist epistemology. Critical constructive epistemology is a multidimensional approach, as journalists are required to analyse and address various factors which form the roots of the crisis, which must be informed to the international community if and when diplomatic interventions are needed. Thus, the primary role of human rights journalists within a critical constructivist epistemology is to establish a *prima facie* case by reflecting social reality informed by socio, political, cultural, ethical and moral foundations.

Social constructivism is an evolved concept based on constructivism. It discourages maintaining neutrality and unbiasedness in journalism, as construction of reality is a consequence of 'consciousness', which is not distinct from perceived reality. According to constructivist epistemology, cosmos is a formation of 'human construction—a social creation' (Kincheloe 2007, p. 8).

Another school of study follows the rationalistic paradigm with a focus on objectivistic epistemology. This approach states that tangible objects exist independent of the perceiver, and therefore truth pertaining to them is absolute, and cannot be subjected to interpretations. This absolute truth can be found out through experimentation and is assessed on the basis of their resemblance to *true reality*. Constructivist approach attempts to study the various philosophical, cultural, and historical factors which have led to the social phenomena, by analysing its natural contexts. Critical constructivists also analyse the social, cultural, philosophical and theoretical factors in understanding the social construction. The distinguishing factor of this approach is the dimension of 'critical theory' being central to its philosophy (ibid.).

Constructivism does not believe in the idea of neutrality, as it stresses that consciousness is not the only element which erases absolute truth (ibid., pp. 8–10). Instead, what is perceived to be objective reality or truth, is in fact still a construct of the human mind. Thereby, how an event or an object is perceived even at first glance, is dependent on the observer's social context and background. Therefore social reality changes from person to person, negating the concept of absolute truth. Analysing HRJ in this context exposes its problems as an HR journalist's background determines their depiction of the crisis. The same differentiator may prove to be advantageous in HRJ practices, as journalists hailing from different socio, cultural and historical backgrounds can join together and give a multidimensional analysis of a human rights crisis with different factors taken into consideration.

Therefore, the inclusion or exclusion of cultural dimensions in news coverage of a crisis, varies with each situation. The problem of conflicting constructions of reality by different HR journalists can be combatted by including the aspect of 'critical engagement' in news reporting. This aspect of 'critical engagement' in constructivist approach gives birth to the approach of 'critical constructivism', which is proposed as the 'epistemological basis' of HRJ. This critical engagement of HR journalists with regard to human rights issues allows them to delve deeper into understanding the dynamics of power dominance which the elites use as a tool manipulate the society. Kincheloe has stated that critical engagement is a reflective process which builds self-knowledge, along with cultural and educational critique (ibid., p. 10).

Kincheloe's take on critical constructivism provides us with another advantage with HRJ, as it allows journalists to be more self-aware as different theories of critical approaches discuss 'consciousness, the process by which their consciousness was constructed' (ibid., p. 11). Following the reality construction process, the steps that must be taken, can be decided by taking into consideration the context of socio, political, cultural, ethical and moral and political conditions of the causes and effects of human rights violations. Following critical constructivism, enables the HR journalists to mimic the principles of 'critical consciousness', thereby perceiving the world outside of the conventional norms by taking into consideration factors such as the nature of news values, the relationship of journalism to power, the dependence on news sources and language.

This detachment factor is a defence against claims that the practices of HRJ and PJ are not antithetical to objectivity, which is considered to be an indicator of good journalism (Loyn 2007). This detachment, which is a consequence of critical theories attempting to understand the factors influencing social reality is the 'objectivity pursued' of news reporting within the concept of 'inseparability of the knower and the known'. This reasoning aligns with what Ward (2008, p.77) calls 'pragmatic objectivity'. Ward defines pragmatic objectivity as a means to the goals of truth, fair judgement and ethical action. Moreover, Ward (1999, p. 7) says,

> The neutral journalist is seen as a detached chronicler, taking no sides, drawing no conclusions, however horrific the event may be...Pragmatic objectivity regards the journalist as a participant in society with a vested interest in the health of its institutions, including the institution of journalism.

Thus, the critical constructivist epistemology provides a deeper understanding of the 'pragmatic objectivity' concept, and becomes pivotal to the practice of HRJ. HR journalists hence become capable of answering questions such as why? Who? What? Where? And How? Of a conflict, by using critical constructivism as a tool. The model empowers them to analyse and assess the human rights violation process and the direct and indirect causes, enabling them to reconstruct socio-political and economic power structures. These factors make HRJ an appropriate medium to achieve social justice, emancipation, equality and democracy. The information produced is culture and context-specific after being analysed critically, in comparison to objectivist knowledge produced through positivist approach in conventional journalism.

Kincheloe states that the critical constructivists do not focus as much on subject–object dualism, as they pay heed to subjugated knowledge. HR journalists therefore aim to voice out the victim's perspectives within the framework distinguishing the knower (subject) and the known (object). This knowledge would better equip them to challenge the power of the relationship of domination which is the focal point of the methodology of the conventional objective journalism. Mc Ginty points out that this relationship of domination dictates both the natural processes and the manipulation of human beings as passive responders to social engineering (cited in Kincheloe 2007, p. 14). The presence of these two binaries of the knower and the known, in objective journalism, places the journalists in a context where 'power domination' is amplified. The journalists often succumb to these dynamics, and serve the interest of power elites thereby contributing to the power imbalance. In conventional journalism, lack of 'inseparability of the knower and the known' makes the model fall prey to the manipulation of the political and economic elites to serve their interests. This is why, in the contexts of war conditioned by propaganda strategies and technologically assisted activities/manipulations, conventional journalism fails to leave a mark. This lack of 'inseparability of the knower and the known' refrained the conventional journalism to adapt itself to cope up with the modern-day warfare conditions. Ward argues that this reactive and passive approach is incompatible with the values of journalism:

> Both the proponents and opponents of objectivity get objectivity wrong. Both define objective knowledge as belief based firmly on neutral facts and absolute standards of logic and reason. Objective knowledge is knowledge of reality that is independent of anyone's perspective. The skeptic has little difficulty casting doubt on such strong claims and therefore objectivity is too easily refuted and the real issues are missed. (Ward 1999, p. 3)

The concept of co-dependency of the knower and known compared to detached concept of objective journalism, believes that victims play an important role in reflecting the social reality. This model thus acts as a counter-hegemonic model to balance the power imbalance of the society. Michel Foucalt's power concept is relevant in understanding this idea. He states that, a researcher's understanding of the society and social reality is shaped by discourse referred to as a body of relations which is impacted by various sources of power, thereby reflecting the existing power relations. Foucault defines discourse as a culturally built representation of social reality, but is distinct from a mirror image. Knowledge is constructed through discourse, and this discourse processing dictates what should be spoken and what should not be spoken. Therefore, the discourse process produces and reproduces both knowledge and power concurrently (Foucault 1970, 1972).

This reiterates the power media holds, in terms of persuasion. Van Dijk explains that this is the ability to influence the minds of the audience (1996, p. 10). He further adds that power is not just the influencer of media, but also includes the role media play within the context of its social, cultural, political or economic power structures of society (ibid., 1996, p. 9). 'Media power' as he elaborates is 'generally symbolic and persuasive'. Meanwhile, media 'effect' are multifold including change of public opinion, agenda setting and framing of an issue etc. This media 'effect' has the potential to directly impact policy level decision-making (Love 2008, p. 266).

Van Dijk stresses on the importance of having access to discourse in analysing the power media holds. Mass media are a tool which produces discourse, thereby it is common for those who want to exert power, to become a part of this fraternity. While theoretically ordinary public has the opportunity to use mass communication channels to contribute to the discourse production, it rarely materialises into reality. Therefore, they do not participate in discourse production (1996, pp. 11–12). Allan (2013) disagrees, stating that the rise in technological innovations like the internet, have empowered the general public to play an active role in the discourse production process with their 'citizen witnessing'. As Downman and Ubayasiri (2017, p. 10), illuminate, the digitally empowered information gathering has had profound impacts on the ways people engages with news. Digital technology has opened a plethora of avenues for journalists and citizens, 'from reporting war crimes on mobile phones to providing eyewitnesses accounts of refugees seeking asylum'.

Conversely, elite groups have better access to these new-age communication channels with better reach as their opinions garner more attention from the media channels and are better able to influence the news production. This adroitness of elite groups to access discourse empowers them to influence the masses. On the other hand, media has the power to control the 'elite discourse', thereby making the elite group depend on them to mould their power and strengthen it. In this manner, media institutions tend to function as the 'institutions of elite power and dominance', as they construct the reality of the known without any critical analysis. Meanwhile, HR journalists follow the critical engagement process, trying to negate this harmful construction of reality within the understanding of socio, political, ethical and moral foundations. This is where the difference between the ability of conventional journalism and HRJ to construct various facets of power becomes evident.

To quote Van Dijk, 'the more people are affected, the larger the scope of the enactment of discursive power. More specifically, public discourse may affect the minds of many people' (1996, p. 13). In other words, higher access to media directly impacts the power levels of the elite. Fortunately, the information disseminated by the media may not always be influential, as the masses, with their access to various forms of communicative events and discourses, have learnt to reject or refuse the persuasive narrative of the media. Therefore, as Van Dijk illuminates, 'in the same way as forms or modes of discourse access may be spelled out, the ways in which the minds of others may indirectly be accessed through text and talk should also be examined' (ibid.).

Fairclough explains it is a continuous cycle, wherein the society is shaped by discourse while simultaneously setting restricts on it, and discourse is also influenced by social practices (Fairclough 2002). Fairclough's idea of discursive order becomes highly relevant here. He (2002, p. 9) explains that there are always multiple discourses at play in every society, sometimes reinforcing each other and sometimes conflicting each other. He refers to these set of discourses as *discursive orders*. These orders of discourse are the breeding grounds for power plays.

Castells (2009), in his *Communication Power*, focuses on communication network power-making in society, with special reference to political power-making. He defines power as 'the relational capacity that enables a social actor to influence asymmetrically the decisions of other social actor(s) in ways that favour the empowered actor's will, interest and values' (ibid., p. 10). He believes that communication power-making is an outcome of various social actors of a network.

In this context of communication power-making, media can disseminate information of a conflict by voicing out stories of victims, human rights and humanitarian organisations, civil society, and diplomats. Such a narrative will help create compassion and establish *prima facie* case to intervene against, or address human rights violations as well as investigate their causes. The media can do this using HRJ model, which aims to promote designing and implementation of interventions amongst relevant stakeholders, by aiding in the construction of reality of a crisis. This is the power HR Journalists hold in addressing the power imbalance of a conflict- ridden society, while conventional journalism reinforces the power imbalance of a society towards a zero-sum outcome.

This power can be a better understanding of a situation constructed by the analysis of the crisis within critical constructivist epistemology. It also helps improve human security at all levels by addressing power imbalance and addressing human insecurity that 'involves transforming the social and political environment that fosters intolerable inequality, engenders historical grievances, and nurtures adversarial interactions' (ibid., p. 236).

In this premise, HRJ within the critical constructivist epistemology is explored as a mirror for the international community to understand the true nature of things such as the violence in socio, economic and cultural contexts of a conflict. Understanding the stakeholders and characteristics of a conflict, human rights violations and their causes within critical constructivist epistemology enables the concerned authorities to choose proper interventions. Within the realm of political communication, HRJ as a human rights agenda-setting mechanism is well defined and operationalised within the critical constructivist epistemology. It enables HRJ to impact people's perceived behavioural control to aid its human rights agenda and empower them to respond to distant suffering.

3.6 Summary

In the first part of this chapter, light has been shed on the media's power and capacity to protect, promote and guard human rights, and prevent mass atrocities. The second part focused on the agenda-setting process and media's capacity to pursue a human rights-based agenda in times of humanitarian crises. The discussion in the third part highlighted the proactive role of HRJ as a watchdog of human rights violations. Drawing insights from the concept of the spectatorship of distant suffering, the discussion highlighted HRJ's functional propensity to influence the audiences' responses to distant suffering. Finally, the fourth part discussed HRJ within the critical constructivist epistemology, to reflect the true state of affairs in the socio, economic and cultural contexts of a conflict. Juxtaposing HRJ with the critical constructivist paradigm defended many of the criticisms against the former such as its argument for journalists' moral responsibility towards human rights and seeking to redress the plights and empower the victims.

Bibliography

Ajzen, I. (2002). Perceived Behavioral Control, Self-Efficacy, Locus of Control, and the Theory of Planned Behaviour. *Journal of Applied Social Psychology, 32*(4), 665–683. https://doi.org/10.1111/j.1559-1816.2002.tb00236.

Ajzen, I., Brown, T. C., & Carvajal, F. (2004). Explaining the Discrepancy Between Intentions and Actions: The Case of Hypothetical Bias in Contingent Valuation. *Personality and SocialPsychology Bulletin, 30*, 1108–1121.

Allan, S. (2013). *Citizen Witnessing: Revisioning Journalism in Times of Crisis Key Concepts in Journalism*. Malden, MA: Polity Press.
Anderson, P. J. (2007). Competing Models of Journalism and Democracy. In P. J. Anderson & G. Ward (Eds.), *The Future of Journalism in the Advanced Democracies*, (pp. 39–49). Aldershot: Ashgate Publishing.
Baehr, P. R. (1999). *Human Rights: Universality in Practice*. London: Palgrave Macmillan.
Balabanova, E. (2015). *The Media and Human Rights: The Cosmopolitan Promise*. London: Routledge.
Berry, V., & McChesney, A. (1988). Human Rights and Foreign Policy-Making. In R. O. Matthews & C. Pratt (Eds.), *Human Rights in Canadian Foreign Policy* (pp. 59–76). Kingston: McGill-Queen's University Press.
Boltanski, L. (1999) *Distant Suffering: Morality, Media and Politics* (G. Burchell, Trans.). Cambridge: Cambridge University Press.
Carey, S., Gibney, M., & Poe, S. (2010). *The Politics of Human Rights: The Quest for Dignity*. Cambridge: Cambridge University Press.
Castells, M. (2009). *Communication Power*. Oxford: Oxford University Press.
Chouliaraki, L. (2006). *The Spectatorship of Suffering*. London: Sage.
Chouliaraki, L. (2008). The Mediation of Suffering and the Vision of a Cosmopolitan Public. *Television and New Media, 9*(5), 371–391.
Chouliaraki, L. (2013). *The Ironic Spectator: Solidarity in the Age of Post-Humanitarianism*. Cambridge: Polity Press.
Chouliaraki, L., & Fairclough, N. (2004). The Critical Analysis of Discourse. In W. Carroll (Ed.), *Critical Strategies for Social Research* (pp. 262–271). Toronto: Canadian Scholar's Press.
Cismas, I. (2004) The Intersection of Economic, Social, and Cultural Rights and Civil and Political Rights. In E. Riedel, G. Giacca, & C. Golay (Eds.), *Economic, Social, and Cultural Rights in International Law: Contemporary Issues and Challenges* (pp. 448–472). Oxford: Oxford University Press.
Claude, R. P., & Weston, B. H. (2006). *Human Rights in the World Community: Issues and Action* (3rd ed.). Philadelphia: University of Pennsylvania Press.
Cole, W. M. (2010). No News Is Good News: Human Rights Coverage in the American Print Media, 1980–2000. *Journal of Human Rights, 9*(3), 303–325.
Coleman, R., McCombs, M., Shaw, D., & Weaver, D. (2009). Agenda Setting. In K. Wahl-Jogensen & T. Hanitzsch (Eds.), *The Handbook of Journalism Studies* (pp. 147–160). New York: Routledge.
Cottle, S. (2017). Journalist Killings and the Responsibility to Report. In U. Carlsson & R. Pöyhtäri (Eds.), *The Assault on Journalism: Building Knowledge to Protect Freedom of Expression* (pp. 129–141). Gothenberg: Nordicom.
Cottle, S. (2019). Humanitarianism, Human Insecurity, and Communications: What's Changing in a Globalised World? In S. Cottle & G. Cooper (Eds.),

Humanitarianism, Communications and Change. New York: Peter Lang Publishing Inc.
Dearing, J. W., & Rogers, E. M. (1996). *Agenda-Setting*. Thousand Oaks, CA: Sage.
De Burgh, H. (2000). *Investigative Journalism: Context and Practice*. London: Routledge.
Dhir, K. S. (2007). Stakeholder Activism Through Nonviolence. *Corporate Communications: An International Journal, 12*(1), 75–93.
Donelly, J. (1989). *Universal Human Rights in Theory and Practice* (p. 1989). Ithaca: Cornell University Press.
Donnelly, J. (1998). *International Human Rights*, 2nd ed. Boulder, Oxford: Westview Press.
Downman, S., & Ubayasiri, K. (2017). *Journalism for Social Change in Asia: Reporting Human Rights*. Basingstoke: Palgrave Macmillan.
Dunleavy, P., & O'Leary, B. (1987). *Theories of the State: The Politics of Liberal Democracy*. Basingstoke: Macmillan.
Fairclough, N. (2002). Discourse as Social Practice. In M. Toolan (Ed.), *Critical Discourse Analysis Critical Concepts in Linguistics* (pp. 1–22). London: Routledge.
Foucault, M. (1970). *The Order of Things: An Archaeology of the Human Sciences*. London: Tavistock.
Foucault, M. (1972). *The Archaeology of Knowledge*. London: Tavistock.
Foucault, M. (1974). Human Nature: Justice Versus Power. In E. Fons (Ed.), *Reflexive Water: The Basic Concerns of Mankind* (pp. 135–197). London: Souvenir Press.
Foucault, M. (1977). *Discipline and Punish: The Birth of the Prison*. London: Allen Lane.
Galtung, J. (1996). *Peace by Peaceful Means: Peace and Conflict, Development and Civilization*. London: Sage.
Galtung, J., & Ruge, M. H. (1965). The Structure of Foreign News. *Journal of Peace Research, 2*(1), 64–91.
Gamson, W. (1989). News as Framing: Comments on Graber. *American Behavioural Scientist, 33*(2), 157–161.
Gamson, W., & Lasch, K. (1983). Evaluating the Welfare State: Social and Political Perspectives. In S. Shimon & E. Yuchtman-Yaar (Eds.), *Evaluating the Welfare State: Social and Political Perspectives*. New York: Academic Press.
Gilboa, E. (2005). The CNN Effect: The Search for a Communication Theory of International Relations. *Political Communication, 22*, 27–44.
Gowing, N. (1994). *Real-Time Television Coverage of Armed Conflicts and Diplomatic Crises: Does It Pressure or Distort Foreign Policy Decisions?* (Harvard Working Paper). Available at: http://shorensteincenter.org/wp-content/uploads/2012/03/1994_01_gowing.pdf. Accessed 5 May 2019.

Hallin, D. (1994). *We Keep America on Top of the World*. New York: Routledge.
Hanitzsch, T. (2007a). It Should Be Fair to Criticize Even Noble Ideas: A Response to Jake Lynch and Samuel Pele. *Conflict and Communication Online, 6*(2), 1–4.
Hanitzsch, T. (2007b). Situating Peace Journalism in Journalism Studies: A Critical Appraisal. *Conflict and Communication, 6*(2), 1–9.
Harcup, T. and D. O'Neill. (2001). What Is News? Galtung and Ruge Revisited. *Journalism Studies, 2*(2), 261–280.
Heinze, E., & Freedman, R. (2010). Public Awareness of Human Rights: Distortions in the Mass Media. *The Journal of Human Rights, 14*(4), 491–523.
Herman, E. S., & Chomsky, N. (1988). *Manufacturing Consent: The Political Economy of the Mass Media*. New York: Pantheon.
Higgins, E. T. (1996). Knowledge Activation: Accessibility, Applicability, and Salience. In E. T. Higgins & A. W. Kruglanski (Eds.), *Social Psychology: Handbook of Basic Principles* (pp. 133–168). New York: Guilford Press.
Höijer, B. (2004). The Discourse of Global Compassion: The Audience and Media Reporting of Human Suffering. *Media, Culture and Society, 26*(4), 513–531.
Höijer, B., Nohrstedt, S. A., & Ottosen, R. (2002). The Kosovo War in the Media—Analysis of a Global Discursive Order. *Conflict & Communication Online, 1*(2), 1–18.
ICHRP (The International Council on Human Rights Policy). (2002). *Journalism, Media and the Challenge of Human Rights Reporting*. Available at: http://www.ichrp.org/files/reports/14/106_report_en.pdf. Accessed 17 Jan 2020.
Iyengar, S. (1990). The Accessibility Bias in Politics: Television News and Public Opinion. *International Journal of Public Opinion Research, 2*, 1–15.
Keck, M. E., & Sikkink, K. (1998). *Activists Beyond Borders: Advocacy Networks in International Relations*. Ithaca: Cornell University Press.
Kim, S. H., Carvalho, J. P., Davis, A. G., & Mullins, A. M. (2011). The View of the Border: News Framing of the Definition, Causes and Solutions to Illegal Immigration. *Mass Communication & Society, 14*(3), 292–314.
Kim, S. H., Han, M., Choi, D-H., Kim, J-N. (2012). Attribute Agenda Setting, Priming and the Media's Influence on How to Think About a Controversial Issue. *International Communication Gazette, 74*(1): 43–59.
Kim, S., Scheufele, D., & Shanahan, J. (2002). Think About It This Way: Attribute Agenda Setting Function of the Press and the Public's Evaluation of a Local Issue. *Journalism & Mass Communication Quarterly, 79*, 7–25.
Kincheloe, J. L. (2007). Critical Constructivism and Post Formalism: New Ways of Thinking and Being. In J. L. Kincheloe & R. Horn (Eds.), *The Praeger*

Handbook of Education and Psychology (Vol. 4, pp. 855–863). California: Green Publishing Group.

Kiousis, S. (2004). Explicating Media Salience: A Factor Analysis of New York Times Issue Coverage During the 2000 U.S. Presidential Election. *Journal of Communication, 54,* 71–87.

Lippmann, W. (1922). *Public Opinion*. New York: Free Press.

Littlejohn, S. (2002). *Theories of Human Communication*. Albuquerque: Wadsworth.

Livingston, S. (1997). *Clarifying the CNN Effect: An Examination of Media Effects According to Type of Military Intervention* (Harvard Research Paper R-18). Joan Shorenstein Barone Center on the Press, Politics and Public Policy, Harvard University, Cambridge, MA.

Livingston, S., & Eachus, T. (1995). Humanitarian Crises and US Foreign Policy. *Political Communication, 12*(4), 413–429.

Love, M. C. (2008). The New Bully Pulpit: Global Media and Foreign Policy. In M. J. Rozell. & J. D. Mayer. (Eds.), *Media Power, Media Politics*. (pp. 257–88) Lanham: Rowman and Littlefield.

Loyn, D. (2007). Good Journalism or Peace Journalism. *Conflict & Communication Online, 6*(2), 1–10.

Lusgarten, A., & Debrix, F. (2005). The Role of the Media in Monitoring International Humanitarian Law During Military Interventions: The Case of Kosovo. *Peace and Change, 30*(3), 359–397.

Lynch, J., & McGoldrick, A. (2005). Peace Journalism: A Global Dialog for Democracy and Democratic Media. In R. A. Hackett & Y. Zhao (Eds.), *Democratizing Global Media* (pp. 269–288). Lanham: Rowman and Littlefield.

Manheim, J. B., & Albriton, R. B. (1984). Changing National Images: International Public Relations and Media Agenda Setting. *American Political Science Review, 78*(3), 641–657.

McCombs, M. (2003). *The Agenda-Setting Role of the Mass Media in the Shaping of Public Opinion*. University of Texas at Austin [Online]. https://www.infoamerica.org/documentos_pdf/mccombs01.pdf. Accessed 12 Feb 2020.

McCombs, M. (2004). *Setting the Agenda: The Mass Media and Public Opinion*. Cambridge: Polity Press.

McCombs, M. (2005). A Look at Agenda-Setting: Past, Present, and Future. *Journalism Studies, 6,* 543–557.

McCombs, M. E., & Shaw, D. L. (1972). The Agenda-Setting Function of Mass Media. *Public Opinion Quarterly, 36,* 176–187.

McCombs, M. E., Shaw, D. L., & Weaver, D. H. (1997). *Communication and Democracy: Exploring the Intellectual Frontiers in Agenda-Setting Theory*. Mahwah, NJ: Erlbaum.

McGregor. J. (2002). Terrorism, Lions and Sex Symbols: Restating News Values. In J. McGregor & M. Comrie (Eds.), *What's News? Reclaiming Journalism in New Zealand*. Palmerston North: Dunmore Press.

McLaughlin, G. (2002). *The War Correspondent*. London: Pluto Press.

Moeller, S. D. (1999). *Compassion Fatigue: How the Media Sell Disease, Famine, War and Death*. London: Routledge.

Mutua, M. (2007). Standard Setting in Human Rights: Critique and Prognosis. *Human Rights Quarterly, 29*(3), 547–630.

Ovsiovitch, J. S. (1993). Human Rights Coverage in the Media: A Quantitative Content Analysis. *ETD Collection for University of Nebraska—Lincoln*. AAI9406087. https://digitalcommons.unl.edu/dissertations/AAI9406087. Accessed 25 Mar 2020.

Pan, Z., & Kosicki, G. (1993). Framing Analysis: An Approach to News Discourse. *Political Communication, 10*(1), 55–75.

Pollock, J. C. (2014). Illuminating Human Rights: How Demographics Drive Media Coverage. *Atlantic Journal of Communication, 22*(3–4), 141–159.

Price, V., & Tewksbury, D. (1997). News Values and Public Opinion: A Theoretical Account of Media Priming and Framing. In G. Barnett & F. J. Boster (Eds.), *Progress in Communication Sciences* (Vol. 17, pp. 173–212). Greenwich, CT: Ablex.

Ramos, H., Ron, J., & Thoms, O. N. T. (2007). Shaping the Northern Media's Human Rights Coverage, 1986–2000. *Journal of Peace Research, 41*(4), 385–406.

Robinson, P. (1999). The CNN Effect. *Review of International Studies, 25,* 301.

Robinson, P. (2000). The Policy Media Interaction Model: Measuring Media Power During Humanitarian Crisis. *Journal of Peace Research, 37*(5), 625–645.

Robinson, P. (2013, September 17). Media as a Driving Force in International Politics: The CNN Effect and Related Debates. *E-International Relations*. Available at: http://www.e-ir.info/2013/09/17/media-as-a-driving-force-in-international-politics-the-cnn-effect-and-related-debates/. Accessed 8 Dec 2019.

Ron, J., Ramos, H., & Rodgers, K. (2005). Transnational Information Politics: NGO Human Rights Reporting, 1986–2000. *International Studies Quarterly, 49,* 557–587.

Sampaio-Dias, S. (2016). *Reporting Human Rights*. New York: Peter Lang.

Savirimuthu, J. (2013, November). John Locke, Natural Rights and Intellectual Property: The Legacy of an Idea. *Journal of Intellectual Property Law & Practice, 8*(11), 892–894 [Online]. https://doi.org/10.1093/jiplp/jpt168. Accessed 11 Feb 2020.

Scheufele, D. A. (1999). Framing as a Theory of Media Effects. *Journal of Communication, 49*(4), 103–122.

Schirch, L. (2002, March). *Human Rights and Peacebuilding: Towards Just-peace*. Paper presented to 43rd Annual International Studies Association Convention, New Orleans, Louisiana.

Schirch, L. (2008). Strategic Peacebuilding: State of the Field Peace Prints. *South Asian Journal of Peacebuilding, 1*(1), 1–17.

Schirch, L. (2013). *Conflict Assessment and Peacebuilding Planning: Toward a Participatory Approach to Human Security*. Boulder: Kumarian Press.

Schudson, M. (1995). *The Power of News*. Cambridge: Harvard University Press.

Selvarajah, S. (2016). Threat Image Construction in the Sri Lankan Media and Its Implications for Peace Communication. In A. Amarasingam & D. Bass (Eds.), *Sri Lanka: The Struggle for Peace in the Aftermath of War* (pp. 73–87). London: Hurst.

Selvarajah, S. (2019). Identifying Obstacles to Peace Journalism in Sri Lanka and Nepal. *Journalism Practice*. http://doi.org/10.1080/17512786.2019.1695536. Accessed 28 May 2020.

Shaw, M. (1999). Global Voices: Civil Society and Media in Global Crises. In T. Dunn & N. Wheeler (Eds.), *Human Rights in Global Politics* (pp. 214–232). Cambridge: Cambridge University Press.

Shaw, I. S. (2012). *Human Rights Journalism: Advances in Reporting Distant Humanitarian Interventions*. Basingstoke: Palgrave Macmillan.

Shaw, I. S., & Selvarajah, S. (2019a). Introduction: Reporting Conflicts, Human Rights and Peacebuilding: Critical and Global Perspectives. In I. S. Shaw & S. Selvarajah (Eds.), *Reporting Human Rights, Conflicts, and Peacebuilding: Critical and Global Perspectives*. Basingstoke: Palgrave.

Shaw, I. S., & Selvarajah, S. (2019b). Human Rights Journalism: Towards a Critical Constructivist Epistemological Approach. In I. S. Shaw & S. Selvarajah (Eds.), *Reporting Human Rights, Conflicts, and Peacebuilding: Critical and Global Perspectives*. Basingstoke: Palgrave.

Tester, K. (2001). *Compassion, Morality and the Media*. Buckingham: Open University Press.

United Nations. (1948, December 10). *Universal Declaration of Human Rights*. Adopted and Proclaimed by General Assembly of the United Nations, Resolution 217A (III).

Van Belle, D. (2009). Media Agenda Setting and Donor Aid. In P. Norris (Ed.). *Public Sentinel: News Media and Governance Reform*. Washington: The World Bank.

Van, M. C. (2008). The New Bully Pulpit: Global Media and Foreign Policy. In M. J. Rozell & J. D. Mayer (Eds.), *Media Power, Media Politics* (pp. 257–288). Lanham: Rowman and Littlefield.

Van Dijk, T. A. (1996). Power and the News Media. In D. Paletz & C. Vinson (Eds.), *Political Communication in Action*. Cresskill, NJ: Hampton Press.

Van Dijk, T. A. (2004). Politics, Ideology and Discourse. In K. Brown (Ed.), *Encyclopaedia of Language and Linguistics* (Vol. 9, 2nd ed., pp. 728–740). Oxford: Elsevier.

Ward, S. J. A. (1999). *Pragmatic News Objectivity: Objectivity with a Human Face*. Cambridge, MA: The Joan Shorenstein Center on the Press, Politics and Public Policy, Harvard University.

Ward, S. J. A. (2008). Truth and Objectivity. In L. Wilkins & C. G. Christians (Eds.), *The Handbook of Mass Media Ethics* (pp. 71–83). New York: Routledge.

Ward, S. J. A. (2010). Inventing Objectivity: New Philosophical Foundations. In C. Meyers (Ed.), *Journalism Ethics: A Philosophical Approach* (pp. 137–152). Oxford: Oxford University Press.

Weaver, D., McCombs, M., & Shaw, D. L. (2004). Agenda-Setting Research: Issues, Attributes, and Influences. In L. L. Kaid (Ed.), *Handbook of Political Communication Research* (pp. 257–282). Mahwah, NJ: Erlbaum.

Wellman, C. (2000, August). Solidarity, the Individual and Human Rights. *Human Rights Quarterly, 22*(3), 639–657. Published by Johns Hopkins University Press. https://doi.org/10.1353/hrq.2000.0040. Accessed 8 June 2020.

Weston, B. H. (1992). Human Rights. In R. P. Claude & B. Weston (Eds.), *Human Rights in the World Community: Issues and Action*. Philadelphia: University of Pennsylvania Press.

Wolfsfeld, G. (1997). *Media and Political Conflict*. New York: Cambridge University Press.

Wolfsfeld, G. (2004). *Media and the Path to Peace*. Cambridge: Cambridge University Press.

CHAPTER 4

The Nexus Between Responsibility to Protect (R2P) and Human Rights Journalism (HRJ)

4.1 Introduction

This chapter studies the relationship between the evolving norms of the 'Responsibility to Protect' (hereafter R2P) and Human Rights Journalism (hereafter HRJ), to better understand the role of media in humanitarian interventions. Social scientists (Lazarsfeld et al. 1944) have long been interested in the impact media has on public opinion and policy. The focus eventually shifted to the relationship between media and public affairs, and the need to understand the role of media in impacting attitudes and behaviours directed the scholarly interest towards the world of politics (e.g. Blumler and Gurevitch 1981; Nimmo 1964; Sigal 1973; Strömbäck 2005; Livingston 1997; Wolfsfeld 1997; Jones and Baumgartner 2005) and social change (Chouliaraki 2006; Downman and Ubayasiri 2017; Pollock 2014; Sampaio-Dias 2016; Cottle 2017; Gies 2015; Balabanova 2014). Despite the huge body of literature available on human rights protection and promotion within the context of media, contemporary researchers (Shaw 1996; Robinson 2000; Cottle 2013; Hammond 2007; Shaw 2012) began to pay more attention to the media's influential power with regard to massive military and humanitarian interventions

The original version of this chapter was revised: Incorrect reference in the bibliography and abstract has been updated. The correction to this chapter is available at https://doi.org/10.1007/978-3-030-49072-0_11

S. Selvarajah, *Human Rights Journalism and its Nexus to Responsibility to Protect*, https://doi.org/10.1007/978-3-030-49072-0_4

in some of the world's hot spots in recent decades. Sadly, there are very few successful humanitarian interventions in history, and of them is, as Martin Shaw (1996, p. 88) put, 'the virtually unprecedented proposal for Kurdish safe havens' was feasible by the empathetic media coverage of Kurdish refugees fleeing from Saddam Hussein's forces. This was swiftly followed by the Operation Restore Hope in Somalia.

Chomsky (1999), Hammond and Herman (2000) and Shaw (2012), interpret Western interventionism more realistically, explaining it as another form of traditional power politics in which the Western parties exploit the 'humanitarian' label to pursue their own selfish interests. Shaw (2012) referred to this phenomenon as the 'politics of humanitarian intervention' as national or geopolitical interests drive the moment, and not genuine concern for human suffering. Shaw argued that many humanitarian interventions fail as a consequence of such lack of empathy and suggested that mainstream media remains complicit in the equation. Habermas argued that 'enlightened, rational communication can be the panacea for human exploitation, ignorance, and repression' (cited in Tumber 2007, p. 24). Yet, some media scholars (Allan 2004; Carruthers 2000; Shaw 2012, 2016; Lynch 2008) termed media as the tool of powerful institutions in the framing of conflicts and human suffering. This form of journalism, which caters to the needs of the powerful, was called human wrongs journalism by Shaw (2012). He also proposed its opposite, human rights journalism, to address this imbalance. Despite this increasing scholarly interest in the role of the media in the promotion and protection of human rights, including humanitarian interventions in the context of HRJ as articulated above, there has been no attempt to critically explore this with regard to the R2P doctrine. In this chapter, I aim to address this gap by proposing the HRJ-R2P nexus as a conceptual functional framework of the role of media in humanitarian interventions.

Through the exploration of human rights violations and the underlying causes behind the conflict, the media can act as a human rights watchdog and campaigner, directly contributing to the conflict prevention strategy within R2P. Against this backdrop, human rights-oriented reporting (otherwise termed as HRJ) can facilitate the implementation of R2P as a 'rights based' approach. Human rights journalist can communicate the reality of a crisis situation thereby providing a *prima facie* case for R2P. Thus, the HR journalists contribute in enhancing the participation of the international community/responsibility holders in collectively dealing with the crisis situation without engaging in petty political agendas. This argument strengthens Allan Thomson's call for journalists to assume the role of 'Responsibility to Report' (R2R) to expose human rights violations and attempt to cease the same. This chapter is divided into three sections: the first section briefly presents the development of the R2P within the context of humanitarian interventions; the second provides a functional theoretical framework of the emerging human rights journalism model and its epistemological foundations and the final section explores the key elements that define the nexus between HRJ and R2P and show how they justify the role of media in successfully implementation of the latter.

4.2 Humanitarian Interventions and Responsibility to Protect (R2P)

Humanitarian Intervention (HI), including R2P, are rooted in a war theory which thereby becomes their moral philosophical foundation. It encompasses the moral issues pertaining to the acceptable time to wage war (jus ad bellum) and the limitations of waging war (jus in bello) (Potter 1973).

4.2.1 Just War, Humanitarian Intervention and International Relations

Justification of recourse to force where there was a 'just cause' can be traced from religious writings of 'just war' period (c330 BC–AD 1650) to scholarly writings and international laws and agreements of United Nations Charter period (p. 11). This justification evolved as a just war doctrine over time. Philosopher Aristotle (384 BC–322 BC) was the first writer who supported restricted recourse to force if there was a just cause. In his work of political philosophy Politics, Aristotle defended waging war for creating 'good life' for a community remarking that 'war must therefore be regarded as only a means to peace' (Arend and Beck 1993, p. 12).

Greatest Christian theologian Augustine (354 AD–430 AD) also justified the use of force to promote peace and eliminate evils. Nine hundred years later philosopher and theologian Thomas Aquinas further developed Augustine Christian's war doctrine and provided three conditions to recourse force: proper authority, just purpose and right intentions. Writers in the sixteenth and seventeenth centuries developed jus ad bellum principles (a criterion that must be met before engaging in war) (ibid., pp. 12–16; Fixdal and Smith 1998, pp. 286–287). Since then, the just war philosophers, legal scholars and practitioners further developed a set of threshold conditions in the event of recourse to force.

The concept of Humanitarian Intervention (HI), which has its roots in the just war tradition (see Hehir 2013), was widely recognised after the end of the cold war in 1990s, due to numerous intra state wars across the globe posing serious threats to human rights.

Arend and Beck define Humanitarian Intervention as, 'the use of armed forces by a State (or States) to protect citizens of the target State from large scale human rights violations' (Arend and Beck 1993, p. 113). For Holzgrefe (2003), HI is a forcible action which does not seek the consent of the sovereign states, as it aims to prevent mass atrocity crimes and human rights violations.

In this manner, the just war tradition evolved to become HI which is a modified, functional tool. Contrastingly, there was a parallel development of the concept of non-interventionism to suit the changing world order which was accommodating more and more sovereign States. The treaty of Westphalia signed in 1648, led to the emergence of State systems which eventually progressed to develop the concept of sovereignty (Arend and Beck 1993, pp. 12–16).

The development of HI which is rooted in the just war tradition, and non-interventionism grounded in the Westphalian paradigm are conflicting demands, which creates tension between the concepts and often becomes a barrier in implementing HI in times of humanitarian crisis and human rights violations. Non-interventionism functions as a tool in restricting the abuse of the HI. Therefore, this tension allows the international community to effectively develop a legitimate intervention in the context of international relations and international law.

International relations theories such as realism, Pluralism and solidarism provide better determine the conditions under which the legitimate intervention be considered.

Origin of the theory of realism goes back to the period of Thucydides (460–411 B.C.E). For realist thinkers, states which focus on the national security with an aim to protect and promote their national interests and power, are the primary players in the international arena.

Thus ethics is not considered as important as sovereignty of the states (Ozdemir 2011, pp. 107, 114). However, not all the thinkers of realism blindly ignore the value of ethics in international relations. While the initial realist scholars were critical of moralism, they did not entirely reject the ethical dimension in international politics. They emphasised on the need for cautiousness in political actions to avoid disorder in international systems (Korab-Karpowicz 2013). Thus, realists deem interventions as legitimate when national security is at stake and there is an imbalance in power on an international platform (Almeida 2002, pp. 158–161; Ozdemir 2011).

Pluralism and solidarism are two distinct but mutually influencing concepts of the English School of international relations. International society is the centre of the approach of the English school (Keating 2013; Ludlow 2009). According to Bull, international society denotes (Bull 1977, p. 13) a group of states which form a society and are bound by a common set of rules, due to their common interests and values.

From a pluralist perspective, these common interests are their philosophies rooted in the concepts of sovereignty and non- intervention of the Westphalian model. They oppose interventions due to their concern for the world order as they believe that: (1) Interventions contribute to war crisis and anarchy. (2) Maintaining the power balance and international order trump the need for protecting minority rights and preventing humanitarian crisis. (3) International consensus in determining a legitimate intervention is imperative and therefore implanting interventions without such consensus will destabilise the international order (Almeida 2002, pp. 162–163; Keating 2013).

Pluralists also reject interventions as it is detrimental to a state's sovereignty and disrespects their domestic sphere of jurisdiction through external interference. Thereby, they believe that intervention is wrong in terms of legal and moral standards. Thirdly, intervention mechanisms can be abused by powerful countries to either expand territorially or to fulfil other selfish interests. Consequently, interventions with the right intentions may later become self-serving (Almeida 2002; Keating 2013; Ludlow 2009).

The problem of selectivity is another reason why pluralists oppose intervention as powerful countries, due to their national interests, may consider interventions based on their own selfish interests (ibid.).

Despite their strong opposition to intervention, pluralists also support conducting minimal humanitarian intervention when national security is at stake. Mass atrocity crime is one of the situations, which according to pluralists can call for a legitimate intervention, though it is not to be considered an obligation. The want such interventions to be an effect of a careful assessment of political circumstances (ibid., p. 164; Ludlow 2009).

Contrastingly, solidarists' view of international society has a broader vision, giving significant weight to cooperation, coexistence and individual rights within the context of international law. Therefore, solidarists view sovereignty and non-interventionism as less important. Thus, it longs for equal rights to everyone; thereby transforming individual states juridical towards an international cosmopolitan society (Costa 2014).

Solidarists argue that allowing injustice within a country to respect sovereignty and the principle of non-intervention, is a gross ignorance of moral responsibility of the international society. They argue that the international community is morally obliged to prevent violation of human rights. This is why they want to link both human rights and humanitarian intervention within the principle of cosmopolitan morality, basic natural rights and global society (Almeida 2002; Ludlow 2009).

After the end of the cold war, the solidarist approach was attracted by legal and moral considerations. While HI was considered to be a legal and moral method under the solidarist tradition, the 'just cause' element of the solidarist concept made it a supreme humanitarian intervention, thereby promoting the idea of moral responsibility within the international community with regard to preventing human rights violations across borders. This moral responsibility allows for HI, with its genuine aim to promote human rights in a sovereign state, to be legitimate under the legal consensus of the international community. In other words, HI is a morally accepted violation of the principles of sovereignty and non- intervention (ibid.).

Solidarist concept agrees with the pluralist standpoint, in terms of the reasons for the requirements of HI. As in the case of pluralism, (1) HI is a moral requirement. (2) HI is a legal requirement. (3) A transition to the world's society. As for the second question of who, it can be either a collective-authorised intervention based on international consensus or unilateral HI based on strong moral ground. Like in pluralism tradition, the third question of political power draws the attention to the maintenance of international order (ibid.).

The international community's current position, with regard to HI, is bent towards pluralism in terms of practices and towards solidarism in terms of will. The existence of these two traditions in the current international order creates a tension which is varyingly destructive and constructive. However, the political actions of the global states, with regard to the HI in the contemporary world setting, is to some extent within the solidarist order.

We will now briefly discuss the history and development of R2P.

4.2.2 *The Idea of Responsibility to Protect (R2P)*

Humanitarian interventions led by the United States and NATO in Somali in 1992 and Bosnia in 1999, respectively were partly a failure because they were not authorised by the UN. Moreover, the international community's failure in preventing the horrifying humanitarian crises such as the ones in Rwanda, Congo and Sudan, forced the UN Secretary General Kofi Annan to appeal to the world leaders to take urgent action, at the UN General Assembly in 1999. The UN General Assembly at the Millennium Summit in the year 2000 suggested implementing alternative mechanisms to prevent mass atrocities in conflict-ridden countries in an appropriate and cooperative manner, instead of methods grounded in the philosophies of sovereignty and non- intervention (Gierycz 2010, p. 112).

In response to Kofi Annan's appeal, the Canadian government appointed the International Commission on Intervention and State Sovereignty (ICISS) in 2000, comprising of eminent individuals, to prepare a plan to prevent future mass human rights violations (Dharmapuri 2012, p. 242). The result was the report 'The Responsibility to protect' (R2P) published by the ICISS in December 2001. Hence, it can be said that the R2P was designed as a response to the criticisms of the failing concept of Humanitarian Intervention.

The R2P comprises of three specific responsibilities: responsibility to prevent, responsibility to react and responsibility to rebuild. The responsibility to prevent primarily focuses on preventing mass atrocity crimes and the prevention of potential crimes before they transpire. While this emphasises on the importance of addressing direct and indirect causes, as well as immediate and long-term consequences of intra-state conflicts and other such crises, it puts the populations at risk. This 'responsibility to react' supports 'interventions' during crisis situations through the implementation of sanctions and international prosecutions, and in extreme cases via military interventions. 'Responsibility to rebuild' emphasises on the role of the international community to extend relief, rehabilitation, reconstruction and reconciliation assistance, once the coercive intervention ceases (ICISS 2001, p. XI).

Defending the option of military intervention, the commission argued that the international community's responsibility to take coercive measures supersedes territorial sovereignty of a state, in times of serious humanitarian needs (ibid.; Wheeler and Egerton 2008). The philosophy of this argument is based on the groundbreaking book published by renowned Sudanese scholar Francis Deng and his associates at the Brooking Institute: 'Sovereignty as Responsibility: Conflict Management in Africa'. This book argues against the 'Treaty of Westphalia', by point out that when states fail to conduct their internal matters in compliance with international standards, 'other nations not only have the right, but also have a duty, to intervene' (Deng et al. 1996; Etzioni 2006, p. 71). It iterated that the right of sovereignty of states is lawful as long as they protect their own population and their rights, denoting that sovereignty is not unconditional, and can be dishonoured if human rights are not adequately protected (Deng 2009a, b). In this way, the ICISS report shifted the position of sovereignty from 'unconditional' to 'conditional' and shifted its role from 'impunity' to 'responsibility'. In this way, as we can see, the ICISS gives significant importance to protecting human rights by recognising the moral acceptance of HI in sovereign states.

The United Nations General Assembly in the World Summit 2005 unanimously adopted the R2P concept with an inclusion of a 'protection clause' in its document at 138 and 139 paragraphs (World Summit Document 2005). Paragraph 138 clearly states the following: 'Each individual State has the responsibility to protect its populations from genocide, war crimes, ethnic cleansing and crimes against humanity'. Meanwhile, paragraph 139 emphasises that the international community, holds the responsibility of implementing appropriate peaceful means, in accordance with the Charter, to protect various minorities from human rights violations and other such crimes against humanity.

Thereby, the World Summit Document advanced the R2P to make it operational, and even authoritative. The document also clarified the nature and scope of the term 'responsibility', with regard to sovereign states and the international community (ibid.; Bellamy 2009). This may be an intentional attempt to ease the tension between the traditions of pluralism and solidarism, by recognising the juridical capacity of the sovereign states and giving them the right and the responsibility to address their internal issues first. Meanwhile, by giving the initial responsibility to the states and by recognising their sovereignty, the World Summit Document embraces the potential abuser as a partner in the process and thereby makes it more cooperative in the international context. The UN Security Council in April 2006, reaffirmed the agreement reached by the world leaders at the previous World Summit, on the collective 'responsibility to protect', and made the document more authoritative (Gierycz 2010, p. 114).

In 2009, newly elected Secretary General Ban Ki-moon presented his report 'Implementing the Responsibility to Protect' to the UN General Assembly, reaffirming the 2005 World Summit Document. The document refined the 'protection clause' into three pillars of the R2P: (1) The protection responsibilities of the State (2) International assistance and capacity-building (3) Timely and decisive response. The first pillar placed the primary responsibility on the State to protect its populations from genocide, war crimes, crimes against humanity and ethnic cleansing, along with their incitement. The second pillar stressed on the responsibility of the international community to encourage and assist the States in fulfilling their responsibility. Finally, the last pillar placed the responsibility on the international community to use diplomatic, humanitarian and other feasible means, including military intervention in extreme cases, when a state manifestly fails to protect its population (Implementing R2P 2009, pp. 4, 8–9).

Clearly, by placing the responsibility of protecting human rights on just the state and the international community, the R2P doctrine ignored the role media and some other actors play in such conflict situations. I aim to address this deficit in the R2P doctrine, by proposing a nexus between its principles and HRJ as a functional theoretical framework, to depict the role media plays in humanitarian interventions.

R2P may be appropriately categorised as 'truth-oriented', as it seeks to propose responses after thorough information analysis. This resonates with senior United Nations official Dorota Gierycz's idea of the 'assessment of human rights record' of States, to design an appropriate response. In other words, it calls for the establishment of a *prima facie* case (see Williams et al. 2012, p. 490). Gierycz emphasises that a monitoring mechanism must be established to analyse the states under their protection obligations, anchored in international legal instruments, to determine the appropriate 'protection clause' that must be applied (2010, p. 119). This is where journalists, performing their role of a watchdog, can play a vital part in establishing a *prima facie* case and consequently mobilising the support required for humanitarian intervention within the R2P framework, to prevent humanitarian catastrophe.

Despite this truth dimension, R2P like mentioned earlier, draws inspiration from both pluralist and solidarist traditions, thereby resonating with the cooperative aspects mentioned in its first two pillars. This cooperative aspect reduces the pluralists' conflict with the idea of transformative cosmopolitan agenda. In case of failure of the first two pillars, its third pillar suggests a rights-based approach. However, R2P's three responsibilities remain rooted in the principles of conflict transformation. Conversely, the conflict transformation dimension becomes prominent within the three progressive stages of obligation (preventing, reacting, rebuilding) (Galtung and Fischer 2013) of the R2P doctrine.

This discussion identifies R2P as a right based, multidimensional approach anchored in the just peace framework. Moral Philosopher Breakey's (2012) five-dimensional rights-based analysis of norms also validates the argument that R2P provides multi-layered rights protection. According to Hugh Breakey, R2P is multi-pronged approach which aims to protect human rights through its use of backup mechanisms along with open-ended duties. This backup protection is highlighted in its three pillars and the first backup requires the State to perform the role of a protector, failing which, it obligates the international community to assist it in fulfil its responsibility. In case the state fails completely, then the third backup action requires the international community to take over as the primary protector (ibid., pp. 33–34).

4.3 Human Rights Journalism and Humanitarian Interventions: Some Epistemological Theoretical Frameworks

The media has the capacity and the power to educate people of their rights and allow them to express their concerns and alert the international community, if such rights are violated. Despite the numerous human rights violation in conflict situations, the media doesn't give adequate priority to addressing them, and merely reports them. Several studies address the limitations attached to the mass media when it comes to explaining the violence along with its context (Tuchman 1972; Carey 1986). What is also well-documented in the literature is the phenomenon of 'spectacularisation' of crisis situations in the presentation of news and the reasons behind the emergence of this style (Debord 1983; Knight 1989).

As has been explained in this book earlier, some studies (Lynch and McGoldrick 2005; Lynch 2008; Shaw 2012) have criticised the failure of traditional journalism in covering conflicts and human rights violations in a conflict-sensitive manner. Lynch and McGoldrick (ibid.) proposed peace journalism as an alternative to the mainstream war journalism which they criticised to be violence-oriented, propaganda-oriented, elite-oriented and victory-oriented. Lynch and McGoldrick (2005, p. 5) define PJ as 'a set of tools, both conceptual and practical, intended to equip journalists to offer a better public service' and provide society at large 'to consider and value non-violent responses to conflict'. In his book 'Human Rights Journalism: Advances in the Reporting of Distant Humanitarian Interventions' published in 2012, Shaw argues that human rights journalism is very similar to Peace Journalism (PJ) as they both focus on reaching a win-win solution through constructive dialogue and demonstration of empathy for all cultures and peoples; and are orientated towards truth and solutions instead of propaganda (lies) and problems (conflicts). Shaw (2012, p. 46) defines HRJ as a diagnostic style of reporting, which critically analyses the victims' experiences and the needs of the perpetrators of human rights violations which is holistically defined, to better identify the underlying causes of conflict and prepare measures to prevent or mitigate them.

In short, HRJ is a style of journalism which promotes the concept of universal human rights for all and is against divides such as United States and THEM. HRJ is even better than PJ, as it operates on achieving a triple win situation as opposed to PJ's win-win. While PJ tries to resolve the conflict in a way that is beneficial to the two protagonists involved in the conflict, HRJ also takes into account the third-party bystanders, who are not directly involved (Shaw 2016, p. 33). Shaw (2012, p. 72) argues that there are multiple reasons why HRJ problematizes and categorises mainstream journalism as Human Wrongs Journalism (HWJ). Some of the reasons include its orientation towards selective justice, its bias against vulnerable voices, its reactive methods, and it detachment from the victims of human rights. Contrastingly, HRJ is more proactive, global, unbiased and attached to the victims in its approach.

The rest of this section will explore some important theoretical frameworks which support HRJ as a functional model for the role of media in the R2P framework, and underline its 'responsibility to report' role as advocated by media scholar and journalist Allan Thompson (2007). These theoretical frameworks are Kant's global justice (1963); Galtung's (1996)

ABC conflict Triangle; Parlevliet's Iceberg Metaphor (2002), Dugan's Nested Paradigm (1996) and Schirch's Just Peace (2002).

4.3.1 *Global Justice*

Shaw (2012) refers to Immanuel Kant's cosmopolitan principle of global justice to support HRJ as a radical alternative to the traditional war journalism because of its approach of identifying and dissecting the aspects of cultural and structural violence, to prevent or mitigate the incidence of direct political violence (Shaw 2012, p. 227). Kant (1963) believed in both peace and human rights and their mutual dependency. He preferred peace over war due to the latter's impact on human rights.

Based on Kant's eighteenth-century philosophy of cosmopolitanism, contemporary philosophers have come up with theories which address the challenges faced by the contemporary world. James Griffen sees human rights as a means of protecting the individual wellbeing (Griffin 2008), John Rawls constructed the theory of international society where people enjoy full just and peaceful relations (Rawls 1999), Jurgen Habermas builds his conception of global civil society (Habermas 1999, 2001), Pogges establishes his notion of human rights as moral claims on the global institutional order (2002).

Notably, in a series of articles written in the post-1989 period, Habermas reconstructed Kant's theory of cosmopolitan to suit the contemporary world's reality. A difference between Kant and Habermas are their thoughts about 'State sovereignty' in relation to the concept of human rights protection in cosmopolitan society. Kant's defence of State sovereignty in the context of the eighteenth-century world order looks irrelevant. Habermas disagrees with Kant's opinion that the State sovereignty is unchallengeable and instead supports rejection of national sovereignty during times of cosmopolitan injustice (Habermas 1999, 2001). In light of Habermas's theory of cosmopolitanism, the solidarist theory of humanitarian intervention is legitimate to reject State sovereignty, when the violation of human rights within a state is so appalling.

Moreover, Kant conceives the cosmopolitan community as an association of states devoid of their distinct political and economic institutions, and thus doesn't view them as a group of 'non-world citizens'. He takes a neutral stance when placed between the conflicting groups of liberals and realists, Universalists and pluralists. Whereas, Habermas looks at the liberal solidarism only as a step in the process of a true cosmopolitan legal order, and favours a stronger version of liberal cosmopolitanism. Consistent with the Solidarist thoughts on humanitarian intervention, Habermas argues that the existence of the UN is a proof of the possibility of transcending the states' systems. He also argues that UN as a body, can only be consistent with the universal human rights, if the body is an intermediate arrangement towards a world federation guaranteeing the rights of individuals rather than states under cosmopolitan law (ibid.).

Jürgen Habermas's advocacy of UN as a rights-based body which overrides sovereignty to ensure cosmopolitan justice, strongly resonates his theory of global justice with the human rights journalist's role of proactively working towards humanitarian interventions instead of being a detached witness, which is typical of traditional reporting of crisis.

4.3.2 *The ABC Conflict Triangle*

The holistic approach of HRJ which, according to Shaw (2012), involves reporting all forms of human rights violations, including direct, visible forms of violence such as murder, and indirect, implicit forms of violence such as poverty and deprivation, resonates with Johann Galtung's ABC (Attitude, Behaviour and Contradictions) Conflict Triangle (see Fig. 4.1).

Galtung (1996) argues that peace does not necessarily mean only the absence of direct violence, which is characterised by some behaviour causing damage, like in case of a war. Instead, he develops the alternative concept of positive peace, which addresses indirect means of violence

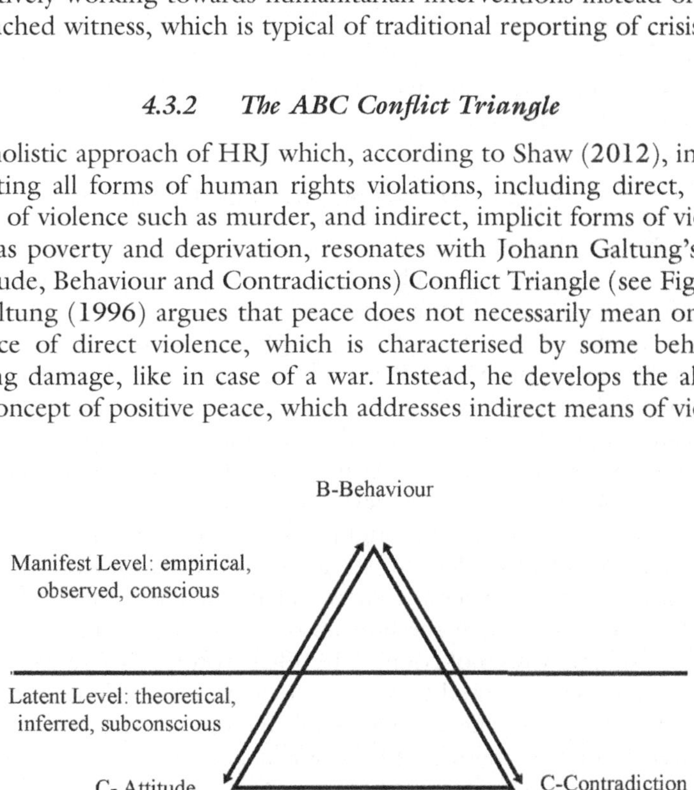

Fig. 4.1 The ABC Conflict Triangle

like cultural (Attitudes) or structural (Contradiction) violence as the 'best protection against violence' (Galtung 1996, p. 32). Galtung's ABC Conflict Triangle, like Shaw's HRJ, therefore takes a holistic approach to peace, as they take into account that direct violence (manifest level) is often a consequence of indirect violence (latent level). It is important to recognise the resonance between Galtung's holistic peace approach and the idea of a holistic human rights approach which is inclusive of both First Generation Rights (negative civil and political rights) and Second Generation Rights (positive economic, social and cultural rights), both of which are enshrined in the 1966 Twin Covenants of the UN, along with the Third Generation Rights (group rights) like those adopted in the 1993 Vienna World Conference as universal, indivisible, interdependent and interrelated (Shaw 2017). Galtung's idea of positive peace and positive rights, on one hand, and negative peace and negative rights, on the other hand, is largely related to Kant's idea of the overlaps between peace and human rights.

4.3.3 The Iceberg Metaphor Theory

Parlevliet's metaphor of an iceberg, based on Galtung's Conflict triangle theory, is extremely useful in illustrating how violations of human rights function as both causes and consequences of violent conflict (see Fig. 4.2). The top corner of the triangle (iceberg), seen above the waterline, portrays human rights violations resulting from violent conflict. It is evident from the diagram that these violations are visible, and may include attacks and intimidations, rape, forcible evictions, abductions, land grabbing, summary executions, disappearances, torture and censorship, etc. by state and non-state actors (Parlevliet 2002, 2010).

Violations of civil and political rights are not the only causes behind the occurrences of violent conflicts. Instead, lack of access to education, food and health care, can also act as factors fuelling violent conflicts. The area just below the waterline, at the bottom of the iceberg, depicts violations of human rights as causes of conflict. In other words, it is an area of latent (invisible) conflict (s) caused by systematic denial of human rights, within the societal structures. This is often determined by the structure of states, the power devolution models and the system of governance, etc. (ibid.).

The two arrows in the topmost triangle depict the interaction between the two different levels of the violent conflict/rights relationship, in a constant manner. Denial of human rights as a cause of conflict is

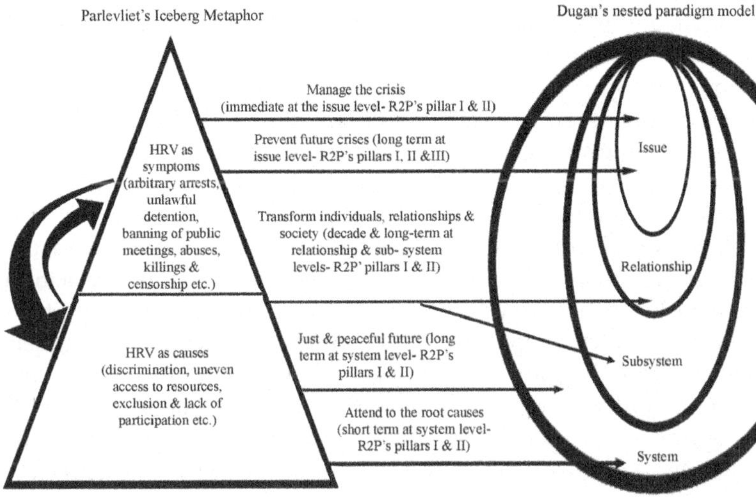

Fig. 4.2 Integrated diagram of Parlevliet's Iceberg metaphor, Dugan's nested paradigm and R2P

proportional to human rights violations. Meantime, as Parlevliet points out, a particular trend of violations such as systematic torture, land grabbing, forcible evictions, abductions, indiscriminate killings, if unaddressed, eventually become 'structural conditions in themselves', thereby inflaming the conflict (ibid.).

Thus, the iceberg diagram better illustrates human rights violations encompassing both their causes and symptoms. It draws insights from the studies of the 'identity-based conflicts' (Azar 1990; Azar and John 1986; Galtung 1990; Galtung and Wirak 1977). These theories explain the role identities play in the context of ethnic conflicts, and the impact of violation of human rights on various aspects of human needs, including protecting and maintaining identity, security, freedom and welfare, etc. which may create room for violent behaviour (Osaghae 1996; Parlevliet 2002). These studies have established a definitive link between human rights violations and violent responses, arguing that internal conflicts concerning the First and Second generations of human rights often elicit violence. Among the various factors which transform latent conflicts into manifest ones, state repression has been identified as one of the most potent ones (Thoms and Ron 2007).

This discussion stresses on the importance of understanding the role various aspects of human rights violations such as injustice, discrimination, inequality and exploitation play in causing violent conflicts. It also emphasises on the necessity of taking into account the state, its structures, and the system of governance to understand the conflicts and the need to consider all forms of violence in the conflict transformation efforts.

The iceberg diagram aids us in designing interventions which can mitigate violations and conflicts, depending on the levels and the nature of human rights violations. For example, when human rights violations are identified by visible symptoms such as violence, the immediate focus should be to protect people from such physical violence and mitigate the conflict through humanitarian interventions. On the other hand, when a latent conflict is identified, efforts should be made to address the underlying structural and cultural causes by means of institution-building, power sharing, reconstruction and development, etc. (Parlevliet 2010).

4.3.4 The Nested Paradigm Model

Lederach's study on the levels of response while dealing with conflicts, informed by Marie Dugan's 'Nested Paradigm Model' (Dugan 1996; Lederach 1997, 2003), helps us understand Parlevleit's iceberg metaphor regarding the causal relationship between direct and indirect forms of human rights violations. Dugan's Nested Paradigm model aids us in analysing conflicts using a single diagram, which examines the relationship of the conflicts with causes and the symptoms in an innovative manner. The analysis uses four varying, but interrelated levels of a conflict analysis model to study conflict situations: issue, relationships, sub-system and system.

In this Nested Model, Lederach identifies the issues that exist in a particular relationship, which can also exist within the larger context of subsystems, and ultimately in the society-wide systems. As Dyck (2000; see Toews 2013, p. 197) argues, this model better articulates the steps required to achieve the five goals of restorative justice practice: (1) Manage the crisis (immediate response at the issue level); (2) Attend to the root causes (short-term response at system level); (3) Prevent future crises (long-term response at issue level); (4) Transform individuals, relationships and society (decade and long-term response at relationship and sub-system levels); (5) Envision a just and peaceful future (long-term response at system level).

Although, it is important to consider interventions at both the issue and the system level, as Lederach emphasises, conflict mitigation measures need to be taken into account at the relationship and sub-system levels, as they have the potential to resolve the conflict in a sustainable manner and promote positive peace (1997). Linking both nested paradigm and iceberg models to the three responsibilities and three pillars of R2P provides us with a picture (see Fig. 4.2), which helps in understanding the various levels of conflict and the proper ways to address them with R2P, within human rights and conflict transformation principles (Dugan 1996, pp. 9–20; Lederach 1997).

The above diagram depicts a novel way of analysing and handling a conflict at four different, interconnected levels, within the principles of human rights and conflict transformation, to achieve the five goals of restorative justice. It also emphasises on the importance of applying various interventions at different levels for an integrated approach, particularly at issue and system levels, to protect people from human rights violations, including war crimes, crimes against humanity, and genocide, and create sustainable peace. The 'rights-based' practice of HRJ, which is guided by the Universal Declaration of Human Rights, is capable of functioning as a pacemaker to complement the 'Integrated Diagram of Parlevliet's Iceberg metaphor, Dugan's nested paradigm and R2P' below. To function as a pacemaker of the 'Integrated Diagram', HRJ must be able to identify human rights violations and conflict as a response of such violations, and at the same time recognise human rights violations as symptoms of violence, which is further explained in the next section.

4.3.5 Just Peace Theory

Shirch (2002) developed the concept of just peace as a hybrid of human rights and peace, to provide solutions when the entities are in disagreements sometimes due to their incompatible goals. The human rights worker may ask the peace worker: how can you work for peace without incorporating the concept of justice for the victim?' The peace worker might ask back: 'peace without justice is better than no peace at all: How will we ever move forward if we insist on punishing offenders?' (Schirch 2002, p. 210). Thus, the goal of 'just peacebuilding', as Schirch (ibid.) emphasises, is to address the human needs and human rights of all the groups involved (both of the victims and perpetrators) at different levels of the conflict, through a variety of short-term, intermediate and long-term approaches.

As Schirch (2013, p. 227) points out in her handbook, Strategic peace-building requires implementation of an approach locally, and inclusion of all the stakeholders involved, from various levels in a systems approach, in the decision-making process which is implemented openly and transparently, very similar to Kant's global justice, Galtung's ABC conflict triangle, Parlevleit's iceberg and Dugan's nested paradigm theories. A systems approach seeks to explain violence as a consequence of varying levels of attitudes and contradictions between different people, which are influenced by local, social, economic, political, cultural and historical conditions. Peace-building strategies should therefore be sensitive to this complex system of factors and processes and must aim to reduce differences and divisions, balance the imbalance of power relations and promote peaceful and just relationships between groups.

4.3.6 Key Elements of HRJ and R2P Nexus

This final section explores the key elements that evolve out of these theoretical frameworks which define the nexus between HRJ and R2P, and also justify the indispensable role of the media in facilitating the successful implementation of the latter: (1) Just Cause and global justice Advocacy (2) Human Rights-based approach (3) Just peace, peacebuilding and conflict prevention (4) Monitoring and accountability (5) Empowering, mobilising and intervening.

4.3.7 Just Cause and Global Justice Advocacy

As reiterated above, both R2P and HRJ unequivocally advocate for preventing human rights violations including mass atrocity crimes, and protecting civilians in times of crisis and thereby contribute to creating the conditions for sustainable peace. This relates to the theory of 'Just cause', which argues for interventions, including restricted recourse to force when there is just cause. It is at this point that a symbiotic connection is established between the concepts of R2P and HRJ, in terms of their objective, which is justified under the criteria of jus ad bellum.

R2P has two functions: firstly, it is about 'political commitment to prevent and halt genocide and mass atrocities accompanied by a policy agenda in need of implementation' (Bellamy 2010, p. 158). Secondly,

R2P is seen as a 'speech act and catalyst for action'. It means that R2P is a 'label that can be attached to particular crisis in order to generate the will and consensus necessary to mobilise a decisive international response' (ibid., p. 160). This is where the role of HRJ comes into help materialise these two functions of R2P.

The expectation is derived from the cosmopolitan context of global justice, which regards a society as a global community where everybody is equal and deserves equal protection, and human rights violation is a common concern for every member of this community (Anderson-Gold 2001, p. 22). This moral obligation necessitates media to focus on human rights without discriminating against any individual, and work towards an inclusive human rights-based justice (Shaw 2012). It also emphasises on the moral responsibility that the journalists must shoulder, which includes raising awareness about human rights violations across borders and mobilising appropriate policy response to end or prevent such violations, for peace to be realised. This conceptualisation grounded in the philosophy of 'global justice', according to Shaw, underpins the role of journalists in disseminating the information of human suffering with the view to serve 'both as a means and as an end to the promotion and protection of human rights and peace''. Communicative actions of journalists 'can contribute to the creation of peace, which can also be indispensable for human rights promotion and protection' (ibid., pp. 12–13). For example, in a number of humanitarian crises, like the Rwandan genocide (1994), the final phase of the Sri Lankan civil war (2009), the Libyan crisis (2011 to date) and the worsening Syria conflict (2011 to date), the international media could be criticised for failing the just cause and global justice advocacy role in exposing the human rights violations and mass atrocity crimes, which was needed to trigger international humanitarian intervention in the context of R2P.

4.3.8 *Just Peace, Peace Building and Conflict Prevention*

The factors which drive the R2P intervention, as the ICISS report highlights, are 'universal human rights' and 'common humanity'. Similarly, HRJ draws its inspiration and features from the Universal Declaration of Human Rights. On this basis, the importance of Shaw's HRJ approach is its holistic approach which involves both negative peace and positive peace, which have been explained above, as well as positive rights and negative rights, informed by Article 1 of the Universal Declaration of

Human Rights (1948), which in its preamble stresses on the importance of recognising the equal rights of every individual in establishing freedom, justice and peace in the world. The core principles of human rights initially recognised in UDHR, such as universality, interdependence and indivisibility, equality and non-discrimination, are crucial in achieving justice.

Shaw argues that this preventive and proactive role of HRJ resonates with the theories of mass communication, human rights and peace. In other words, it agrees with the earlier discussed 'just peace framework' which was advocated by the peacebuilding scholar Lisa Schirch (2002, 2008). Hence, the features that form the framework of Schirch's 'strategic peacebuilding' are similar to the aspects of R2P and HRJ, particularly those which address the root causes of conflict.

Developing a communication approach which incorporates the principle of human rights-oriented reporting, can aid Rapid Response mechanisms in intervening and ensuing in conflict prevention or mitigation as per the R2P doctrine. Further, it will also assist efforts by religious and traditional Peacekeepers who operate on a community level, by bridging them with the UN and other relevant responsibility holders. While it precedes and enhances preventive diplomacy at Track 01, 02 and 03 levels, coverage of local mediation efforts will amplify their voices which will be heeded in policy discussions.

It is within this premise that HRJ has the potential of functioning as a pacemaker of the 'Integrated Diagram of Parlevliet's Iceberg metaphor, Dugan's nested paradigm and R2P' (Fig. 4.2) with its ability to identify human rights violations and their role in causing a conflict, and in depicting human rights violations as symptoms of violence. It is with this aim that HRJ tries to demonstrate a political function, to bring to the attention of the world the suffering of the people, human rights abuses and their underlying causes, so that it enables the international community to act as a cosmopolitan community of humanity and respond in accordance with the three responsibilities and three pillars of R2P.

Thus, media ought to play a diagnostic and prognostic role in terms of 'providing information by covering the national, geopolitical and humanitarian angles of the news, paying more attention to analysing its political context; that it puts emphasis on explaining why things went wrong up to the crisis, instead of just telling the story as it is' (Shaw 2012, p. 96). Therefore, the HR journalists are not only expected to report about a crisis, but also analyse the its underlying causes by drawing insights from the concepts of conflict analysis and transformation, thereby enabling the international community to respond to the crisis in accordance with the R2P criteria.

4.3.9 Empowering, Mobilising and Intervening

R2P is a normative approach, aiming for a 'pre-given', natural, self-evident and indisputable set of rights which are equal to everyone. Similarly, HRJ is a normative journalistic practice, characterised as an inclusive rights-based journalism (Shaw 2011). According to Cudd (2006, p. 4), a normative concept is driven by a social theory describing the concept and its use in the society. In other words, normative concepts are derived from ideal theories and must be the centre of aspiration for societies and institutions. It is under this impression that the nexus between R2P and HRJ as an approach to intervene in a war or conflict, to end or prevent them, is guided by the theories of conflict analysis, conflict transformation and human rights.

This rationale clearly shows HRJ's 'normative capacity' to provide a facilitating role for the function of the 'Integrated Diagram of Parlevliet's Iceberg metaphor, Dugan's nested paradigm and R2P'. HRJ characterises the broad spectrum of roles inscribed in Parlevliet's iceberg metaphor illustrated above (rules; structures and institutions; relationships and process), and the relevance of Parlevliet's multidimensional approach in dealing with conflicts. Thus, it shows its own relevance and effectiveness in facilitating the R2P norm.

The diagnostic style of reporting of HRJ places great deal of importance on addressing power imbalance in the society, to achieve a positive social change. As Parlevliet (2002, p. 26) explains, it is important to analyse the asymmetry of power and resources in conflict-ridden societies and also understand the impact of such an asymmetry on conflicts, by analysing various aspects of the state and its institutions, to design interventions which can tackle structural violence, political marginalisation and socio-economic injustice. Asymmetry of power and resources in societies which directly impacts access to institutions and the protection of identity, creates an antagonistic nature of relationships between parties in conflict. Therefore, intervention efforts should focus both on addressing the imbalance of power and resources, and relationships. As Lederach (1997) argues, preventive and peacebuilding strategies are unlikely to eliminate problems and create positive social change, if they do not address asymmetry of power and resources in society.

Another possible destructive impact of power imbalance, particularly in situations of mass atrocity crimes, is the resistance of the powerful and authoritative figures against the efforts aiming towards positive change, as they often perceive such demands related to human rights as a threat or nuisance (Parlevliet 2010). Thus, they are more likely to reject calls from the international community despite their legally binding to respect international human rights treaties and instruments which aim to protect human rights through their authority. When geopolitics is involved, one nation's hoods are another's soul- mates, which further complicates the process of upholding international human rights norms. To enable states to fulfil their obligation of upholding these norms, Parlevliet suggests applying considerable and sustained public pressure along with offering political impetus to challenge their resistance.

Explicably, this discussion is all about invoking the three underlying responsibilities of R2P through its pillar approach. This underlines the positive role HRJ plays in addressing the power imbalance, which is concentrated in the hands of a few sections, and challenging the status quo which restricts them from violating the rights of the weak, which conventional war journalism fails to do. On the other hand, the diagnostic and prognostic role of HRJ, based on critical/empathy, diagnostic, pro-activism, interventionism and peace journalism frames, 'challenges, not reinforces, the status quo of the powerful dominant voices of society against the weak and marginalised ones in the promotion and protection of human rights and peace' (Shaw 2012, p. 46). As opposed to Human Wrongs Journalism, HRJ aims to challenge society's power imbalance by addressing both direct and indirect forms of violence, and prioritises the use of empathy critical frames to promote caring, proactive, interventionist attitudes and approaches to promote and protect human rights.

These five frames of HRJ are interconnected and mutually reinforcing across the dimensions of human rights and conflict transformation. For example, the empathy critical frames, expose the problems of victims in a conflict, reinforcing the diagnostic frames to reflect social reality, which aids in constructing '(global) compassion', which is explained by Hoijer (2004) or the 'cosmopolitan spectatorship' elucidated by Chouliaraki (2006, 2008). This type of critical framing enables the audience to remain proactive to facilitate the goals of interventionism framework;

this framework is needed to influence policy response and pro-activism framework to address direct and indirect violence, and in that way balance the social imbalance.

4.3.10 *Human Rights-Based Approach*

All the frames of HRJ aim to safeguard and foster human rights and peace, by creating public pressure, compassion or by balancing the power relationships, and heavily rely on the construction of reality based on information of the direct and indirect causes of conflict. Conversely, factors such as the nature of news values, the relationship of journalism to power, the dependence on news sources and the language used to describe war, enable conventional journalism to create distorted versions of reality and contribute to reinforcing the status quo of the powerful. As Sonwalker describes, 'it nurtures and reinforces a power geometry that is inherently unfair-some versions of reality are routinely presented as normal' (cited in Shaw 2012, p. 99).

As Shaw notes, diagnostic reporting of HRJ, analyses all factors that influence a conflict 'at the personal, institutional, and structural-cultural level, power relations and relations of power within a socio-cultural and political context' (Shaw 2012, p. 99), thereby constructing a social reality and aid in designing human rights and peace-building strategies.

In other words, for human rights and peace-building strategies to be successful, actors should understand the true nature of events and their effects. HRJ, as a 'rights-based multidimensional' approach is capable of fulfilling this task in terms of establishing a *prima facie* case within a critical constructivist epistemology, from which, appropriately along the lines of its three pillars, R2P can be invoked.

Critical constructive epistemology enables human rights journalists to understand and inform the social, cultural, political, ethical and moral foundations of a crisis. This knowledge enables the international community to assess the crisis situations that require international response in terms of interventions, peace-making, etc. Thus, the primary role of human rights journalists within a critical constructivist epistemology is to establish a *prima facie* case through the construction of social reality informed by social, political, cultural, ethical and moral foundations, to achieve the end goal of establishing human security.

4.3.11 Monitoring and Accountability

As mentioned earlier, Parlevliet (2010, p. 23) believes that human rights must be dealt with using a multidimensional approach, and she identifies four important dimensions in dealing with conflicts: rules; structures and institutions; relationships and processes. Rights, which are legally recognised on national and international platforms, are inalienable from human beings. Rights as structures and institutions, not only signify the division of a society based on structures and resources, but also the applicable societal mechanisms to resolve conflicts which arise as a result of these divisions. Rights as relationships refer to the relevance of rights to regulate and govern the 'top to bottom' and 'bottom to top' level interaction between the various parties in a society. Rights as processes underline the importance to take into account the dignity, participation, inclusion, protection and accountability, to ensure a holistic method of addressing the problems of access, protection and identity.

These four different human rights dimensions of Parlevliet ease the application of the three responsibilities of R2P, which in turn complement its 'three pillar' methodology. Taking into account the conceptual relationship between Parlevliet's Iceberg Metaphor and Dugan's 'Nested Paradigm Model', abuses which take place within the relationship and sub-system contexts, can be addressed through R2P's three responsibility approach considering human rights violations as symptoms (at the issue-specific level) and causes (at the system level) of conflict in a holistic manner. HRJ plays the role of monitoring and assessing the implementation of R2P to ensure and strengthen the transparency and accountability of its operations and actions. It is particularly important to monitor the actions of those who are granted the permission to intervene in the crisis by the Security Council. For instance, in the context of the Libyan crisis, the so-called R2P intervention in February 2011, which was deployed to protect the Libyan population, instead participated in aiding the rebel forces to facilitate regime change, and R2P therefore failed in ending the Libyan crisis, and building peace and reconciliation. This failure to regulate the actions of those who were in charge of the R2P operations in Libya is a reason for the failure to act in Syria (Bellamy 2014), and this bitter experience has increased the reluctance of states towards implementing R2P. Similarly, R2P failed to offer meaningful protection in Darfur due to its lack of holistic appraisal as the political conflict was extremely complex. In both these cases, media appears to have failed in its monitoring and accountability role (Badescu and Bergholm 2009).

4.4 Scrutinising Media's Role of Responsibility to Report (R2R)

The concept of R2P states the measures the international community must take when human rights are extremely violated including mass killings crimes and genocides. R2P not only respectfully recognises the states' responsibility of protecting their citizens, but also provides assistance to the states when required. It offers the provision of international intervention when a state completely fails in its obligation to protect the rights of its citizens, despite the assistance offered by the international community. Military interposition is also allowed as a method of international intervention as a last resort. However, a range of measures are taken in a nonviolent manner keeping in mind the three responsibilities in order to avoid military interference (Weiss 2004). Hence, the implementation of R2P can be viewed as a legal obligation and the international community can only act upon it as a moral responsibility (Bolton 2005). But as argued above it is clear from the discussion that the concept of R2P as a 'rights based' approach within the 'just peace' framework can be pushed towards Habermas's cosmopolitan project where necessary, by establishing a *prima facie* case.

Establishing a *prima facie* case serves as a procedural mechanism to invoke the three underlying responsibilities of R2P through its pillar approach. This is where the above identified five key elements which define the nexus between HRJ and R2P underline the indispensable role of the media in facilitating the successful implementation of R2P within its three responsibilities and three pillars framework. As elaborated above, the five parameters that define the R2P-HRJ nexus are (1) Just Cause and global justice Advocacy (2) Human Rights-based approach (3) Just peace, peacebuilding and conflict prevention (4) Monitoring and accountability (5) Empowering, mobilising and intervening. In other words, these five key elements define media's 'Responsibility to Report' (R2R) emphasised by Allan Thompson (2007) in his edited volume 'The Media and the Rwanda Genocide' (hereafter these five elements are referred as 'the elements of R2R'). Thomson (ibid.) expects media's function of R2R will work in tandem with the global community's adopted safeguarding principles with respect to genocide and mass atrocities. He also wants to observe R2R for development of a new model concerning individual journalists' behaviour. He urges journalists to exercise their moral principles to fulfil their responsibilities of report mass atrocities, when they are constrained by structural forces such as money, resources and time, as well as institutional structures, such as ownership and management, as elucidated in the previous chapters. Thus, the R2R role of the media is positioned both within human rights legal tradition and social accountability framework.

According to Susana Sampaio-Dias (2016, p. 24), there have been modifications in the international laws to incorporate mechanisms which advance current practices of prevention of human rights violations and contributed to the creation of principles of R2P. This principle could be the determinant of the relational basis of R2R for journalists, who, as pointed out in contemporary theories of sociology and politics, function in a cosmopolitan and globalised scenario. Therefore, it is imperative that journalism is viewed in terms of its social role, specifically within media and journalism studies, when concerning human rights issues. With the rise in technology, and consequently globalisation, there has also been an increase in discourse over global public sphere, along with global social ethic for human rights (ibid., p. 21). She also stresses on the importance of media in the construction and reflection of this new global reality, especially within the context of human rights, to educate and raise awareness enabling promotion of a sense of social relationship towards the 'other'.

In recent times, there has been an increased promotion by human rights policy to adopt 'responsibility' towards the other. Therefore, to better understand the relationship between human rights and journalism, it is necessary to understand this change in terms of 'R2R'. 'Legitimate expectation' is a legal term which denotes implementation of fairness and rationale, in a situation where a person has an expectation or interest, regarding a public body either retaining an age-old practice or keeping a promise. This is a procedural term of law which emphasises on an institution's durable standards or moral foundations leading to the development of legitimate expectations from that institution. With respect to journalism, people develop an inherent belief and expectation of media, that it will portray the societal 'wrongs' in the process of which it will expose both the violations that take place and their perpetrators. Therefore, the public predetermines the roles and responsibilities of the role of journalism, attaching to it an innate expectation concerning ethics, despite the increasing distrust and disbelief in media (ibid., pp. 32–33). It is within the social expectation that Allan (2007) expects journalists to act along the line of R2P to report if they observe something unacceptable human rights violations and crimes against humanity happening. Let us now see how media can play its R2R role to facilitate the implementation of R2P.

Although Allan's call for journalists to cover stories of human rights violations go unnoticed falls within proactive and humanistic perspectives, the HR Journalists' R2R role goes beyond just preventive practise, giving them the tools they need to perform multidimensional and multimodal functions and invoking the three underlying responsibilities of R2P through its pillar approach.

Highlighting the role of media in facilitating R2P doctrine, Simon Cottles (2019, pp. 172–174) elucidates how local and international media can play a critical role in its implementation. He argues that the first pillar of the R2P can be easily facilitated by using the media as a tool. The first pillar requires the state to take responsibility of protecting its citizen's rights against various crimes against humanity. The media can enable the first pillar by reporting about the potential risks and dangers, and by urging the powerful and the general public to fulfil their obligations, while also educating and warning the society about the changing conditions which are moving towards violence on the ground.

Similarly, to exercise of the pillar two, Cottle states, that the media can shine a spotlight on the conflict situations with assistance from decision makers around the world, and it can alert the world about the serious violence. It can also devise appropriate interventions and remind publics and international powerholders of their obligations to encourage and assist the States in fulfilling their responsibility. In this way, the media can play an influential role in ensuring that human rights violations do not go unnoticed and unpunished (ibid.).

With respect to the pillar three, media's main role includes constructing a public discourse and dialogue on the responsibility of the international community of implementing a decisive action, in case the state fails to fulfil its responsibilities and conflicts progress to become mass atrocity crimes. The criteria which encompass such military interventions under the R2P, should also inform such reporting. The criteria require the violence to be large-scale in nature, with regard to threatened or actual loss of life or ethnic cleansing; the intervention must aim to cease the suffering or prevent it; military force must be used in the worst-case-scenario; the means must be proportionate to the ends; the probability of the success of such an intervention must be high. Media must actively examine and debate about the policy options during such crises. This can check the need for the use of such democratic force, and also ensures that the action taken is proportionate to the crises and there is no generation of surplus violence. This monitoring by the media must continue in the face of rising or receding atrocity, and even after the processes of civil society are restored (ibid.).

These requirements of R2P and HRJ's power to provide a way out were highlighted during our earlier discussion, which recognised that the diagnostic style of reporting of HRJ has the ability to identify human rights violations and the consequential conflict, and also identify human rights violations as symptoms of violence, and functions as a pacemaker of the 'Integrated Diagram of Parlevliet's Iceberg metaphor, Dugan's nested paradigm and R2P' to facilitate the implementation of R2P. Conversely, we have also highlighted the functional capacities of the five key mutually reinforcing elements in sustaining media's role of R2R to invoke the three underlying responsibilities of R2P through its pillar (first pillar, second pillar and third pillar) and responsibility approach (the responsibility to prevent, the responsibility to react and the responsibility to rebuild). As explained above, '*Just peace, peace building and conflict prevention*' element precedes and enhances preventive diplomacy at Track 01, 02 and 03 levels, '*Empowering, mobilising and intervening*' element addresses power imbalance in the society, '*Just Cause and Global Justice Advocacy*' argues for interventions, including restricted recourse to force when there is a just cause, '*Human Rights-based approach*' establishes a *prima facie* case of human rights violations and '*Monitoring and accountability*', monitors the actions of both the abusers and the interveners at all stages.

Importantly, the 'Monitoring and accountability' and 'Just Cause and Global Justice Advocacy' elements can play a crucial role in reinforcing and legitimising the R2P concept by establishing a *prima facie* case of mass atrocity crimes as well as in determining the appropriate intervener by mediating between the pluralist and solidarist traditions. 'Assessment of human rights record' of States, as Gierycz (2010, p. 119) stresses, can serve as a basis for an appropriate legitimate response to mass atrocities. She elaborates that employing a human rights monitoring methodology to scrutinise the states under their protection obligations, anchored in international legal instruments can be an assessment tool to decide on the application of the 'protection clause' in an appropriate manner (2010, p. 119). This is where, HRJ's Monitoring and accountability element as a truth seeking tool can play a vital role in establishing ***prima facie*** case of a violent situation.

On the other hand, concerning the qualification of the intervener, in order to ensure genuine protection through the identification of relevant obliged responsible holder (s), R2P leaves this process open. As Breakey (2012, pp. 33–34) explains, R2P, as a paradigm of a rights-based norm, anchors itself on 'Responsibility' and identifies a set of agents whose roles are to protect the rights. Nevertheless, although the World Summit Document of 2005 entrusts the responsibility to the Security Council as the appropriate legitimate body, it doesn't clarify who exactly holds the obligations and how they should exercise their responsibility in a particular situation (ibid.). Hence, this aspect of identifying 'relevant obliged responsible holders' and the path of execution remains an important part of the process, which has been left open for it to be resolved situationally and contextually. HRJ's Just Cause and Global Justice Advocacy element can play a very important role in creating a discursive order of setting the conditions for a relevant responsible holder to be identified.

Scholars in the recent years have argued that the Security Council cannot be held as the only responsible body for the implementation of R2P. While acknowledging the coordinating role of the United Nations and the requirement for the authorisation of the Security Council in the case of a military intervention, scholars have argued that a relevant obliged responsible holder can be determined in terms of two properties: effectiveness and legitimacy (Pattison 2009, 2010). Political Scientist James Pattison in his groundbreaking book 'Humanitarian Intervention and the Responsibility to Protect: Who Should Intervene?' argues the point that effectiveness and legitimacy are the determinants which must decide on the qualification of an intervener in any case involving a large-scale violation of human rights. The interveners can be states, coalitions of states, international bodies such as NATO, etc. (2010, pp. 74–75). Characterising legitimacy as a scalar concept, Pattison explains legitimacy as a 'morally justifiable power' can determine an 'intervener possessing full legitimacy and intervener possessing an adequate degree of legitimacy' (ibid., p. 32). The degree of legitimacy is decided by a number of qualities such as effectiveness, representativeness, legality, etc. On the other hand, as Pattison elucidates, an intervener can also have varying degrees of these qualities, of which 'effectiveness' is considered as the most important quality to be a legitimate actor. In this manner, James Pattison's elucidation to the question of 'who is entitled to intervene' is a very creative way of moving the position of R2P from pluralist (collective or unilateral interventions with the approval of UN) to solidarist (collective or unilateral interventions with the approval of UN or a collective authority or strong morality without the approval of UN). This situation expects more responsible and indispensable role from the media to identify the relevant responsible holder(s) who must intervene the situation legitimately and appropriately. Establishing a strong *prima facie* case, in turn would complement Just Cause and Global Justice Advocacy element to create a genuine global discursive order to rightly identify the responsible holder to intervene.

4.5 Summary

This chapter explored the nexus between HRJ and R2P and dealt with some important epistemological theoretical frameworks which support HRJ as a functional model of the role of the media in the R2P framework. These epistemological theoretical frameworks are Kant's global justice (1963); Galtung's ABC conflict Triangle; Parlevliet's Iceberg Metaphor (2002), Dugan's Nested Paradigm (1996); and Schirch's Just Peace (2002). These theoretical frameworks identified five key elements that define the nexus between HRJ and R2P and also utilised them to justify the indispensable role of the media in facilitating the successful implementation of the R2P within its three responsibilities and three pillars framework. The five parameters that define the R2P-HRJ nexus are (1) Just Cause and global justice Advocacy (2) Human Rights-based approach (3) Just peace, peacebuilding and conflict prevention (4) Monitoring and accountability (5) Empowering, mobilising and intervening. The discussion also showed how these five key elements resonate with Allan Thompson', which in turn describe Allan Thompson's (2007) emphasis on R2R in times of mass atrocity crimes.

Bibliography

Allan, S. (2004). The Culture of Distance: Online Reporting of the Iraq War. In S. Allan & B. Zelizer (Eds.), *Reporting War: Journalism in Wartime* (pp. 347–364). Abingdon: Taylor and Francis.

Almeida, J. M. (2002). International Political Theory and the Issue of Legitimate Intervention. *Verão*. Instituto da Defesa Nacional. 2ª Série; N° 102 [Online] http://hdl.handle.net/10400.26/1300. Accessed 11 Nov 2018.

Anderson, M. C., & Robertson, C. L. (2011). *Seeing Red: A History of Natives in Canadian Newspapers*. Winnipeg: University of Manitoba Press.

Anderson-Gold, S. (2001). *Cosmopolitanism and Human Rights*. Cardiff: University of Wales Press.

Arend, A. C., & Beck, R. J. (1993). *International Law and the Use of Force: Beyond the UN Charter Paradigm*. London: Routledge.

Azar, E. E. (1990). *The Management of Protracted Social Conflict: Theory and Cases*. Aldershot: Dartmouth Publishing Company.

Azar, E. E., & John, W. B. (Eds.). (1986). *International Conflict Resolution: Theory and Practice*. Sussex, England: Wheatsheaf Books.

Badescu, C. G., & Bergholm, L. (2009). The Responsibility to Protect and the Conflict in Darfur: The Big Let-Down. *Security Dialogue, 40*(3), 287–309. https://doi.org/10.1177/0967010609336198.

Balabanova, E. (2014). *The Media and Human Rights: The Cosmopolitan Promise*. London: Routledge.

Bellamy, A. J. (2009). *The Responsibility to Protect: The Global Effort to End Mass Atrocities*. Cambridge: Polity Press.

Bellamy, A. J. (2010). The Responsibility to Protect-Five Years On. *Ethics and International Affairs, 24*(2), 143–169.

Bellamy, A. J. (2014). From Tripoli to Damascus? Lesson Learning and the Implementation of the Responsibility to Protect. *International Politics, 51*(1), 23–44.

Breakey, H. (2012). Protection Norms and Human Rights: A Rights-Based Analysis of the Responsibility to Protect and the Protection of Civilians in Armed Conflict. *Global Responsibility to Protect, 4*(3), 309–333.

Blumler, J. G., & Gurevitch, M. (1981). Politicians and the Press: An Essay on Role Relationships. In D. Nimmo & K. Sanders (Eds.), *Handbook of Political Communication* (pp. 467–493). Beverly Hills, CA: Sage.

Bolton, J. R. (2013). Letter from John R. Bolton, Representative of the United States of America to the UN, to Jean Ping, President of the UN General Assembly. 30 August 2005. Available at http://www.responsibilitytoprotect.org/files/US_Boltonletter_R2P_30Aug05%5B1%5D.pdf. Accessed 22 Aug 2016.

Bull, H. (1977). *The Anarchical Society: A Study of Order in World Politics*. London: Macmillan.

Carey, J. W. (1986). Why and How?: The Dark Continent of American Journalism. In R. Manoff & M. Schudson (Eds.), *Reading the News* (pp. 146–196). New York: Pantheon.

Carruthers, S. L. (2000). *The Media at War: Communication and Conflict in the Twentieth Century*. Basingstoke: Macmillan.

Chomsky, N. (1999). *The New Military Humanism*. London: Pluto Press.

Chouliaraki, L. (2006). *The Spectatorship of Suffering*. London: Sage.

Chouliaraki, L. (2008). The Mediation of Suffering and the Vision of a Cosmopolitan Public. *Television and New Media, 9*(5), 371–391.

Costa, B. F. (2014). The English School and Regional International Societies: Theoretical and Methodological Reflections. In A. Karmazin., F. B. Costa., Y. Zhang, & F. Merke (Eds.), *Regions in International Society: The English School at the Sub-Global Level* (pp. 22–44). Brno: Masaryk University.

Cottle, S. (2009). *Global Crisis Reporting: Journalism in the Global Age*. Maidenhead: Open University Press.

Cottle, S. (2013). Journalists Witnessing Disasters: From the Calculus of Death to the Injunction to Care. *Journalism Studies, 14*(2), 232–248.

Cottle, S. (2017). Journalist Killings and the Responsibility to Report. In U. Carlsson & R. Pöyhtäri (Eds.), *The Assault on Journalism: Building Knowledge to Protect Freedom of Expression* (pp. 129–141). Gothenberg: Nordicom.

Cottle, S. (2019). Humanitarianism, Human Insecurity, and Communications: What's Changing in a Globalised World? In S. Cottle & G. Cooper (Eds.), *Humanitarianism, Communications and Change*. New York: Peter Lang Publishing Inc.

Cudd, A. (2006). *Analysing Oppression*. Oxford: Oxford University Press.

Debord, G. (1983). *Society of the Spectacle*. Detroit, MI: Black and Red Press.

Deng, F. M. (2009a). The Evolution of the Idea of "Sovereignty as Responsibility. In A. Adebajo (Ed.), *From Global Apartheid to Global Village: Africa and the United Nations* (pp. 191–213). Scottsville: University of KwaZulu-Natal Press.

Deng, F. M. (2009b). Frontiers of Sovereignty a Framework of Protection, Assistance, and Development for the Internally Displaced. *Leiden Journal of International Law, 8*(2), 249–286.

Deng, F. M., Kimaro, S., Lyons, T., Rothcild, D., & Zartmann, I. W. (1996). *Sovereignty as Responsibility: Conflict Management in Africa*. Washington: The Brookings Institution.

Dharmapuri, S. (2012). Implementing UN Security Council Resolution 1325: Putting the Responsibility to Protect into Practice. *Global Responsibility to Protect, 4*(2), 241–271.

Downman, S., & Ubayasiri, K. (2017). *Journalism for Social Change in Asia: Reporting Human Rights*. Basingstoke: Palgrave Macmillan.

Dugan, M. (1996). A Nested Theory of Conflict. *A Leadership Journal: Women in Leadership, 1*, 9–19.

Dyck, D. (2000). Reaching Toward a Structurally Responsive Training and Practice of Restorative Justice. *Contemporary Justice Review, 3*(3), 239–265.

Etzioni, A. (2006). Sovereignty as Responsibility. *Orbis, 50*(1), 71–85.

Fixdal, M., & Smith, D. (1998). Humanitarian Intervention and Just War. *Mershon International Studies Review, 42*(2), 283–312.

Galtung, J. (1969). Violence, Peace and Peace Research. *Journal of Peace Research, 6*(3), 167–191.

Galtung, J. (1990). Cultural Violence. *Journal of Peace Research, 27*(3), 291–305.

Galtung, J. (1996). *Peace by Peaceful Means: Peace and Conflict, Development and Civilization*. London: Sage.

Galtung, J. (2000). *Conflict Transformation by Peaceful Means*. New York: United Nations.

Galtung, J. (2002). Peace Journalism: A Challenge. In W. Kempf & H. Luostarinen (Eds.), *Journalism and the New World Order, Studying War and the Media* (pp. 269–272). Nordicom: Göteborg.

Galtung, J. (2004). USA, the West and the Rest After September 11 and October 7 2001. In S. A. Nohrstedt & R. Ottosen (Eds.), *U.S. and the Others: Global Media Images on 'the War on Terror'* (pp. 57–76). Göteborg: Nordicom.

Galtung, J., & Fischer, D. (2013). *Pioneer of Peace Research*. London: Springer.

Galtung, J., & Ruge, M. H. (1965). The Structure of Foreign News. *Journal of Peace Research, 2*(1), 64–91.

Galtung, J., & Wirak, A. H. (1977). Human Needs and Human Rights: A Theoretical Approach. *Bulletin of Peace Proposals, 8*, 251–258.

Gies, L. (2015). *Mediating Human Rights: Media, Culture, and Human Rights Law*. New York, NY: Routledge.

Gierycz, D. (2010). From Humanitarian Intervention (HI) to Responsibility to Protect (R2P). *Criminal Justice Ethics, 29*(2), 110–128.

Griffin, J. (2008). *On Human Rights*. Oxford: Oxford University Press.

Hammond, P. (2007). *Framing Post-Cold War Conflicts*. Manchester: Manchester University Press.

Habermas, J. (1999). Kant's Idea of Perpetual Peace: At Two Hundred Years' Historical Remove. In C. Cronin & P. de Greiff (Eds.), *The Inclusion of the Other: Study in Political Theory* (pp. 167–201). Cambridge: The MIT Press.

Habermas, J. (2001). The Postantional Constellation and the Future of Democracy. In J. Habermas (Ed.), *The Postnational Constellation: Political Essay* (pp. 58–112). (M. Pensky, trans.). Cambridge: The MIT Press.

Hammond, P., & Herman, E. S. (Eds.). (2000). *Degraded Capability: The Media and the Kosovo Crisis*. London: Pluto Press.

Hehir, A. (2013). *Humanitarian Intervention: An Introduction* (2nd ed.). New York: Palgrave Macmillan.

Hoijer, B. (2004). The Discourse of Global Compassion: The Audience and Media Reporting of Human Suffering. *Media, Culture and Society, 26*(4), 513–531.

Höijer, B., Nohrstedt, S. A., & Ottosen, R. (2002). The Kosovo War in the Media—Analysis of a Global Discursive Order. *Conflict & Communication Online, 1*(2).

Holzgrefe, J. L. (2003). The Humanitarian Intervention Debate. In J. L. Holzgrefe & R. O. Keohane (Eds.), *Humanitarian Intervention: Ethical, Legal, and Political Dilemmas* (pp. 15–52). Cambridge: Cambridge University Press.
ICISS (International Commission on Intervention and State Sovereignty). (2001). *The Responsibility to Protect: Report of the International Commission on Intervention and State Sovereignty*. Ottawa: The International Development Research Centre. Available at http://responsibilitytoprotect.org/ICISS%20Report.pdf. Accessed 20 Dec 2017.
Implementing the Responsibility to Protect. (2009). *Report of the Secretary-General at Sixty-Third Session*. Available at http://responsibilitytoprotect.org/implementing%20the%20rtop.pdf. Accessed 22 Mar 2018.
Jones, B., & Baumgartner, F. (2005). *The Politics of Attention. How Government Prioritizes Attention*. Chicago: University of Chicago Press.
Kant, I. (1963/1784). *Idea for a Universal History from a Cosmopolitan Point of View* (L. W. Beck, Trans. and Ed.). New York: Macmillan.
Keating, T. (2013). Pluralism and International Society. *E-International Relations*. Available at http://www.e-ir.info/2013/05/15/pluralism-and-international-society/. Accessed 20 Dec 2017.
Klein, J. (1986). *Lectures and Essays*. The MIT Press Classics Series. Cambridge, MA: The MIT Press.
Knight, G. (1989). The Reality Effects of Tabloid Television News. In M. Raoby & P. A. bruck (Eds.), *Communication for and Against Democracy*. Montreal: Black Rose Books.
Korab-Karpowicz, J. (2013). Political Realism in International Relations. *The Stanford Encyclopedia of Philosophy*. Available at: http://stanford.library.usyd.edu.au/entries/realism-intl-relations. Accessed 18 Dec 2019.
Lazarsfeld, P. F., Berelson, B., & Gaudet, H. (1944). *The People's Choice: How the Voter Makes Up His Mind in a Presidential Campaign*. New York: William Morrow.
Lederach, J. P. (1997). *Building Peace: Sustainable Reconciliation in Divided Societies*. Washington, DC: United States Institute of Peace.
Lederach, J. P. (2003). *The Little Book of Conflict Transformation*. Intercourse: Good Books.
Livingston, S. (1997). Clarifying the CNN Effect: An Examination of Media Effects According to Type of Military Intervention. *Harvard Research Paper* R-18, Joan.
Ludlow, D. R. L. (2009). Humanitarian Intervention and Rwandan Genocide. *The Journal of Conflict Studies*, *XIX*(1). Available at: http://journals.hil.unb.ca/index.php/jcs/article/view/4378/5055. Accessed 21 Dec 2019.
Lynch, J. (2008). *Debates in Peace Journalism*. Sydney: Sydney University Press.
Lynch, J., & McGoldrick, A. (2005). Peace Journalism: A Global Dialog for Democracy and Democratic Media. In R. A. Hackett & Y. Zhao

(Eds.), *Democratizing Global Media* (pp. 269–288). Lanham: Rowman and Littlefield.

Nimmo, D. D. (1964). *Newsgathering in Washington*. New York: Atherton.

Osaghae, E. E. (1996). Human Rights and Ethnic Conflict Management: The Case of Nigeria. *Journal of Peace Research, 33*(2), 171–188.

Ozdemir, R. (2011). Invasion of Iraq: A Reflection of Realism. *Turkish Journal of Politics, 2*(2), 103–115.

Parlevliet, M. (2002). Bridging the Divide: Exploring the Relationship Between Human Rights and Conflict Management. *Track Two, 11*(1), 8–43.

Parlevliet, M. (2010). Rethinking Conflict Transformation from a Human Rights Perspective. In V. Dudouet & B. Schmelzle. *Human Rights and Conflict Transformation: The Challenges of Just Peace* (pp. 15–46). Berlin: Berghof Conflict Research.

Parlevliet, M., Lamb, G., & Maloka, V. (2005). Introduction: Understanding Conflict and Its Relationship with Human Rights. In M. Parlevliet, G. Lamb, & V. Maloka (Eds.), *Defenders of Human Rights, Managers of Conflict, Builders of Peace? National Human Rights Institutions in Africa* (pp. 9–32). Cape Town: University of Cape Town.

Pattinson. J. (2010a). *Humanitarian Intervention and the Responsibility to Protect*. Leiden: Martinus Nijhoff Publishers.

Pattinson, J. (2010b). *Humanitarian Intervention and the Responsibility to Protect: Who Should. Intervene?* Oxford: Oxford University Press.

Pattison, J. (2009). Humanitarian Intervention, the Responsibility to Protect and Jus in Bello. *Global Responsibility to Protect, 1*(3), 364–391.

Pattison, J. (2010). *Humanitarian Intervention and the Responsibility to Protect: Who Should Intervene?* (pp. 44–180). Oxford University Press.

Pogge, T. (2002). *World Poverty and Human Rights*. Cambridge: Polity Press.

Pollock, J. C. (2014). Illuminating Human Rights: How Demographics Drive Media Coverage. *Atlantic Journal of Communication, 22*(3–4), 141–159.

Potter, R. B. (1973). The Moral Logic of War. In C. R. Beitz & T. Herman (Eds.), *Peace and War* (pp. 203–233). San Francisco: W.H. Freeman.

Rawls, J. (1971). *A Theory of Justice*. Cambridge: Harvard University Press.

Rawls, J. (1999). *The Law of People*. Cambridge: Harvard University Press.

Robinson, P. (2000). The Policy Media Interaction Model: Measuring Media Power During Humanitarian Crisis. *Journal of Peace Research, 37*(5), 625–645.

Sampaio-Dias, S. (2016). *Reporting Human Rights*. New York: Peter Lang.

Schirch, L. (2002). *Human rights and Peacebuilding: Towards Justpeace*. Paper presented to 43rd Annual International Studies Association Convention, New Orleans, Louisiana, March 2002.

Schirch, L. (2008). Strategic Peacebuilding: State of the Field Peace Prints. *South Asian Journal of Peacebuilding, 1*(1), 1–17.

Schirch, L. (2013). *Conflict Assessment and Peacebuilding Planning: Toward a Participatory Approach to Human Security*. Boulder: Kumarian Press.

Shaw, M. (1996). *Civil Society and Media in Global Crises: Representing Distant Violence*. London: Pinter.

Shaw, M. (1999). Global Voices: Civil Society and Media in Global Crises. In T. Dunne. & N. Wheeler (Eds.), *Human Rights in Global Politics* (pp. 214–232). Cambridge: Cambridge University Press.

Shaw, I. S. (2011). 'Human Rights Journalism': A Critical Conceptual Framework of a Complementary Strand of Peace Journalism. In I. S. Shaw, J. Lynch, & R. Hackett (Eds.), *Expanding Peace Journalism: Comparative and Critical Approaches* (pp. 96–121). Sydney, NSW: Sydney University Press.

Shaw, I. S. (2012). *Human Rights Journalism: Advances in Reporting Distant Humanitarian Interventions*. London: Palgrave Macmillan.

Shaw, I. S. (2016). *Business Journalism: A Critical Political Economy Approach*. Taylor and Francis. London.UK: Routledge.

Shaw, I. S. (2017). Media, Culture and Human Rights: Towards an Intercultural Communication and Human Rights Journalism Nexus. In H. Tumber & J. Waisbord (Eds.), *Routledge Companion to Media and Human Rights*. London.UK: Routledge.

Shaw. I., Lynch. J., & Hackett, R. (2011). *Expanding Peace journalism: Comparative and Critical Approaches*. Sydney: Sydney University Press.

Sigal, L. V. (1973). *Reporters and Officials: The Organization and Politics of Newsmaking*. Lexington, MA: D.C. Health.

Strömbäck, Jesper. (2005). In Search of a Standard: Four Models of Democracy and Their Normative Implications for Journalism. *Journalism Studies, 6*(3), 331–345.

Thompson, A. (Ed.). (2007). *The Media and the Rwanda Genocide*. London: Pluto Press.

Thoms, O. N. T., & Ron, J. (2007). Do Human Rights Violations Cause Internal Conflict? *Human Rights Quarterly, 29*(3), 674–705.

Toews, B. (2013). Justice and Peace in Restorative Justice: A Path to Interdependence. In F. Enns, A. Mosher, & O. F. Tveit (Eds.), *Just Peace: Ecumenical, Intercultural, and Interdisciplinary Perspectives*. Eugene, OR: Pickwick Publications.

Tuchman, G. (1972). Objectivity as Strategic Ritual: An Examination of Newsmen's Notions of Objectivity. *The American Journal of Sociology, 77*(4), 660–679.

Tumber, H. (2007). The Media and International Conflict: Theoretical Overview. In H. Nossek, A. Sreberny, & P. Sonwalkar (Eds.), *Media and Political Violence*. London: Routledge, Taylor & Francis.

Weiss, T. G. 2004. The Humanitarian Impulse. In D. M. Malone (Ed.), *The United Nations Security Council After the Cold War* (pp. 37–54). Boulder, CO: Lynne Rienner.

Weiss, G. (2011). *The Cage: The Fight for Sri Lanka and the Last Days of the Tamil Tigers*. London: The Bodley Head.

Wheeler, N. J., & Egerton, F. (2008). The Responsibility to Protect: "Precious Commitment" or a Promise Unfulfilled? *Global Responsibility to Protect, 1*(1), 114–132.

Williams, P. R., Ulbrick, J. T., & Worboys, J. (2012). Preventing Mass Atrocity Crimes: The Responsibility to Protect and the Syria Crisis. *Case Western Reserve Journal of International Law, 45*(1/2), 472–503.

Wolfsfeld, G. (1997). *Media and Political Conflict*. New York: Cambridge University Press.

Wolfsfeld, G. (2004). *Media and the Path to Peace*. Cambridge: Cambridge University Press.

World Summit Document. (2005). Resolution adopted by the General Assembly', 25 October. Available at http://www.un.org/womenwatch/ods/A-RES-60-1-E.pdf. Accessed 22 Mar 2017.

CHAPTER 5

Analysing Feature Detection of Media Representations Via Framing Matrix and Multimodal Discourse Analysis Matrix

5.1 Introduction

This chapter has two primary purposes. The first one is to propose a 'Human Rights Journalism (HRJ)- Responsibility to Protect (R2P) Nexus Conceptual Model', consolidating the knowledge we gained in the previous chapters. The idea is to illuminate how HRJ can demonstrate its power and capabilities under the agenda-setting framework to protect, promote and fulfil human rights of rights-holders. This, on the other hand underlines the importance of a robust analytical framework to evaluate the practice of HRJ as well as its capacity to construct a human rights-focused discourse through the agenda-setting process to protect and reinforce human rights. Therefore, the second purpose of this chapter is to propose a research framework named 'Framing Matrix and Multimodal Discourse Analysis Matrix' (FMMDAM), integrated into the coding manual of the content analysis framework to analyse the practice of HRJ. The capacity of using the FMMDAM is based on its ability to analyse a large number of news stories of a particular event over a long period of time and examine the accessibility and applicability effect of the agenda-setting process to assess the performance and the conditions of the practice of HRJ. This chapter is an innovative methodological contribution on the operationalisation of the analytics of mediation and the framework of pity and protection within a quantitative research project. Understanding this framework will prove to be beneficial for undergraduate and postgraduate

S. Selvarajah, *Human Rights Journalism and its Nexus to Responsibility to Protect*, https://doi.org/10.1007/978-3-030-49072-0_5

students within the sphere of media, journalism and mass communication studies, especially those interested in the intersection between media, human rights, conflicts and peace building.

5.2 A Research Framework for Analysing the Practise of HRJ

Our discussion in Chapter 3 highlighted the HRJ's ability to pursue a human rights agenda, within the critical constructivist epistemology. Our discussion in Chapter 4 identified five key elements which characterise the nexus between HRJ and R2P, while also elaborating how they functionalize media's (Responsibility to Report) R2R role, thereby facilitating the implementation of R2P. The knowledge that has thus been acquired through our previous discussions, aids us in developing a conceptual model to understand the complementation of the five key elements with the application of R2P, within the agenda-setting framework (Fig. 5.1).

Clearly, the functional dynamism of the five key elements of R2R is better illustrated in the below 'HRJ- R2P Nexus Conceptual Model', within the agenda-setting framework. Chapter 3 highlighted the three components of the agenda-setting process: media agenda, public agenda and policy agenda. Media agenda merely relates to the issues discussed in the media. Public agenda refers both to the issues discussed in the media and their impact over the public's thoughts pertaining to an issue or an event. Policy agenda is concerned with the issues that the public is made aware of by the media, which consequently draws the attention of the policymakers. We also discussed two characteristics of agenda-setting which are external (visibility) and internal (valance), that make the media salient. Visibility of a news story depends on the frequency and the prominence attributed to an issue or an event in the media. Whereas, valence is the perceptual attributes of media content including positivity, neutrality and negativity. These two kinds of 'transfer of salience' are also categorised as the first level (visibility) agenda-setting and second level (valence) agenda-setting. The first level of agenda-setting refers to the perceived importance of an issue (what to think about) and the second level focusses on the relative salience of the various attributes of an issue (how to think about it). We have also discussed the concepts of accessibility and applicability, and their parallels to the first and second levels of agenda-setting. Accessibility identifies the ease with which one can find or access information about an issue along with its capacity to activate

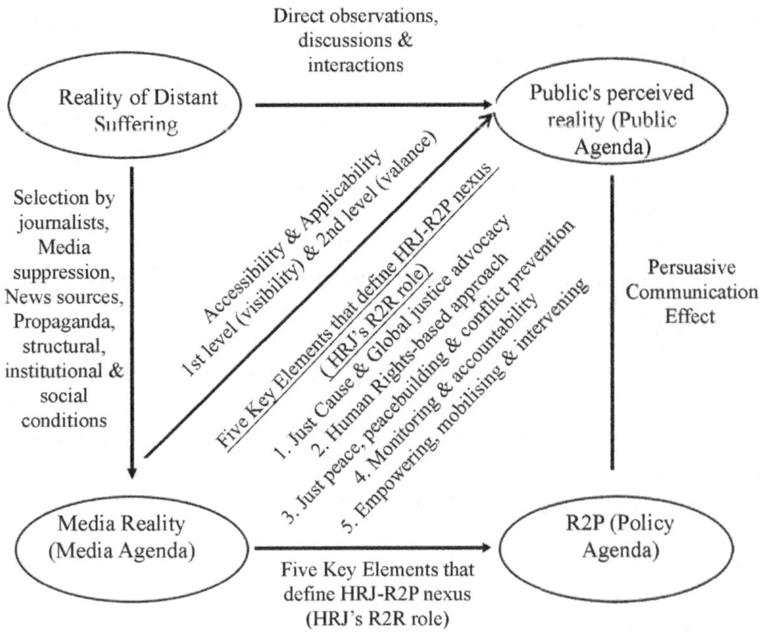

Fig. 5.1 HRJ-R2P Nexus Conceptual Model

the pre-existing knowledge in an individual's memory pertaining to the same subject. Conversely, applicability refers to establishing a connection between the two concepts (attributes of a message and the stored ideas or knowledge of an individual). Moreover, the discussion also highlighted the parallelism between agenda-setting and accessibility, as well as framing and applicability, in terms of processing messages.

Warring parties try to manipulate the media to portray the issue in a manner which complements the way they want the general public to perceive the reality of that conflict. Meanwhile, human rights organisations and peace organisations expect the media to expose the suffering of the people stuck in conflict as they see it and reflect the truest form of reality so that the world can act to end the suffering. On one hand, the warring parties engage in propaganda campaigns to exert control over media's discourse production, which would aid them in impacting the perception of the distant others, about the conflict and the suffering, in a manner that is favourable to them. On the other hand, they take legal and extra-legal measures such as media suppression, intimidation, a ban on journalists entering the conflict zone, and censorship, to prevent true portrayal of the situation by the media. Conversely, as discussed in Chapter 2, factors such as the nature of news values, the relationship of journalism to power, the dependence on news sources and the language used to describe war, enable conventional journalism to reinforce the status quo of the powerful through distorted versions of reality.

It is because of this control over the media, by various actors in a conflict, that we see different types of discourses surrounding each conflict existing parallelly, and subsequently construct a discursive order (Fairclough 2002) as explained in the preceding chapters. Whoever, creates a formidable discourse in the discursive order through their communicative actions, would be able to influence the behaviour and the responsiveness of the distant others, with respect to the distant suffering. Although the same logic applies to the human rights organisations and peace organisations, this seldom happens in practice due to the aforementioned failings of conventional journalism, which produces news that distorts the representation of reality. Moreover, in some instances where conventional journalism brings out the sufferings of the distant people, it ironically constructs a mindset of 'feel good' activism (Chouliaraki 2013) and compassion fatigue (Moeller 1999) among the distant news consumers. Thus, alternative journalism models such as PJ and HRJ have been proposed for journalists covering humanitarian crises, mass atrocities and other forms of human rights violations. This would enable the creation of powerful peace and human rights discourse in an organised and systematic manner to help take control over the situations and to end the suffering.

In this premise, as discussed in Chapter 3, the concept of HRJ as a 'rights-based multidimensional' approach aiming to protect and promote human rights and prevent mass atrocities, has been proposed within a critical constructivist epistemology. We also recognised the ability and the power of HRJ to pursue a human rights agenda, and particularly, how the five key elements that define the nexus between HRJ and R2P can perform R2R role within the agenda-setting mechanism.

The above 'HRJ- R2P Nexus Conceptual Model', throws light upon the HRJ's potential to influence the public agenda and create options for R2P interventions, to respond to distant sufferings. As illustrated in the above diagram, the general public's perceived reality of the actual reality of a distant suffering, is the essence of the agenda-setting process and is created in two ways. Firstly, people who directly observe the suffering and experience the suffering (victims) would create the perceived reality of that suffering. Media reporting of that suffering would also influence the construction of the perceived reality. However, the former's perceived reality of the suffering wouldn't be very different from the actual reality. Conversely, in the case of the distant others, media plays a key role in determining their perceived reality of the distant suffering. Although their pre-existing knowledge of the suffering can influence their perception to some extent, the information acquired through the media has a greater influence on them. It is within this premise, that Chouliaraki (2006), in her research of spectatorship of suffering, underlined media's power in creating a sense of immediacy by connecting the readers to the distant sufferers, and categorised the news reports based on their potential of creating immediacy. This emphasises HRJ's ability to activate the five key elements of R2R to invoke the three underlying responsibilities of R2P through its pillar approach, and also evaluate its effectiveness to do so in terms of the frames of HRJ and the typology of the news stories. In other words, the role HRJ plays in the construction of the perceived reality among the distant news consumers, to establish a *prima facie* case to construct the reality of the humanitarian crisis and evoke R2P intervention, can be evaluated based on the five frames of HRJ and the typology of the news stories. Because, the expectation from HRJ is that it would help the distant news consumers to develop a perceived reality, by establishing a *prima facie* case of distant suffering that would not differ much from the actual reality, within the critical constructivist epistemology. That is, for human rights and peace-building strategies to be successful, actors should understand the true nature of events and their effects. HRJ, as a 'rights-based multidimensional' approach, has great potential to fulfil this task in relation to establishing a *prima facie* case within a critical constructivist epistemology, from which R2P can be invoked- however, appropriately along the line of three pillars.

As Shaw describes, diagnostic reporting of HRJ analyses all the factors which influence a conflict, 'at the personal, institutional, and structural-cultural level, power relations and relations of power within a socio-cultural and political context' (2012, p. 99), and thus constructs a social reality to aid in designing human rights redress strategies.

Against the backdrop of our discussion in Chapter 4 on the nexus between HRJ and R2P, human rights-oriented reporting and media's role of a watchdog have huge potential to facilitate the implementation of R2P as a 'rights-based' approach, by communicating the reality of a crisis and thereby establishing a *prima facie* case for R2P. Thus, it enables the international community/responsibility holders/UN to deal with the crisis based on global consensus and collective commitment, without pursuing petty political agendas.

Based on the above understanding of the 'HRJ- R2P Nexus Conceptual Model', any analysis of the practice of HRJ concerning distant suffering from the R2P perspective, should articulate its analysis within the agenda-setting mechanism. This means, the analysis as indicated above, has to take into account both the accessibility and the applicability of the agenda-setting process in terms of the quantity of news coverage of a distant suffering, and the qualitative effect (framing effect) of the same. As expressed already, accessibility is the magnitude of information provided to an individual about a distant suffering through news sources. This is also referred as the first level (visibility) agenda-setting process, which conditions the audiences regarding 'what to think about', in terms of the salience of the issues or the events reported in the media. In contrast, the concept of applicability explains the nexus between the attributes of a distant suffering and the audiences' stored ideas or knowledge. This is described as the second level (valence) of agenda-setting, which conditions the audiences to determine 'how to think about' a distant suffering. This is where Chouliaraki's spectatorship of distant suffering can immensely aid us to understand the capacity of the practice of HRJ in creating immediacy by connecting the readers with distant sufferers. As we underlined in Chapter 3, the five frames of HRJ are interconnected and mutually reinforcing across the dimensions of human rights and conflict transformation. For example, the empathetic critical frames, on one hand, expose the sufferings and problems of the victims in a conflict, reinforcing the diagnostic frames to construct a social reality, which in turn helps to construct '(global) compassion' which is explained by Hoijer (2004) or the 'cosmopolitan spectatorship' elucidated by Chouliaraki (2006). This impacts the audiences who become active with a strong moral commitment to facilitate the goals of interventionism framework and influence policy responses and pro-activism framework, to address both direct and indirect violence to balance the social imbalance.

As illustrated in the above diagram, the process of 'media agenda' is influenced by several factors such as news selection by journalists, media suppression, news sources, propaganda of the warring parties, structural, institutional and social conditions which were described in Chapter 3. Therefore, in addition to the quantitative and qualitative analysis of media content, conducting interviews, surveys and questionnaires to collect data and information from journalists would be extremely helpful in understanding the challenges that confronted them in the course of their reporting, which in turn would complement the analysis of media content. Similarly, as we can see from the above diagram, policy agenda is fashioned by both public agenda and media agenda, because actors involved in the public policy-making process can be directly influenced by news coverage of a distant suffering and also by the persuasive communication effect of the public agenda. Therefore, conducting interviews, and circulating surveys and questionnaires among policymakers and humanitarian responders would help us understand the extent to which the practice of HRJ created persuasive communication effect and its effect on policymakers to evoke the R2P. Persuasive communication effect can be understood as a change that the news consumers undergo as a consequence of receiving messages through communication processes including both direct observation and media. Nevertheless, the focus of this chapter is solely on proposing a research framework that innovatively creates a matrix for the analysis of HRJ frames (Frame Analysis Matrix) and typology of news stories (Multimodal Discourse Analysis Matrix), and integrating them into the coding manual of the content analysis to scrutinise the practice of HRJ.

Theoretical reflections (Shaw 2012; Boltanski 1999) emphasise on the role media plays in constructing reality regarding conflict situations, human rights violations and the underlying causes, with an aim to develop solutions for peacebuilding and human rights interventions in conflict situations. While there is increasing research on the mediation of distant suffering, there is limited research on the empirical analytical tools to understand and scrutinise it. Although Chouliaraki (2006) identifies typology of news stories, which centres on the obligations of the spectators to realise, feel and react, her multimodal analysis framework lacks comprehensive evaluation tools which can capture a big sample size over a long time period corresponding with the theories of news production. Likewise, using the Frame Analysis for media content of a larger sample size to analyse the 'human rights discourse' perceived by the practise of HRJ, when dealing with media content organised by the facts framed by the journalists, poses similar problems.

This chapter aims to address this scholarly deficit, by proposing 'Framing Matrix and Multimodal Discourse Analysis Matrix' (FMMDAM), integrated into the coding manual of the content analysis framework. A great advantage of using FMMDAM, integrated into the coding manual of the content analysis framework, is its ability to analyse a large number of news stories concerning a specific event, over a long period of time. It allows the use of multiple variables such as the types of news sources, articles, the mode of news coverage & its sections, and the number of photographs and their sizes. It also lets analysts identify patterns and helps scrutinise what exists and matters in news reporting, by identifying the relationship between the frames/variables. Multimodal analysis helps identify media's distinct role in reporting, concerning what spectators/readers feel and do, and their responses to watching/reading the news stories about human suffering, with respect to the mode of presentation of the news text, the correspondence between the text and the image and the aesthetic quality of the news text. Meanwhile, Critical Discourse Analysis (CDA) investigates the mediation between the spectators and the distanced victims, and the conditions connecting both the parties, specifically concerning the factors that form immediate reality/immediacy. Similarly, Frame Analysis aids in understanding the method of presentation of a news story to the audience ('the frame') and its influence on the choices people make, specifically those who are receptive to this news story. There can be HRJ and/or HWJ frames in a news story, which are shaped and produced based on the information that is conveyed and disseminated.

Let us take an example to better understand the discussion. We will use the same case study of the humanitarian crisis in Sri Lanka in 2009 that has been presented in Chapters 6 and 7 of this book. The purpose of this case study is to examine the practice of HRJ in the humanitarian crisis in Sri Lanka in 2009, with regard to the international newspapers, and its agenda-setting effect from the R2P perspective. To optimise this research, as enlightened in the above 'HRJ- R2P Nexus Conceptual Model', it is pertinent to design the analytical framework within the principles of both HRJ and the spectatorship of distant suffering. Meanwhile, the research outlook has to be carefully designed to try and uncover the extent to which the practice of HRJ created options for R2P intervention in the humanitarian crisis in Sri Lanka in 2009, within the agenda-setting framework. Based on this premise, the following research questions were formulated:

1. What was the extent of coverage of the humanitarian crisis in Sri Lanka in 2009 by the international newspapers?
2. What specific sources were heavily and frequently relied upon for reporting the issue?
3. What was the extent of coverage of human rights violations and suffering in the international newspapers?
4. To what extent the frames of HRJ were expressed in the reporting?
5. How and why the international newspapers failed/succeeded in drawing the attention of the global state actors, for their action/failure to act on the distant suffering in Sri Lanka?
6. How and to what extent did the international press create the 'accessibility effect' of the agenda-setting?
7. How and to what extent did the international press create the 'applicability effect' of the agenda-setting?
8. To what extent did the international newspapers expose the issues of human rights, to construct options for R2P intervention in terms of 'accessibility' and 'applicability' effects?

To answer these questions, the challenge lies in identifying the international press coverage of the humanitarian crisis in Sri Lanka in 2009, in terms of both their quantitative and qualitative aspects. The idea is to determine the extent of their practice of HRJ in terms of the accessibility and applicability effects. It is also equally important to assess the quality of the discourse in question, to determine the 'effect' it has had in terms of the construction of options for R2P. Answering the first six questions in the aforementioned set requires uncovering the volume of news coverage in the international press concerning human rights violations, sources mentioned, number of HRJ frames and accessibility level, etc. during the period of one month. This necessitates a quantitative analytical method to objectively assess the practice of HRJ. Content analysis is one such method which has gained wide application, especially in media content studies.

Conversely, some of the above questions, such as the framing effect of HRJ, accessibility and applicability effect, etc. need a qualitative analytical approach to unearth the answers. Although qualitative methods such as Frame Analysis and Discourse Analysis can be applied to answer these questions, they cannot be used distinctly as it would be a time-consuming, space-consuming, and an inefficient approach. Moreover, it also wouldn't help in understanding the relationship, connection and implication between the research findings of these methods. More importantly, Frame Analysis and Discourse Analysis are qualitative research methods, and thus they cannot be applied on a bigger sample size. For example, in the case of the Sri Lankan humanitarian crisis, the Sri Lankan government formally started its military offensive in 2007 in the Vanni region, which was the last remaining LTTE-controlled area; but it turned into a severe humanitarian crisis in September, 2008, when the United Nations was asked by the Sri Lankan government to withdraw from the LTTE-controlled areas in Vanni. Therefore, in order to get a full picture of the mass atrocities that occurred during the final war, it is necessary to analyse the international newspaper coverage of this crisis from September, 2008 till the end of the war in May, 2009. In total, this study analysed 1290 news stories including news reports/articles/columns published during the final war period in Sri Lanka in 6 international newspapers: *The Independent (UK), The Times (UK), The Washington Post (US), The New York Times (US), The Times of India (India)* and *The Hindu (India)*. This is a large amount of media content. If the duration of the crisis was longer, the sample size would have further increased. Therefore, development of a quantitative—qualitative content analysis framework is required to overcome these limitations, without compromising on the qualitative values of these methods. In the context of the analytical challenges outlined above, this chapter offers FMMDAM as an integrated research framework that addresses these expectations. The discussion will now dwell on the way in which FMMDAM can be developed and used to answer the aforementioned questions.

5.3 Quantitative and Qualitative Content Analysis

As previously explained, the best way to approach the study of the practice of HRJ from the agenda-setting perspective is to initially scrutinise the volume of news coverage of a distant suffering, through content analysis. This would require an analysis of the magnitude and the method of reporting of human rights violations and suffering of the humanitarian crisis in the (international) newspapers. Such an analysis will also involve an evaluation of the extent of expression of the frames of HRJ in the reporting and the specific sources that were most frequently relied upon for the same. Furthermore, we also need to evaluate the extent to which the issues of human rights, within the agenda-setting framework, helped construct options for R2P. The quantitative-qualitative framework would be the most suitable tool to articulate the research subject for the following reasons:

1. As already mentioned, due to the nature of this research, a large number of published media content will be taken into consideration, including news reports/articles/columns published international newspapers. Analysing all of these news stories in a qualitative manner using discourse analysis and frame analysis will be highly problematic, keeping in mind the time constraints and the word count limitation for the study.
2. Although some of the news stories' features including their type, the section of the newspaper, number of pictures, their nature and their size, type of coverage and the sources of news, can be scrutinised in a qualitative manner, quantitative method is more reliable to understand the trends, relationships and patterns among and between these features.
3. The nature and the scope of such aforementioned research questions require the articulation of the frame analysis and the multimodal discourse analysis to scrutinise HRJ frames and the typology of news stories within the agenda-setting framework.

To combat the issues pertaining to the study and achieve the aims, research must be carried out diligently. This chapter, therefore, proposes to create separate matrices for the analysis of HRJ frames (Frame Analysis Matrix) and typology of news stories (Multimodal Discourse Analysis Matrix) and integrate them into the coding manual of the content analysis.

These two matrices will be used to analyse news stories/articles in a quantitative manner by integrating the framing analysis matrix and multimodal discourse analysis matrix into the content analysis coding manual. This will enable comparisons between different variables, and trends can also be observed among them with regard to the distance suffering.

The following discussion focuses on the method of preparation of content analysis framework and the articulation and integration of the frame analysis matrix and multimodal discourse analysis model into the coding manual of the content analysis framework. Examples are shown from the case study of the humanitarian crisis in Sri Lanka in 2009 presented in Chapters 6, 7, and 8.

5.3.1 Content Analysis Coding Manual

A coding guide and coding manual can be prepared by identifying the categories such as the total news, section of the newspaper, type of news stories, number of pictures, their nature and their size, type of coverage, type of story and news sources. The news entries can be filtered by reading them and the Microsoft Excel spreadsheet or Data Analysis Software SPSS can be used to analyse the data. The definitions of the categories such as news report, column, news feature and editorial are explained in Chapter 6 (Table 5.1).

Content analysis facilitates both the quantitative and qualitative investigations. Quantitative content analysis enables us to examine the manifested content within the news stories such as frames, function of news sources, aesthetic quality and agency. Meanwhile, the latent message within the content can be analysed in an interpretative manner, to uncover the hidden, implied and connotative meanings. Therefore, the investigative process aiming to uncover the above sample questions necessitates the use both quantitative and qualitative content analysis in a systematic manner. The purpose of the content analysis serves two purposes:

1. To get a clear picture of the newspaper coverage of the humanitarian crisis by comparing a number of variables. For example please find table data as below (Table 5.2).
2. Further, the research inquiry inevitably has to strengthen its analysis in a quantifying manner, within the theoretical principles of HRJ and spectatorship of suffering. Hence, it is necessary to create a Frame Analysis Matrix for HRJ and Multimodal Discourse Analysis Matrix for typology of news stories and integrate them into the content analysis coding manual. This helps us understand their emphasis, identify the patterns, analyse what exists and happens and what matters in news reporting. It also helps in identifying the relationship and nexus between the frames and the variables.

The discussion below focuses on the theoretical underpinnings for these two matrices within a framing context.

Table 5.1 Content analysis coding guide

Category	*Coding*	*Category*	*Coding*
Name of newspaper	1 = The Washington Post 2 = The New York Times 3 = The Independent 4 = The Times 5 = The Hindu 6 = Time of India	Type of story	1 = Ongoing War related 2 = (Other) War Related
Type of article/report	1 = News Report 2 = Editorial 3 = Column 4 = News Feature 5 = Cartoon/illustration 6 = Letter 7 = Weekly news summary 8 = News in brief	Type of coverage	1 = Embedded/spot 2 = Distant coverage (stationed in Sri Lanka, but not in war zone) 3 = Distant coverage (stationed abroad) 4 = Agency story, 5 = Desk/Newsroom coverage
Section of newspaper	1 = Lead story 1st page 2 = Sub story 1st page 3 = Inside lead story 4 = Inside sub story 5 = Op-ed	Quoted/mentioned sources	0 = None 1 = Military Officials 2 = Government Officials 3 = LTTE Officials 4 = UN/Foreign Officials 5 = Victims 6 = Civil Society/NGOs/Human Rights Groups 7 = Indian Politicians
No of photos/graphics	0 = 0 1 = 1 2 = 2 3 = More than 2	Noteworthy war incidents	0 = none of them 1 = UN Withdrawal in September 2008 2 = Mass exodus and plight of people 3 = Attacks in No Fire zone 4 = Bombing on Hospital 5 = Human Shield by LTTE 6 = Blockade of food and medical aid 7 = White flag Incident

(continued)

Table 5.1 (continued)

Category	*Coding*	*Category*	*Coding*
Size of main photo	1 = 1 Column 2 = 2 Column 3 = 3 Column 4 = 4 Column 5 = 5 Column 6 = 6 Column 7 = NA	Key frame	1 = Human Wrongs Journalism 2 = Human Rights Journalism
Nature of photo	1 = Current 2 = File 3 = Info Graphic 4 = Cartoon	1 = Human Wrongs Journalism, 2 = Human Rights Journalism	1 = Empathy Distance Frame 2 = Evocative Reporting 3 = Reactive 4 = Non-interventionist 5 = War Journalism 6 = Empathy Critical Frame 7 = Diagnostic Reporting 8 = Proactive 9 = Interventionist 10 = Peace Journalism

5.4 Frame Analysis

Goffman's (1974) *Frame Analysis* was integrated into content analysis to articulate the qualitative part of the research. In this way, the qualitative aspects of the Frame Analysis are assessed in a quantitative manner due to reasons established in the preceding paragraphs. Kuypers (2006, p. 8) explains framing as a process in which some individuals, establish a certain perspective concerning a situation, either intentionally or unintentionally, which also influences the interpretation of facts by others regarding the same situation. Frames operate on four levels: stating the problems, assessing the underlying reasons, judging on the basis of moral frameworks and recommending solutions. Frames are usually centred on an issue or an event and are often the principle formative idea.

Frame Analysis helps in understanding how a news story is presented to the audience ('the frame') the influence of such a way of presentation on the choices of those who are receptive to this news story. There can be several frames in a news story which are shaped and produced by the

Table 5.2 Variables for Content Analysis

1. Type of Articles vs. All published news
2. Sections of Newspaper vs. All published news
3. a. Total number of news items with photos vs. All published news. b. Of them how many with '1', '2' and 'more than 2' photos?
4. Photo sizes vs. Main photo
5. Nature of pictures vs. All published news with photos
6. Type of stories vs. All published news
7. Type of coverages vs. All published news except Editorial
8. Quoted or mentioned sources vs. All published news
9. Noteworthy War incidents vs. All published news
10. Key Frames vs. All published news
11. Key Frames vs. Sub-frames
12. Key Frames vs. Type of Articles
13. Key Frames vs. Type of coverage
14. Key Frames vs. Non-Photo News/ Photo News
15. Key Frames vs. Quoted or mentioned sources
16. Key Frames vs. Noteworthy War incidents
17. Sub- frames vs. Non-Photo News/ Photo News
18. Sub- frames vs. All published news
19. Sub- frames vs. Quoted or mentioned sources
20. Sub Frames vs. Type of coverage
21. Sub Frames vs. Type of Articles
22. Sub Frames vs. Noteworthy War incidents
23. Typology of News stories vs. All published news
24. Typology of News stories vs. "Key Frames"
25. Typology of News stories vs. "Sub-frames"
26. Typology of News stories vs. Non-Photo News/ Photo News
27. Typology of News stories vs. Quoted or mentioned sources
28. Typology of News Stories vs. Type of Articles
29. Typology of News stories vs. Type of coverage
30. Typology of News stories vs. Noteworthy War incidents
31. Period vs. All published news
32. Period vs. Nature of picture
33. Period vs. Type of Articles
34. Period vs. Type of coverage
35. Period vs. Quoted or mentioned sources
36. Period vs. Key Frames
37. Period vs. Sub Frames
38. Period vs. Noteworthy War incidents
39. Period vs. Typology of News stories
40. Key Authors vs. Key Frames
41. Key Authors vs. Sub Frames
42. Key Authors vs. Typology of News stories
43. Typology of News story vs. Mode of Presentation
44. Typology of News story vs. The correspondence between text & image
45. Typology of News story vs. The aesthetic quality of the news text
46. Typology of News story vs. Space–Time (Representation)
47. Typology of News story vs. Agency (Orientation)
48. Sources vs. Space–Time (Representation)
49. Sources vs. Agency (Orientation)
50. Total News vs. Mode of Presentation
51. Total News vs. The correspondence between text & image
52. Total News vs. The aesthetic quality of the news text
53. Total News vs. Space–Time (Representation)
54. Total News vs. Agency (Orientation)

information they convey and disseminate (Goffman 1974; Fairhurst and Sarr 1996; Scheufele 1999).

Kuyper finds frames to be a powerful aspect of a media due to its capacity to influence peoples' imagination and representation of the world in specific ways, prioritising certain aspects of the multidimensional reality of a situation over others. In other words, frames within a text make 'some information more salient than other information' (Kuypers 2009, p. 181).

William Gamson (1989) argues that facts hold no intrinsic meaning, and are practically neutral, until they are set within a frame or a narrative. Certain facts are organised by frames in a conscious or unconscious manner, and as a result achieve coherence and get highlighted over other facts.

Framing is a process, whereby actors organise the facts of a situation in a manner which highlights certain information over other, thereby promoting their viewpoints. In this process the frames tend to highlight a particular reality from within the multidimensional reality of a situation, by identifying the problem and its causes as well as making moral judgments and suggesting remedies (Kuypers 2009, p. 185). As Entman explains, salience and selection are the two important elements of framing. Salience influences the audience to perceive the piece of information they receive as more meaningful, memorable and noticeable (1993, p. 52).

Therefore, Frame Analysis is a suitable qualitative analytical tool to identify and assess the frames of HRJ and their functions, with respect to the international newspaper coverage of a distant suffering. This analytical process will shed light on comprehending the 'reality' perceived by the audience, on the basis of the media content organised by the framing of facts, by the journalists who cover distant sufferings. In other words, as we elaborated in Chapters 3 and 4, this study's central idea revolves around the agenda-setting capacity of HRJ to invoke R2P, where the articulation of Frame Analysis, which is related to the agenda-setting tradition (concept of applicability), becomes inevitable.

The comparative Frame Analysis enables us to better understand the mediated communication of a distant suffering with distance spectators. It will allow us to engage in a cross-national and cross-journalism comparison. The cross-national comparison is comprehended in terms of crisis reporting by different newspapers from various countries, in the context of geopolitical implications. For example, the way the newspapers 'selected' (news selection) and made 'salient' (agenda-setting) the humanitarian crisis. The cross-journalism comparison is a continual comparison between the influence of the features of HWJ and HRJ, as the analysis will shed light in understanding where, why and what was wrong.

Based on the factors discussed above, a '*Framing Matrix*' can be prepared by embracing the framing matrix strategy and framework articulated by Ryan (1991), who argued that framing is decided by a core value or principles that underlies it. Ryan adopted this matrix from the earlier works of Gamson and Lasch (1983), who in this model enabled the frames to characterise core positions, metaphors, images, catchphrases and attributions of responsibility for the problem, and the solution implied by the frame (see Ryan 1991). These six facets define a frame of a news report:

Core position—It describes the main argument in one sentence.

Metaphor—It refers to a familiar character in both text and speech, to describe something which is difficult to understand, but has same characteristics of 'something'.

Catch phrases—Frequently used terms and phrases to strengthen the discourse.

Symbols and Images—Meaning-making of text–image relationship.

Source of problem—Ability of the frame to identify the causes.

Appeal to principle—The individual's core values to which the argument built in the frame appeals.

Aligning the properties/characteristics of the news reports against these five facets in the described manner enables the researcher to identify the relevant frames. Winett, Wallack and others (Winett 1995) further adapted this framing matrix, suggesting the development of a framing memo to list all potential ways in which an issue could be framed (by opponents and proponents of a policy) and attributed. This sheds light on how can identify the frames of HRJ and HWJ in the news reporting of a distant suffering. A framing memo consists of the identified frames of news reporting of an issue/event *vis a vis* the six facets that define a frame. A framing memo of an event/issue can consist of several frames. To prepare a framing memo, a researcher must conduct a systematic research and thoroughly review newspaper articles on the chosen issue. The researcher can further analyse them to identify the way in which each side frames or positions the policy issue. Shaw, in his theory of 'Human Rights Journalism', used a number of case studies to identify the frames of HRJ and HWJ. Thus, further research on identifying the frames that operate in the research discipline of HRJ is not necessary. Nevertheless, preparing a memo consisting of the sub-frames of HRJ and HWJ, identified by Shaw, would help us identify the properties/arguments of newspapers' content in a configuring manner which, in turn, would enable the preparation of a framing matrix. That is, identifying the properties/arguments of newspapers' content in a framing memo in a configuring manner, would produce distinct framing matrices for identifying the sub-frames of HRJ and HWJ, without which a researcher who conducts an HRJ study cannot identify the frames in newspapers' content in a scientific manner.

Content from all the newspapers must be read thoroughly to identify the properties of the *framing memo* that represent each sub- frames of HRJ and HWJ. The completion of this process is indicated by the construction of the *Framing Matrix* to identify the sub- frames of HRJ and HWJ, which is used in the coding manual. Inter-coder reliability/inter-judge reliability is an integral part of content analysis and is essential for objective and valid interpretation of data. Therefore, a researcher must ensure the inter-coder reliability/inter-judge reliability not only in the data coding of the coding manual based on the *Framing Matrix*, but also in the preparation of the *Framing Matrix* (see Allen 2017; Lavrakas 2008).

This framing matrix, integrated into the content analysis, can aid in comparing the emphasis and the function of the frames articulated by journalists in their reporting of a distant suffering.

For example, in the case of the humanitarian crisis in Sri Lanka, the analysis involved more than 1290 news stories from six newspapers in the UK, United States and India. However, scrutiny of every article from such a large sample in a qualitative frame analysis process is impossible, and the study thus engages in a quantitative investigation through HRJ *Framing Matrix* and HWJ *Framing Matrix* prepared. These matrices illustrated below show how they can be used to identify the sub-frames of HRJ and HWJ of the newspapers' reporting of the humanitarian crisis (Tables 5.3 and 5.4).

In a similar manner, we can use Chouliaraki's (2006) Multimodal Discourse Analysis to scrutinise the typology of news stories by preparing a matrix, which is integrated into the content analysis coding manual. The next section of this chapter discusses the underlying theories of the multimodal discourse analysis, and the manner in which it can be articulated in the study of distant suffering.

Table 5.3 Human rights journalism matrix

Frames	*Core position*	*Metaphor*	*Images*	*Catch phrases/words*	*Solution*	*Appeal to principle*
Empathy Critical	Analysing the root causes of the conflict	Rights based approach	Civilian causalities/sufferings, devastation of livelihood/property	Civilians trapped, loss of civilian life; bloodbath; targeting civilians; scores of people dead/wounded; Unattended bodies & injured people; attack on hospitals; barbed wire detention camps, hostage-taking, summary execution, rape, torture, arbitrary arrests and imprisonment, so-called 'No-Fire Zone'; untold suffering; unimaginable humanitarian catastrophic; countless victims; terrible humanitarian situation; slaughter of civilians; civilians caught up; living in bunger	Give voice to the victims	UDHR

(continued)

Table 5.3 (continued)

Frames	*Core position*	*Metaphor*	*Images*	*Catch phrases/words*	*Solution*	*Appeal to principle*
Diagnostic Reporting	Upholding of human rights	Construction of reality	Images of historical background of conflicts, sociocultural damage and psychological damage	Centralisation of power, equality for all, military occupation; High Security Zones; injustice; discrimination; marginalisation; human rights abuses; denial of education and employment; as second-class citizens; resentment and suspicion; vicious civil war; curtailment of freedom of expression; divided country	Critical analysis/engagement	Free speech/Watchdog journalism

Frames	*Core position*	*Metaphor*	*Images*	*Catch phrases/words*	*Solution*	*Appeal to principle*
Proactive	Early warning	Act before it happens	Withdrawing humanitarian agencies; movements of military equipment; presence of children and women in the war zone; places of schools, hospitals & historical artefacts in the area;	War crimes; risk of starvation; in danger of being killed; a bloody endgame would be a disaster; avoid a very large-scale humanitarian crisis; safety of civilians; evolving human tragedy; mounting civilian cost; fired by both parties; ensure the protection and well-being of civilians;	Timely intervention	Responsibility to Prevent

(continued)

Table 5.3 (continued)

Frames	*Core position*	*Metaphor*	*Images*	*Catch phrases/words*	*Solution*	*Appeal to principle*
Interventionist	Draw the attention of the international community	Agenda Setting	Mass atrocities, usage of banned weapons; attacks on hospitals and schools; people dying without food and water; scores of dead bodies and bloodied civilians;	Justice, accountability, humanitarian and human rights law, violating the rules of war; war crimes; crimes against humanity; risk of atrocities; act urgently to protect civilians; declare a truce; situation is now critical; war without witnesses; no access to war zones/refugee camps; war must end; could produce a 'bloodbath'; obligation to act	Construction of the reality of the crisis	Responsibility to React

Frames	*Core position*	*Metaphor*	*Images*	*Catch phrases/words*	*Solution*	*Appeal to principle*
Peace Journalism	Conflict analysis and balanced coverage	Win-win approach	Human & economic cost of war; potential victims; peace efforts of local leaders, civil societies & political leaders; sufferings of civilians; devastation of livelihood	War never brings peace, Nobody can win the war; ceasefire; military restraint and serious negotiation; constitutional reforms; sustainable peace; victory in the battlefield will remain hollow; will sow the seeds of hatred; War may get over soon, but'; through democratic means	Awareness of non-violence and creativity into journalism	Conflict Resolution

Table 5.4 Human wrongs journalism matrix

Frame	*Core position*	*Metaphor*	*Images*	*Catch phrases/words*	*Solution*	*Appeal to principle*
Empathy Distance Frame	War is inevitable	Injection pains, but it cures	Escaped people; victim being cared/assisted by one party; dehumanisation of 'one' party; suicide/terror attacks outside the war zone	Child Recruitment; suicide attacks; trapped civilians; child soldiers surrendered; Human Shield; War for Peace; Humanitarian War	Wipe out the troublemaker	Humanitarian Assistance/Relief
Evocative Reporting	Sensitising public opinion to serve geopolitical interests	Sensationalism/Drama	Stranded victims: mourning for loved ones who had died; mothers holding their babies running; terrified children and women; atrocities of one party	Evacuation of civilians; lack of food, water and medicine; innocent civilians; civilian exodus; escaping civilians; mass exodus; malnutrition; needs of the displaced; provide relief and succour; tragedy without humanitarian assistance	Aid assistance rather than dealing with HR violations	Humanitarian Assistance

Frame	*Core position*	*Metaphor*	*Images*	*Catch phrases/words*	*Solution*	*Appeal to principle*
Reactive	Wait for the violence & causalities to occur	Bystander journalism	Images of casualties and material damage; plumes of bomb debris; scenes of fighting and destruction	Massive assault began; caused severe casualties; lost the battle; unaccounted for; needs of IDPs; caused immense suffering; heavily shelled & bombed; captured strongholds; cornered into a small area	Report facts as we see	Objectivity
Non-Interventionist	Internal issue	Neutral observer	Escaped people; refugees being looked after; humanitarian assistance and relief efforts; presence of international agencies; violence of losing party	Freeing terrorists' clutches: pressure them to surrender uncompromising military secessionism; freeing the remaining civilians; rescue operation; Interfering in internal affairs; they will use the ceasefire; we are more concerned about our own citizens than anyone	Let them sort their own problems out	The Realist School

(continued)

Table 5.4 (continued)

Frame	*Core position*	*Metaphor*	*Images*	*Catch phrases/words*	*Solution*	*Appeal to principle*
War Journalism	If it bleeds, it leads	Zero-sum game	Military operations; causalities; armoury, jubilant troops; scenes of fighting, scary soldiers waving guns; graphics of war preparation/military strength; captured city; hoisting of victory flag; suicide attacks; dehumanising graphics; worthy victims	Victory is not so far away; final assault; overwhelming the remaining; final hours; end game; no holds barred battle; escape routes cut off; hopeless battle; to save top brass; pioneered the use of suicide bombings; suicide squad; internationally banned terrorist outfit; ruthless terrorists; terrorist attacks; lethal and cruel; Pol Potist	Military victory	Objectivity

5.5 Multimodal Discourse Analysis

To analyse 'effect', it is important to understand the power/knowledge configurations in the discourse production concerning humanitarian crisis reporting. The magnitude of depiction of true reality of a distant suffering by international newspapers, to promote global compassion and intervention, must be scrutinised to analyse of the practice of HRJ in humanitarian crisis situations.

To examine the international newspapers' role in invoking 'human rights discourse', understanding the potential of discourse analysis in examining the factors impacting the production of knowledge/power, seems to be an effective method.

Foucault argues that linguistic relations are associated with 'particular systems of "power/knowledge relations" specific to their historical juncture' (1977, p. 27). This power relationship claims a truth through the meaning-making process. Chouliaraki terms it as a 'truth value'—a truth that reconstructs power in the meaning-making process (Chouliaraki 2004, p. 155). Foucault argues that meaning and power are inseparable and are always co-articulated within every social practice (Foucault 1974). He further adds that both meaning and power can be analysed under discourse analysis (ibid.). This argument supports the social constructionist epistemology of the discourse analysis, which treats language as a social activity and not a true mirror of the world (Nikander 2008).

For Van Dijk (1995, p. 18), discourse and social structure are mediated by social cognition, which is defined as 'the system of mental representations and processes of group members' (van Dijk 1995, p. 18). Within the social cultural approach to Critical Discourse Analysis (CDA), Fairclough underlines a three-dimensional model in which 'the connection between text and social practice is seen as being mediated by discourse practice' (1995, p. 133). Chouliaraki (2006) explains CDA as the analysis of space-time aspect of news stories, involving interactions between the victims and readers, to promote action concerning the suffering. Therefore, it helps identify the role of the agency in meaning-making process, through the analysis of media portrayal of the actors within a crisis to reflect the suffering to the world. Analysing news in terms of their functional characteristics and identifying them in line with these characteristics through CDA, can help assess media's construction and representation. This can establish HRJ's contribution to the failure/success of R2P of a distant suffering by analysing media discourses that reflect and construct reality by ascribing meanings to our world.

Chouliaraki emphasises on the importance of analysing images, due to their influence on the spectators/readers' ability to feel and remember the suffering, owing to their aesthetic quality (ibid., p. 76). She uses semiotic analysis, which she articulates as 'Multimodal' and CDA to examine the communicative impact of the images used by the media, and in her studies of distance sufferings.

Through multimodal and CDA, we can analyse the handling and linking of images and texts to produce meaning, and also understand the space-time effect which determines the type of agency used to connect victims and readers. Consequently, we can understand news reporting's impact on readers' compassion and action towards the suffering of others (ibid.; Chouliaraki 2008b).

The outcome of meaning making is reality, and thus how journalists construct the meanings of the distant suffering in their reporting, should be carefully analysed to understand the conditions of the human suffering (Bruner 1996). The influence of specific values and beliefs on the system of communication determines the reality formation of distant suffering. The reality is understood in terms of how knowledge or meaning generated by discourse construction of the media is perceived by the audience. Images, language and symbols also play an important role in this reality formation (Leistyna 2001). According to Leistyna (1996, p. 336), the discourse has evolved into the complex 'ways in which reality is perceived through and shaped by historically and socially constructed ways of making sense, that is, language, complex signs and practices that order and sustain particular forms of social existence'. Thus, meaning which constructs the reality of an event or issue is formed based on 'difference', conditioned by societies' values, beliefs, traditions and history as well as the way images, languages and symbols are used to communicate the message. The differences that constitute the semiotic process are of two types: difference within the semiotic and difference outside the semiotic. The difference within the semiotic is the inherent dissimilarity in the medium of creating meaning. It is determined by how the technology of verbal and visual recording, which uses images and narratives of an event or issue, presents a medium as material reality (Chouliaraki 2006, p. 71). This is hypermediacy. According to Bolter and Grusin (2000, p. 272), hypermediacy is a 'style of visual representation whose goal is to remind the viewer of the medium'. The difference outside the semiotic is in the meaning making based on the interaction between the sufferer and the distant audience outside the medium. This is immediacy (Chouliaraki 2006, p. 71). As opposed to hypermediacy, as Bolter and Grusin (2000, p. 272) define, immediacy is a 'style of visual representation whose goal is to make the viewer forget the presence of the medium and believe that he is in the presence of the objects of representation'. Therefore, a researcher must carry out the study of distant suffering in terms of two grounds: hypermediacy and immediacy. The multimodal analysis is used to analyse hypermediacy and CDA is used to examine immediacy in the media reporting of distant suffering (Chouliaraki 2006, p. 71).

Multimodal analysis focuses on the dissimilarities in the meaning-making process of the distant suffering in media, in terms of articulating the visuals and texts within the content. As Scollon and LeVine 2004, pp. 1–2) argue:

> Language in use, whether this is in the form of spoken language or text, is always and inevitably constructed across multiple modes of communication, including speech and gesture not just in spoken language but through such "contextual" phenomena as the use of the physical spaces in which we carry out our discursive actions or the design, papers, and typography of the documents within which our texts are presented.

Their standpoint underlines the nexus between multimodality and discourse, and highlights discourse information in communication. Moreover, this highlights the processing of information involving more than one mode of communication and emphasises the importance of analysing all aspects of discourse and how people communicate.

Conversely, CDA analyses dissimilarities that are independent to meaning-making process in media, involving the actors of distant suffering such as victims, perpetrators and benefactors. This helps identify pain, pity, feelings and wishes, with regard to the formation of immediate reality or immediacy (Chouliaraki 2006).

In conclusion, through multimodal analysis, a researcher scrutinises the visual and textual meaning-making, consequently identifying the role media plays through its reporting, in impacting what spectators/readers feel, how they perceive, what they do and how they respond when watching/reading news about a human suffering. CDA investigates the mediation and the factors connecting the spectator and the distanced victim, with a moral responsibility to act upon the suffering, based on their understanding of the outcome of the meaning making of the distant suffering, which is reality. The next section aims to explain the analytical process of Multimodal analysis and CDA separately.

5.5.1 *Multimodal Analysis Process*

Multimodality has been considered as a phenomenon (Scollon and LeVine 2004), a domain of research field (O'Halloran 2005) and an analytical method (O'Halloran 2007). As an effective analytical tool, it investigates how the construction of text and image produce meaning in media content, and also evaluates them based on their capacity to reflect reality and cause persuasive communicative effect. Chouliaraki (2006) uses three factors to identify a hierarchical typology of news stories: (1) The mode of presentation of news, (2) The correspondence between the text and image, and (3) The aesthetic quality of the news text.

The mode of presentation includes the location of the reporter, the kind of realism articulated, portrayal of suffering, language usage (Narration or victim's quotation), appeals for compassion among readers, seeking action towards suffering and engagement with the victims. The correspondence between narrative/text and image emphasises on the aesthetics of reporting including portrayal of suffering through different types of images, meaningful interaction between text and image, language usage (description of facts/elements of exposition/narration) and their 'effect'. The aesthetic quality is determined by the semiotic aspects in the news story: Pamphleteering, philanthropy and sublimation. Pamphleteering evokes anger among the spectators, against the perpetrators (centres on perpetrators). Philanthropy encourages the spectators to improve the victims' condition either through charity or other means (centres on victims). Sublimation focuses on the reasons for suffering, its moral implications and spectator's responsibility, thereby emphasising on the underlying reasons for the suffering in order to alleviate it (centres on spectators/readers) (ibid.; see Aaltola 2012).

5.5.2 *Critical Discourse Analysis (CDA)*

As we have discussed earlier, discourses are sources of power (Corbett 1996) due to their capacity to create representations. These representations construct reality by attributing meanings to events and issues. This is why language is considered as both constitutive of the social world and constituted by other social practices (Phillips 2006). According to constructionists, media as producers of discourse require its text to be analysed within its social context (Jørgensen and Phillips 2002).

In this context, CDA involves analysis concerning media reporting of distance sufferings involving representations and orientations. Though both encompass reporting of suffering, they are treated separately in the analysis, to understand their manifestations in the news report (Chouliaraki 2006).

5.5.3 *Representations (Space–Time)*

CDA, while analysing representations, emphasises on space-time dimensions of the sufferings, to understand the closeness between the spectator and victim, and the urgency of action against the suffering. According to Chouliaraki (2006), space-time analysis explores how spectators face distant suffering at different levels and involvements, and scrutinises the sense of immediacy and the kind of moral distance established between the spectator and the sufferer. To quote Chouliaraki 2008a, p. 691):

> In the analysis of representations, CDA then would look into the construal of the scene of mediated action within a specific space and time that separates 'us' from 'them'. The category of 'spacetime' refers to the place and the temporality of action. It tells us how close a specific media event appears to the viewer and how important engagement with or even action on the distant 'other' is. The analysis of 'spacetime', then, shows us how media technologies not only deterritorialise our experience of the world but also, simultaneously, how they re-territorialise such experience, by regulating the degrees of proximity/distance or urgency/finality for each mediated event.

The space-time analysis of a chronotope of suffering involves four characteristics within the context of suffering: concreteness, multiplicity, specificity and mobility. Scrutinising these characteristics help in evaluating the magnitude of 'persuasive communication effect' created through a news report, to make readers feel cosmopolitan by the moral closeness with the victims. Concreteness refers to the concrete physical space of suffering; whereas multiplicity includes multiple physical contexts of suffering. Specificity distinguishes sufferings by providing details of specific locations and person(s). By linking the conditions of readers and victims, mobility tends to establish a 'relationship of action' (Chouliaraki 2006, pp. 85–87).

5.5.4 *Orientations (Agency)*

Chouliaraki argues that humanising the suffering increases compassion of the readers, thereby improving the news reports' potential to invite the readers/spectators regarding a suffering and develops their 'capacity to act' (agency) (ibid., p. 88). As she elaborates, 'in the analysis of orientations, CDA would look into the category of agency. Agency is about who acts upon whom in the scene of mediated action' (Chouliaraki 2008a, p. 691).

Agency role presents the suffering in two ways: agora and theatre. Agora emphasises on the role of humanising the victims (through text and image) which, through the news reports, empowers them to tempt the readers to speak and act on their suffering. Agora depends on the unbiasedness of the readers in their perception of the suffering and the misfortune of the victims. It refers to how active the distant other appears on screen. Conversely, theatrical articulation, uses emotions as the gateway to portray the sufferings, that is, understanding of the distance suffering is mediated by the social relationships. The agency in the news report is galvanised by the role of the 'benefactor' and 'persecutor' (symbolic figures) who communicate the reality of distant suffering by inviting the readers to feel for and identify. It means how other actors present in the scene of action appear to engage with one another (ibid., Chouliaraki 2006, pp. 88–90; 2008b, pp. 223–224).

5.5.5 *Typology of News Stories*

As discussed earlier, through the analysis of the news reports of the distant suffering within the multimodal discourse analysis, Chouliaraki identifies typology of news stories as: ***adventure, emergency*** and ***ecstatic***, in which the obligation of the spectators to realise, feel and react are embedded.

Chouliaraki (2006) explains that adventure news is simple, descriptive, factual reporting of news stories which limit the emotional and moral responses of a viewed suffering. They are based on singular space-times devoid of anecdotes and aftermath which limits the immediacy between the readers and victims. Adventure news fails to construct agency thereby preventing action on the suffering.

Emergency News, evokes pity by constructing categories of the realism of distant suffering through complicated narratives, thereby creating agency for spectators to possibly act, due to a sense of obligation towards those who are depicted as suffering. The categories of realism expected from emergency news are primarily: perceptual, categorical and ideological (ibid., p. 119; Cottle 2009, p. 136).

Perceptual realism involves objectively witnessing a distant suffering in 'real' space and time. Categorical realism is emotionally powerful due to the spectator's sense of omnipresence of threats of natural disasters, starvation and endemic. Ideological realism persuades the readers to side with justice in the context of ideological dilemma and is also emotionally powerful, like categorical realism (Chouliaraki 2006, pp. 127–139; 2008b, pp. 218–219).

There are three links between distance suffering and image-text presentation, which construct unique meaning to determine the kind of realism mentioned above: indexical, iconic and symbolic meaning, which do not always work independently. The capacity of the meaning constructed as a result, determine the aesthetic quality of the news reports and the kind of realism. Indexical meaning establishes the feeling of distance suffering through the principle of resemblance. In the meaning-making process, an 'uninvolved' visual perspective and descriptive narrative (impression of objectivity) in the news reports, create the knowledge of the suffering and constructs the perceptual realism. Iconic meaning creates a cause-and-effect connection of a suffering, using image and text to form categorical realism, such as images of starvation. Symbolic meaning allows the text and image to evoke some idea in an arbitrary manner, devoid of natural links between the suffering and image-text articulation. It convinces the readers of an issue as if it was a 'universal' truth in the context of ideological influence to construct ideological realism (ibid.).

Chouliaraki (2006) articulated the 'typology of news stories' with reference to the television coverage of particularly the distance sufferings. Distinctively, the *ecstatic* news category only pertains to the analysis of the live video coverage of the events. But, the methodological explanation of this chapter is on media content, focusing on the newspapers' coverage of a distant suffering, and it is therefore imperative to understand if 'typology of news stories' can be applied in the case of the newspapers. A careful scrutiny of the features of the typology of news stories insinuates that categories of *emergency* and *adventure* can be adapted to the analysis of newspaper reporting, by commenting on relevant features of newspaper layout that signal various degrees of urgency and proximity in line with two categories. For instance, incidents recorded through a few lines in the inside sections of the paper would count as adventure (sometimes, distant incidents simply appear through captioned photos: no context or explanation, just an aesthetic depiction of the event reported because of its visual value). Meanwhile, incidents that are covered entirely on the frontpage or front-page secondary reports with a small picture and some linguistic reference to the urgency or significance of the incident for a particular group of people, national or regional, can be categorised as 'emergency news'. Thus, considering the relevance of newspaper analysis, only the ***adventure*** and ***emergency*** genres are taken into consideration of the analysis.

Reading through the news reports, a researcher might find that some of the qualities of emergency news are compromised depending on the structure of the news stories such as news layout, presentation, design, nature of images and their location in the newspaper. Hence, we can divide the emergency news into two categories for the analytical purpose: semi emergency and emergency. Although both share the same qualities, their possible 'effects' would be influenced by the structure of the news reports in the newspapers. Below, Multimodal Discourse Analysis matrix illustrations help identify the typology of news stories.

As in the case of the frame analysis, the articulation of the multimodal discourse analysis can take the form of quantitative analysis as opposed to the detailed qualitative analysis articulated by Chouliaraki. The advantage of the quantitative nature of the multimodal discourse analysis is that, it enables us to scrutinise a large number of news stories and analyse their discursive properties between the typology of news stories in a comparative perspective, in parallel to the quantitative frame analysis. A multimodal analysis coding guide (see Table 5.6) can be prepared based on the analytical elements illustrated in the below multimodal discourse analysis matrix (see Table 5.6) to scrutinise them in the coding manual (see Table 5.7). Depending on the scope of the study, the designing of the matrices and coding manual will vary. Additional insights and explanation will be provided in Chapters 6, 7, and 8 (Tables 5.5 and 5.6).

As it can be observed in the Multimodal Discourse Analysis Matrix, a new dimension (communicative property), added in the 'multimodal analysis' matrix under (semi) emergency news category is the 'complicated narratives'. As multimodal analysis is an investigation of the meaning-making of the text–image articulation in news stories, Chouliaraki (2006)

Table 5.5 Coding guide for multimodal discourse

Categories	*Coding*
Typology of News Stories	1 = Adventure News 2 = Semi-Emergency News 3 = Emergency News
Mode of presentation	1 = Simple Narratives-Simple reporting of facts 2 = Questions of why do not appear 3 = Complicated narratives 4 = Complicated multimodal narratives 5 = Meditation of suffering gives credibility and distinct claim to reality 6 = Perceptual realism-facticity 7 = Categorical realism- emotion 8 = Ideological realism-Justice
The correspondence between text and image	1 = Descriptions rather than narrations 2 = Visual: minimal, abstracted representations 3 = Indexical meaning (Perceptual realism-facticity) 4 = Iconic meaning (Categorical realism-emotion) 5 = Symbolic meaning (Ideological realism-Justice)
The aesthetic quality of the news text	1 = Aesthetic distance (Overall semiotic effect-making the readers to feel the suffering) 2 = Pamphleteering—Political condemnation 3 = Philanthropy—Makes the readers to do something in terms of providing charity 4 = Sublimation-Enables to understand the underlying reasons for the suffering
Space–Time (Representation)	1 = Singular Space-Time: An isolated place, a one-off event restricts the possibility of historicity 2 = No connectivity between the suffering & spectators 3 = Hierarchy of place—victims of worthy places 4 = Concrete (suffering in the context of concrete physical space) 5 = Specific (the context of suffering as a singular space by elaborating on its unique properties or individualises the sufferer as a unique person with an array of attributes) 6 = Multiple (moves spectators through the multiple physical contexts of suffering) 7 = Mobile (mobility)

(continued)

Table 5.5 (continued)

Categories	*Coding*
Agency (Orientation)	1 = Void of Agency (Neither empathy nor denunciation, annihilation of the sufferer) 2 = Lack of Agora & Theatre 3 = Hierarchy of human lives-worthy/unworthy victims (void of agents) 4 = Agora (humanization of the sufferers-active sufferers) 5 = Theatre (communicating the reality of distant suffering-active Persecutors & Benefactors)

Table 5.6 Multimodal discourse analysis matrix

Modes of Analysis		*Adventure news*	*Semi-emergency news*	*Emergency news*
Multi-Modality	Mode of presentation	1. Simple Narratives-Simple reporting of facts 2. Questions of why do not appear	1. Complicated narratives/Complicated multimodal narratives 2. Meditation of suffering gives credibility and distinct claim to reality 3. Perceptual realism-facticity 4. Categorical realism-emotion 5. Ideological realism-Justice	1. Complicated narratives/Complicated multimodal narratives 2. Meditation of suffering gives credibility and distinct claim to reality 3. Perceptual realism-facticity 4. Categorical realism-emotion 5. Ideological realism-Justice
	The correspondence between text and image	1. Descriptions rather than narrations 2. Visual: minimal, abstracted representations	1. Indexical meaning (perceptual realism) 2. Iconic meaning (Categorical realism) 3. Symbolic meaning (ideological realism)	1. Indexical meaning (perceptual realism) 2. Iconic meaning (Categorical realism) 3. Symbolic meaning (ideological realism)
	The aesthetic quality of the news text	3. Aesthetic distance	1. Pamphleteering 2. Philanthropy 3. Sublimation	1. Pamphleteering 2. Philanthropy 3. Sublimation
CDA	Space-Time (Representation)	1. Singular Space-Time: An isolated place, a one-off event restricts the possibility of historicity 2. No connectivity between the suffering & spectators 3. Hierarchy of place—victims of worthy places	4 distinct chronotropic properties: 1. Concrete 2. Specific 3. Multiple 4. Mobile	4 distinct chronotropic properties: 1. Concrete 2. Specific 3. Multiple 4. Mobile

(continued)

Table 5.6 (continued)

Modes of Analysis	*Adventure news*	*Semi-emergency news*	*Emergency news*
Agency (orientation)	1. Void of agency (Neither empathy nor denunciation, annihilation of the sufferer) 2. Lack of Agora & Theatre 3. Hierarchy of human lives-worthy/unworthy victims (void of agents)	1. Agora (humanization of the sufferers-active sufferers) 2. Theatre (communicating the reality of distant suffering (active Persecutors & Benefactors)	1. Agora (humanization of the sufferers-active sufferers) 2. Theatre (communicating the reality of distant suffering-active Persecutors & Benefactors)
Structure of the News Stories News Layout, presentation and Design	1. A few lines in the front/inside sections of the paper (news in brief) 2. News reports of facts without images in the front page/inside 3. News reports of facts with map/graphics/file photo in the front page/inside page 3. Captioned photos: no context or explanation, just an aestheticisation of the event reported because of its visual value 4. Editorial with strong semantic usage on dehumanisation of the suffering/devoid of agency	1. Full & total inside page coverage/inside lead story without images, but with strong linguistic reference to the urgency or significance of the incident for a particular group of people 2. Inside page secondary reports with a small picture and some linguistic reference to the urgency or significance of the incident for a particular group of people 3. Editorial with strong semantic usage on humanisation or action on suffering.	1. Full and total front page/lead story and cross-platform coverage with images 2. Full and total inside page coverage/inside lead story with images 3. Front page secondary reports with big images and some linguistic reference to the urgency or significance of the incident for a particular group of people 4. Editorial with strong semantic usage on humanisation and action on suffering

used the term 'complicated multimodal narratives' to refer to the visual–verbal combination. This term in the multimodal analysis, was appropriate in her studies concerning television news reporting of distant suffering. Nevertheless, in many instances, news stories are published without any image but with complicated narratives in the case of newspapers, and they cannot be ignored from the analysis. Although, such text-only news reports can be scrutinised under CDA, it was found convenient to study them along with the news reports published with images for analytical convenience. This is why, a communicative property 'complicated narratives' was added in the mode of presentation in the multimodal analysis matrix, to scrutinise the text-only news stories, enabling the researcher to scrutinise all the news stories under the analytical guidelines of mode of presentation. Moreover, the text-only news stories were treated as 'Not Applicable' under the second genre of the multimodal analysis: the correspondence between narrative/text and image. The Table 5.7 below shows how FMMDAM is integrated into content analysis framework and how Frame Analysis, Multimodal Analysis and CDA are used in a quantitative manner. This is an excerpt from the Washington Post's coding manual of its coverage of Sri Lanka's humanitarian crisis in 2009, which is explained in detail in Chapters 6, 7, and 8 (Table 5.7).

Table 5.7 Content analysis coding manual for FMMDAM

Article number	*Date of publication*	*Author (if any)*	*Name of newspaper*	*Type of article*	*Section of newspaper*	*Number of pictures*	*Size of the main picture*	*Nature of picture*	*Type of story*	*Type of coverage*
1	19/9/08	Ravi Nessman	3	1	4	0	NA	NA	1	2
2	04/10/08	–	3	1	4	0	NA	NA	1	3
3	17/11/08	Andrew Buncombe	3	4	3	1	2	3	1	3
4	26/11/08	Andrew Buncombe	3	4	4	2	2	1	1	3
5	28/01/09	Andrew Buncombe	3	1	3	2	3	2	1	3

Quoted/mentioned sources	*Noteworthy war incidents*	*Key frame*	*Sub frames*	*Typology of news story*	*Mode of presentation*	*Correspondence between text & image*	*Aesthetic quality of the news text*	*Space-time (representation)*	*Agency (orientation)*
1,2,3	0	1	5	1	1,2	NA	1	2	1,2
0	0	1	5	1	1,2	NA	1	2	1,2
1,2,6	1	1	5	1	4,5,6	3	1	5	1,2
1,2,6	2,5	1	5	1	1	1,2	1	5	1,2
1,4,6	2,3	2	6,7,8	3	4,5,6,7	3,4	4	7	5

5.6 Summary

This chapter developed 'HRJ- R2P Nexus Conceptual Model' to understand how the five key elements of R2R facilitate the creation of options for R2P interventions, within the agenda-setting framework. Drawing insights from this conceptual model, this chapter proposed a research framework (FMMDAM) that creates a matrix for the analysis of HRJ frames (Frame Analysis Matrix) and typology of news stories (Multimodal Discourse Analysis Matrix), and integrated them into the coding manual of the content analysis to scrutinise the practice of HRJ. This framework articulates the philosophy and sociology of distant suffering, framing theories and the construction of humanitarian crises by the media. This is a multimodal, longitudinal content analytical strategy, rooted in the fine-grained and theoretically grounded approach of Critical Discourse Analysis at the same time. This is an effective way to reconstitute in a systematic empirical fashion (as opposed to the more frequent superficial story-like accounts), the public emergence and development of a civil war crisis, and its impact on public perceptions and public policies.

Bibliography

Aaltola, E. (2012). *Animal Suffering: Philosophy and Culture*. Basingstoke: Palgrave Macmillan.

Allen, M. (2017). *The SAGE Encyclopedia of Communication Research Methods* (Vols. 1–4). Thousand Oaks, CA: Sage. https://doi.org/10.4135/9781483381411.

Boltanski, L. (1999). *Distant Suffering: Morality, Media and Politics* (G. Burchell, Trans.). Cambridge: Cambridge University Press.

Bolter, J. D., & Grusin, R. (2000). *Remediation: Understanding New Media*. MIT Press.

Bruner, J. (1996). Foreword. In B. Shore (Ed.), *Culture in Mind: Cognition, Culture and the Problem of Meaning*. New York and Oxford: Oxford University Press.

Chouliaraki, L. (2004). Watching 11 September: The Politics of Pity. *Discourse and Society, 15*(2–3), 185–198.

Chouliaraki, L. (2006). *The Spectatorship of Suffering*. London: Sage.

Chouliaraki, L. (2008a). Discourse Analysis. In T. Bennett & J. Frow (Eds.), *The SAGE Handbook of Cultural Analysis* (pp. 674–698). London: Sage.

Chouliaraki, L. (2008b). Mediation, Text and Action. In V. K. Bhatia, J. Flowerdew, & R. H. Jones (Eds.), *Advances in Discourse Studies* (pp. 211–229). London: Routledge.

Chouliaraki, L. (2013). *The Ironic Spectator: Solidarity in the Age of Post-Humanitarianism*. Cambridge: Polity Press.

Chouliaraki, L., & Fairclough, N. (2004). The Critical Analysis of Discourse. In W. Carroll (Ed.), *Critical Strategies for Social Research* (pp. 262–271). Toronto: Canadian Scholar's Press.

Corbett, J. (1996). *Bad Mouthing: The Language of Special Needs*. London: The Falmer Press.

Cottle, S. (2009). *Global Crisis Reporting: Journalism in the Global Age*. Maidenhead: Open University Press.

Entman, R. M. (1993). Framing: Toward Clarification of a Fracture Paradigm. *Journal of Communication, 43*(4), 51–68.

Fairclough, N. (1995). *Critical Discourse Analysis: The Critical Study of Language*. London: Longman.

Fairclough, N. (2002). Discourse as Social Practice. In M. Toolan (Ed.), *Critical Discourse Analysis Critical Concepts in Linguistics* (pp. 1–22). London: Routledge.

Fairhurst, G., & Sarr, R. (1996). *The Art of Framing*. San Francisco: Jossey-Bass.

Foucault, M. (1974). Human Nature: Justice Versus Power. In E. Fons (Ed.), *Reflexive Water: The Basic Concerns of Mankind* (pp. 135–197). London: Souvenir Press.

Foucault, M. (1977). *Discipline and Punish: The Birth of the Prison*. London: Allen Lane.

Gamson, W. (1989). News as Framing: Comments on Graber. *American Behavioural Scientist, 33*(2), 157–161.

Gamson, W., & Lasch, K. (1983). Evaluating the Welfare State: Social and Political Perspectives. In S. Shimon & E. Yuchtman-Yaar (Eds.), *Evaluating the Welfare State: Social and Political Perspectives*. New York: Academic Press.

Goffman, E. (1974). *Frame Analysis: An Essay on the Organization of Experience*. New York: Harper and Row.

Hoijer, B. (2004). The Discourse of Global Compassion: The Audience and Media Reporting of Human Suffering. *Media, Culture and Society, 26*(4), 513–531.

Jørgensen, M., & Phillips, L. (2002). *Discourse Analysis as Theory and Method*. London: Sage.

Kuypers, J. A. (2006). *Bush's War: Media Bias and Justifications for War in a Terrorist Age*. Lanham: Rowman and Littlefield.

Kuypers, J. A. (2009). *Rhetorical Criticism: Perspectives in Action*. Lanham: Lexington Books.

Lavrakas, P. (2008). *Encyclopedia of Survey Research Methods*. Thousand Oaks: Sage. https://dx.doi.org/10.4135/9781483381411.n252.

Leistyna, P. (1996). Glossary. In P. Leistyna, A. Woodrum, & S. Sherblom (Eds.), *Breaking Free: The Transformative Power of Critical Pedagogy* (p. 336). Cambridge, MA: Harvard Educational Review Press.
Leistyna P. (2001). Discourse in Late Modernity: Rethinking Critical Discourse Analysis. *Journal of English Linguistics, 29*(2), 183–189.
Moeller, S. D. (1999). *Compassion Fatigue: How the Media Sell Disease, Famine, War and Death*. London: Routledge.
Nikander, P. (2008). Working with Transcripts and Translated Data. *Qualitative Research in Psychology, 5*(3), 225–231.
O'Halloran, K. L. (2005). *Mathematical Discourse: Language, Symbolism and Visual Images*. London and New York: Continuum.
O'Halloran, K. L. (2007). Systemic Functional Multimodal Discourse Analysis (SFMDA) Approach to Mathematics, Grammar and Literacy. In A. McCabe, M. O'Donnell, & R. Whittaker (Eds.), *Advances in Language and Education* (pp. 75–100). London and New York: Continuum.
Phillips, L. (2006). Doing Discourse Analysis: A Brief Introduction to the Field. In N. Carpentier et al. (Eds.), *Media Technologies and Democracy in an Enlarged Europe* (pp. 285–294). Tartu: Tartu University Press.
Ryan, C. (1991). *Prime Time Activism: Media Strategies for Grassroots Organizing*. Boston, MA: South End Press.
Scheufele, D. A. (1999). Framing as a Theory of Media Effects. *Journal of Communication, 49*(4), 103–122.
Scollon, R., & LeVine, P. (2004). Multimodal Discourse Analysis as the Confluence of Discourse and Technology. In P. LeVine & R. Scollon (Eds.), *Discourse and Technology: Multimodal Discourse Analysis* (pp. 1–6). Washington, DC: Georgetown University Press.
Shaw, I. S. (2012). *Human Rights Journalism: Advances in Reporting Distant Humanitarian Interventions*. New York: Palgrave Macmillan.
van Dijk, T. (1995). Discourse Analysis as Ideology Analysis. In C. Schäffner & A. Wenden (Eds.), *Language and Peace* (pp. 17–36). Amsterdam: Harwood Academic Publishers.
Winett, L. (1995). *Advocate's Guide to Developing Framing Memos*. Berkeley, CA: Berkeley Media Studies Group.

CHAPTER 6

Accessibility Effect: Understanding the Information Politics of the Sri Lankan Humanitarian Crisis

6.1 Introduction

The war between the Sri Lankan state and the Liberation Tigers of Tamil Eelam (LTTE) has a long history dating back to 1970s and continuing till 2009. From 1983 to 2009, the LTTE waged four Eelam wars against the successive Sri Lankan governments (see Rotberg 1999, p. 27; McConnell 2008). The decisive Eelam War IV started in July 2006, and ended in May 2009 with the military defeat of the LTTE.

In September 2008, the Government launched its final move towards Kilinochchi, which was the de facto capital of the LTTE during the war. At the same time the Government ordered the UN to leave from the LTTE-controlled areas as it could no longer guarantee the safety of its staff. Artillery shells originating from the Government forces started attacking the UN compounds in Kilinochchi during the first week of September 2008. The UN recalled all its international staff, which resulted in ending all forms of UN humanitarian assistance in the LTTE-controlled territories (UN Internal Review Report 2012, Para. 14, 26, 31 and 38; Ratner 2012, p. 796). The withdrawal of the UN led to severe curtailment of the humanitarian work in the area at a time when the need for such services was greater than ever. Despite appeals and warnings about severe humanitarian crisis by civil society organisations and human rights organisations, the UN went ahead with its decision to pull out from the LTTE-controlled areas (UN Internal Review Report 2012, Para. 37).

S. Selvarajah, *Human Rights Journalism and its Nexus to Responsibility to Protect*, https://doi.org/10.1007/978-3-030-49072-0_6

The war ended on 19 May 2009; this led to the crushing of decades' long armed struggle led by the LTTE, by the Sri Lankan military, wiping out its entire leadership and destroying the lives of more than 70,000 people and millions of properties. Human rights activists and academicians widely condemned the UN and the international community for their failure to act and prevent war crimes and crimes against humanity. Neither journalists nor aid workers of any non-governmental organisations were given access to the war zone. This war has been described by international commentators as 'a war without witnesses' (Mathesan and Allan 2010, p. 184). According to the UN panel of report, the Sri Lankan forces shelled hospitals and no-fire zones, executed the surrendered people and raped women. The panel also accused the LTTE for preventing the civilians from escaping and using civilians as human shields (Panel of Experts Report 2011, pp. ii–iii).

As Professor Damian Kingsbury (2012, p. 8) writes, the ignorance and passivity of the international community to fulfil their responsibility to invoke R2P doctrine enabled the war to become brutal and to be won by the dominant party—the Sri Lankan military—with the massacre of thousands of people and severe human rights abuses. Gordon Weiss (2011), who was the UN spokesperson in Sri Lanka during the humanitarian crisis in 2009 later wrote a book called 'The Cage' in which he detailed how the UN failed to protect the civilians. He personally believes war crimes were committed during the final stages of the civil war and called for an international investigation. Neither journalists nor aid workers of any non-governmental organisations were given access to the war zone (see UN Internal Review Report 2012).

This is where a question arises as to whether this situation could have been avoided, had the international media constructed a human rights-focused agenda-setting effect and in this way demonstrated its watchdog function to draw international attention. By providing information on certain human rights violations, the media are able to make people think further. When extensive reporting is done on particular matters in a specific way, people tend to notice its importance and that triggers further insight into thinking. This helps determine distant others' awareness and perception of the world, and thereby produce a clear portrayal of the issue to set a public agenda. In chapter three, we differentiated this agenda-setting effect in terms of accessibility and applicability.

The scope of this chapter is limited to the analysis of the accessibility effect of the agenda-setting of the humanitarian crisis in Sri Lanka, and develops the following research question: How and to what extent were the human rights violations and suffering of the humanitarian crisis in Sri Lanka reported in the international newspapers? In other words, the research inquiry requires an analysis of how and to what extent did the international press create an 'accessibility effect' of the agenda—setting process in its coverage of the humanitarian crisis in Sri Lanka in 2009.

Moreover, in addition to constraints that affect the news reporting of a distant suffering such as Galtung and Ruge's (1965) news value theory, Herman and Chomsky's 'anti-ideology filter' (1988) and Hanitzsch's (2007a) structural constraints, there was a total lack of access to information due to the total ban on the journalists and aid organisations to enter the war zone during the humanitarian crisis. This situation is likely to have severely undermined the international news coverage of the humanitarian crisis in Sri Lanka and made the journalists largely depend on the elite news sources to report about the war. It is therefore a hypothesis that remains untested if the lack of access to war zone diminishes the prospects of filing news stories from the battle zone and has a direct effect on the accessibility effect of the agenda-setting of the news reporting of a distant suffering in terms of instigating international humanitarian action.

6.1.1 Methodological Framework and Data Collection

The research question requires us to scrutinise the extent to which and how human rights violations and suffering of the humanitarian crisis in Sri Lanka were reported in the international newspapers. This demands us to analyse the published newspapers content of the humanitarian crisis using a content analysis method.

Content analysis is a widely used quantitative data-collection technique in communication research. It is described as a data-collection technique for the objective, systematic and quantitative description of the manifest content of communication (Wimmer and Dominick 2006). Analysing the newspaper content using content analysis generated a better insight into the way the Sri Lankan humanitarian tragedy was covered in the international newspapers. This study needs to know the volume of news coverage such as human rights violations and sufferings during the war in Sri Lanka in the international press between 8 September 2008 and 20 May 2009. As mentioned in the preceding chapter, the reason for choosing this time frame and using that as the sampling because, the final phase of the last Eelam war started with the complete removal of all humanitarian agencies including the UN in September 2008 and ended in May 2009. It was on 8 September 2008, the Sri Lankan government ordered all humanitarian organisations except ICRC to evacuate Vanni. The war ended on 19 May 2009, crushing the decades' long armed struggle led by the LTTE, wiping out its entire leadership. Although, the war came to an end on 19 May 2009, newspapers published on 20 May 2009 included in the content analysis to scrutinise their coverage of the final day of the war on 19 May 2009.

The quantitative part of analysis of this study involves the following six guiding steps formulated from the research insights gathered from Deacon et al. (2007, p. 75). (1.) Identify the research questions in a coherent manner (2.) Define the total range of content to be scrutinised (3.) Formulate a 'coding manual' (4.) Analyse a sample content (5.) Collate the findings (6.) Critically reflect on the findings.

Only newspapers were chosen in the content analysis. Although, people turn to television for news coverage these days, newspaper readership remains high and the role of newspapers is crucial in setting public discourse and political agenda (Walgrave et al. 2008). The role of newspapers has been proved to be very influential in the media coverage of humanitarian crises, and according to Kepplinger (2007), decision-makers depend more on serious broadsheet papers. Importantly, as per the author's preliminary analysis, the international television coverage of the Sri Lankan crisis during the selected period, compared to the international newspapers, proved very low.

Purposive sampling method was used to select the newspapers and their countries to represent international press. Two newspapers were chosen from the following countries: India, UK and United States. These three countries were actively involved in the Sri Lankan conflict. The newspapers selected for the analysis are: *Times* and *The Independent* (UK), *The New York Times* and *Washington Post* (US) and *Indian Express* and *The Hindu* (India). These are the leading newspapers in these countries and are recognised internationally.

As explained in the preceding chapter, a coding guide and coding manual were prepared by identifying the categories to identify manifest content by counting length, frequency, type of news stories and placement of news stories in the international press. A total of 1290 news stories including news reports/articles/columns published in six international newspapers published between 8 September 2008 and 20 May 2009 were analyzed.

It was in the same coding manual that the Frame Analysis matrix and Multimodal Analysis matrix were integrated, as explained in Chapter 5 to develop FMMDAM.

6.2 Content Analysis: Attention of the Newspapers Towards the Humanitarian Crisis

The Table 6.1 shows the extent to which the six newspapers, *The Times, The Independent, The New York Times, The Washington Post, The Hindu* and *The Times of India* covered the final war in Sri Lanka between 8 September 2008 and 20 May 2009.

Table 6.1 shows the number of types of article against all published news. The total number of news reports published in these newspapers includes both the ongoing war and other war-related news, such as

Table 6.1 Type of articles vs. all published news

Type of Articles	*The Independent*	*The Times*	*The New York Times*	*The Washington Post*	*The Times of India*	*The Hindu*
News Report	23	48	35	10	225	751
Editorial	4	5	2	2	7	12
Column	12	5	2	2	9	11
News Feature	18	1	10	13	10	4
Cartoon/ Illustration	0	0	0	0	0	5
Letter	2	3	0	0	0	0
Weekly News Summary	0	0	0	0	0	0
News in Brief	1	13	9	37	0	0
Total (War News + War Related)	46+14=75	64+11=75	53+4=57	54+10=64	136+115=251	272+511=783

demonstrations and protests outside the war zone, arrests and cordon off, statements of politicians related to war, etc.

Table 6.1 shows the sharp quantitative variances between the newspapers in their coverage of the war. Among all six newspapers *The Hindu* newspaper extensively covered the war compared to other newspapers. *The Times of India* next to *The Hindu* in terms of news coverage, while there is not much variance among other newspapers such as *The Independent, The Times, The New York Times* and *The Washington Post*: 60, 75, 57 and 64. These statistics reveal a fact that in terms of geographical location, the newspapers based in India, *The Times of India and The Hindu* have shown much interest in the final war that took place in Sri Lanka. This tendency is reflected perhaps due to the geographical proximity and the geopolitics associated with the war in Sri Lanka.

As described in chapter two, Galtung and Ruge's news value of cultural proximity is better suited to explain the reason for this discrepancy between the Indian newspapers and the US/UK newspapers in the number of the news coverage. They believed that our perception of what constitutes an event is culturally determined and not a natural occurrence. Galtung and Ruge (1965, p. 53) also believed that it related to 'human culture' and therefore should not vary too much globally. They put forward a system of twelve factors describing events that together are used as a definition of 'newsworthiness': frequency, intensity, unambiguity, proximity, relevance, consonance, predictability, continuity, composition, elite persons and elite nations, negativity and ethnocentricity. As far as the UK and the US newspapers are concerned, the humanitarian crisis in Sri Lanka best satisfies the following two news values out the twelve news values:

1. Negativity: Bad news is more newsworthy than good news.
2. Continuity: A story that is already in the news gathers a kind of inertia.

Although, what happened in Sri Lanka was bad news, as far as the UK and the US newspapers are concerned, this bad news did not qualify other 10 news values, and thus possibly would have made these newspapers to ignore the crisis. Moreover, although there was 'continuity' as the Sri Lankan war had been taking place for more than three decades and the final phase of the war, which was subjected to the analysis of this study had started in August 2006, none of the selected newspapers had their permanent correspondents stationed in Sri Lanka to cover the war process. As revealed through a scrutiny of the by-lines and acknowledgements of the news stories, whenever the violence peaked, these newspapers sent their journalists to cover the incidents. This is accentuated by the constrained caused by economic considerations. As Hanitzsch (2007a, p. 5) emphasises, the war reporting of mainstream news media to a greater extent is constrained by economic considerations. Perhaps, this is the reason why the United States and the UK newspapers to a larger extent ignored the humanitarian crisis in Sri Lanka.

Meanwhile, for Indian newspapers, the news reporting of the humanitarian crisis in Sri Lanka was probably essential, as India is a neighbouring country and a country that has actively been involved in the ethnic conflict in Sri Lanka. This is one of the news values listed by Galtung and Ruge (1965) as 'meaningfulness' for an incident/issue to become news in a media institution. As far as the Indian newspapers are concerned, there is a significant number of Tamil population living across India and one of the states in India 'Tamil Naadu' is almost exclusively of Tamils. Moreover, one of the newspapers selected for this study *The Hindu* has its headquarters in Tamil Naadu. This creates a cultural proximity concerning the humanitarian crisis that took place in the Tamils living province of Sri Lanka. As Galtung and Ruge explain (1965), stories concerned with people, who speak the same language, look the same and share the same preoccupations as the audience receive more coverage than those concerned with people who speak different languages, look different and have different preoccupations. In addition, the Indian newspapers also qualify Galtung and Ruge's news values of negativity and continuity.

Against this theoretical backdrop, during these eight months period between 8 September 2008 and 20 May 2009, the humanitarian crisis was so severe and as described by the UN internal review report, unimaginable human rights violations were committed. The number of civilian casualties within a few weeks in 2009 reached over 70,000 (UN internal review report 2012). Public, trapped inside the schools and places of worship were indiscriminately bombarded and hospitals and dwellings destroyed with no access to any humanitarian aid (Panel of experts 2011). Both sides were accused of committing serious war crimes, crimes against humanity and other violent crimes. In the emerging cosmopolitan world order, the international media should have represented victims of violence. Being part of global voice, they should have made the audience to feel the sufferings of these victims and feel obliged to care for them. In other words, the international media should have created a human right focussed agenda-setting effect to instigate an international humanitarian action to deal with the crisis. However, as revealed in the calculation of the news coverage of *The Independent, The Times, The New York Times* and *The Washington Post,* the total number of news reports published during this eight-month period clearly shows the lack of attention, priority and sympathy of these newspapers with regard to this humanitarian crisis. Conversely, the Indian newspapers, in terms of number, gave importance to this humanitarian crisis and covered them extensively. Nevertheless, regardless of the number of the news coverage, whether these newspapers exposed the human rights violations and constructed an accessibility effect in terms of human rights discourse, is yet to be uncovered in this study.

On the other hand, as Table 6.1 shows, the coverage of the other war-related news, such as the anti- war demonstrations, hunger strikes, political condemnation against the war which occurred in foreign countries such as in India, UK, United States and European Countries, is much higher in the Indian newspapers. This is because the Tamils in Sri Lanka and Tamil Nadu (Tamils living state in India) have umbilical relationship, and there was a higher level of political activism demonstrated by the Tamil political parties, human rights organisations, pro-Eelam Tamil organisations, lawyers and students against the war and demanding the Indian government to intervene to stop the war. In this context, these incidents and activities were considered newsworthy for the Indian newspapers.

All in all, this analysis indicates the direct influential power of the news production theories such as Galtung and Ruge's (1965) news value theory and Hanitzsch's (2007a) structural constraints in conditioning the accessibility effect of the media in crisis situations.

Table 6.2 provides insights into the importance and priority given by these newspapers regarding the Sri Lankan crisis, by detailing how these news items were published in the newspapers according to the sections of the newspapers.

As Table 6.2 discloses, only *The Hindu* newspaper published a significant number of news stories in its front page. Out of its 783 news items published during the eight months period, 53 are lead stories and 99 are sub stories published in the front page. *The Hindu* had also published 145 lead stories in its inside pages. These figures show how much importance

Table 6.2 Sections of newspaper vs. all published news

Section of Newspaper	*The Independent*	*The Times*	*The New York Times*	*The Washington Post*	*The Times of India*	*The Hindu*
1st page Lead story	2	2	2	0	3	53
1st page Sub story	0	2	0	3	22	99
Inside lead story	27	31	21	17	58	145
Inside sub story	31	39	33	44	168	484
Op-ed	0	0	1	0	0	2

and priority *The Hindu* newspaper had given to the coverage of the Sri Lankan crisis. Meanwhile, none of the other newspapers published more than 3 lead stories in their front pages. The total number of lead stories published by *The Independent* during the 8 months period of the worst humanitarian crisis was just 2. This is almost the case with other UK and US newspapers such as *The Times, The New York Times* and *The Washington Post:* 4, 2 and 3. Relatively *The Times of India* published higher number of news stories in its front page, 25. Almost the same trend is observed with regard to the sub stories published in the front page of these newspapers.

Nevertheless, as shown in Table 6.2, compared to the Indian newspapers, the UK and the US newspapers published more prominent stories (opinion/news feature) in their inside pages: *The Independent*—27 (45%); *The Times*—31 (42%); *The New York Times*—21 (37%); *The Washington Post*—17 (27%); *The Times of India*—58 (23%) and *The Hindu*—145 (19%).

This shows that although the Indian newspapers published more lead stories and sub stories in their front pages compared to the United States and the UK newspapers, they published small number of prominent stories (opinion/News feature) in their inside pages. Nevertheless, if there was any reason why the Indian newspapers published more lead stories and sub stories, and what kind of stories they were, is yet to be revealed. In addition, whether these newspapers performed poor level of HRJ/PJ/Watchdog journalism in their coverage given the low level of news stories published throughout the period/low level of news stories published in their front page, or if not, the newspapers (Indian) performed higher level of HRJ journalism, given the higher number of news stories and front-page news, cannot be decided, without a qualitative analysis such as frame analysis/discourse analysis to evaluate the applicability effect. This analysis will be performed in the next chapter using FMMDAM.

However, the quantitative calculation does reveal a fact that this humanitarian disaster was not given due attention and priority in the news coverage of the UK and the US-based international newspapers. There were human rights violations that occurred every day during the final war, and hundreds of people died every day during the final phase of the war (Panel of experts 2011), however, as described above, the coverage of this crisis situation was very low *Vis-a-Vis* the 8 months period of continued humanitarian disaster, which was later described by U.N. Secretary General Ban Ki-moon called the sites 'appalling', after visiting Sri Lanka just 4 days after the end of the war and flying over the site of the last battle. 'I have travelled around the world and visited similar places, but this is by far the most appalling scenes I have seen', Ban told CNN (2009).

Table 6.1 further showed the breakdown of the type of news stories published during the period such as news report, editorial, column, news feature, cartoon/illustration, weekly news summary and News in brief. A news feature is a detailed news story with a fresh angle and is usually longer than a news story. It is about concepts and ideas of specific interest. Opinion column is defined as a persuasive piece positioned towards the middle of the paper. Another type of opinion column is published on the opposite of the editorial page. They express only the opinion of the writer of an issue. Meanwhile, letter is written by those who are not directly involved in news production. The newspaper institutions reserve the right to publish the letters (see Stephenson 1998; Batty and Cain 2010). Editorial is considered as the opinion of the newspaper and much more valuable than any other news stories in creating public opinion, as it stirs the conscience of the readers and influences policy makers on an issue of concern (Lowell 2008).

Out of the 60 stories published by *The Independent*, 23 stories are news reports, 30 stories are news features and columns, and only 2 stories are editorial. Out of the 75 stories published by *The Times*, 48 stories are news reports, 6 stories are news features and columns and 5 stories are editorial. In its total 57 stories, *The New York Times* published 35 stories, 12 news features and columns and 2 editorials. Out of its 64 stories, *The Washington Post* published 10 news stories, 15 news features & columns and 2 editorials. Interestingly, *The Washington Post* published 37 'News in Brief' stories. This '*News* in Brief' is a summary of world news in a few sentences in its inside pages. This is 58% of the total stories published in this newspaper. Some major incidents such as killings of people, attacks in no-fire zone, mass exodus of refugees were also reported in this category of news story, while the same news stories were given importance in other newspapers and published distinctly. This ignorance or lack of due attention towards the distant suffering in Sri Lanka is highly seen in *The Washington Post* than any other newspapers. *The Times of India*, in its total 251 stories, published 225 news reports, 190 news features, 9 columns and 7 editorials. Out of its 783 total news stories, *The Hindu* had published 751 news reports, 4 news features, 11 columns, 5 cartoons/illustrations/graphics and 12 editorials.

Although in varying numbers, the scrutiny of Table 6.1 reveals that all the selected newspapers had written editorials on the Sri Lankan humanitarian catastrophe and this in turn indicates a fact that this situation had got the due attraction from all the selected international newspapers. Nevertheless, the lack of sustained editorial writings particularly in the US newspapers reveals their unwillingness and ignorance in shaking the conscious of the policymakers to intervene in stopping the mass atrocities. Whether the higher number and sustained specific predisposition of editorial writings in the Indian newspapers constructed a human-rights focussed discourse or not was not performed in this chapter. This will be examined through further scrutiny of their framing effect in the next chapter.

The breakdown of photos published in the newspapers presented in above Table 6.3 reveals the interest and importance given by the newspapers in publishing photos with their news stories. Chouliaraki (2006) in her analysis of distance suffering showed the power of the media to create different types of aesthetic values and trigger aid distribution, political condemnation and other forms of global response to the humanitarian crisis by publishing photos taken of the distance suffering events. Influence of the images of suffering in creating pity and empathy towards the distance suffering has been well-documented from the Vietnam War to the ongoing Syrian crisis. Although, a qualitative analysis can help identify and assess the characteristics of the images and their effect, systematic quantitative scrutiny can also help evaluate if the newspapers had shown

Table 6.3 Analysis of published photos

No. of Pictures	*The Independent*	*The Times*	*The New York Times*	*The Washington Post*	*The Times of India*	*The Hindu*
0	26	38	28	41	116	536
1	18	18	22	12	122	235
2	14	16	6	8	6	6
‹2	2	2	2	3	4	3
Size of the main Pic						
1 Column	5	4	7	2	76	79
2 Column	10	12	4	7	49	49
3 Column	10	11	7	4	9	72
4 Columns	4	8	9	6	1	40
5 Column	3	1	2	4	0	6
Nature of Pic						
Current	22	32	24	19	77	143
File	10	2	1	4	52	93
Info Graphic	2	3	5	0	3	5
Cartoon	0	0	0	0	2	5

interest and taken efforts in publishing images of the sufferings in Sri Lanka.

As depicted in Table 6.3 shows, *The Independent* published 34 images in its total 60 stories (57%), of which most of the images are 2 and 3 column size. Out of the published 34 images, 22 of them were (then) contemporary images, 10 of them were file images and 2 of them were infographics. There is not much difference between the newspapers in terms of the images published except *The Hindu* and *The Washington Post*: *The Times* (49%), *The New York Times* (53%), *The Washington Post* (36%), *The Times of India* (53%), *The Hindu* (31%). The reason why *The Washington Post* published low number of images is because, as explained earlier, it published 58% of its news stories as 'News in Brief' with all other international news stories in one or two sentences, where there is almost impossible to publish images. However, in rare instances *The Washington Post* did publish photos with one or two lines captions in its 'News in brief 'section. In the case of *The Hindu*, as observed earlier, it published large amount of news stories related to the political activities in Tamil Nadu, such as the statements of political leaders which do not require photos; however, in some instances, they had appeared with small file photo(s) of the relevant politicians.

The reason why the newspapers were unable to publish images of sufferings in the war zone was due to the ban on the journalists, independent observers and humanitarian workers from entering the conflict zone (UN Internal Review Report 2012). This is further confirmed in Chapter 9, where journalists who had covered the war in Sri Lanka revealed how the lack of access to the war zone affected their reporting of the war. The inability of the newspapers to publish the raw images of distant suffering caused by the lack of access to the war zone, affected the aesthetic quality of the news reports published in these newspapers will be analysed in detail in Chapter 9.

The breakdown of the 'type of news coverage' of every newspaper shown in Table 6.4 below further provides insights into the reason why the newspapers were unable to publish raw images of the war.

The editorial writings were not included in the above Table 6.4 breakdown as they are supposed to be written by the paper's editors or by

Table 6.4 Type of coverage vs. all published news (Except editorial)

Type of Coverage	*The Independent*	*The Times*	*The New York Times*	*The Washington Post*	*The Times of India*	*The Hindu*
Embedded/spot	2	0	1	3	2	37
Distant coverage (stationed in Sri Lanka, but not in war zone)	13	10	17	12	52	265
Distant Coverage (stationed in Sri Lanka)	32	55	28	4	22	23
Agency Story	1	2	10	43	78	18
Events covered in their own countries	7	3	0	0	84	426

one of the staffs at the newspaper in house. Except *The Hindu* newspaper, all the other newspapers contain a lower percentage or ignorable number of embedded/spot news coverage. A closer look at the articles further reveal a fact that none of these stories were classified as embedded/spot news coverage, from the war zone where the tragedy occurred. Despite this fact, a very lower number of news stories were classified as 'embedded/spot news coverage' in *The Independent (2), The Times (0), The New York Times (1), The Washington Post(3) and The Times of India (2)*, because the correspondents who filed these stories had taken their own effort to interview the refugees who fled from the war zone to the nearest town (Vavuniya) to report what actually was going on the inside of the war zone and to hear the untold sufferings of the people. There were only two incidents where *The New York Times* on 6 December 2008 and *The Independent* on 16 April 2009, published a news story, respectively from Vellankulam and Kilinochchi which had been just captured by the government forces from the LTTE, and the military had arranged a tour to the journalists to show these places. This revelation is a clear reflection of the impact of the ban on journalists from entering the war zone by the government. This lack of access to war zone, as it had impacted the prospects of filing news stories from the battle zone, would have certainly obstructed the opportunities for the journalists/newspapers to publish raw images of sufferings of the people and human rights violations to expose the real face of the crisis.

Interestingly, Table 6.4 also reveals that *The Hindu* was able to file considerable number 37 news stories from the war zone. This is because, as *The Hindu's* correspondent Muralidhar Reddy reveals in Chapter 9, its editorial policy was supportive of the Sri Lankan government's war against the LTTE, and thus it had special access to the war zone. This is further discussed and explored in chapter nine during the analysis of the interviews of the journalists who had covered the war for these newspapers. However, the revelation from Table 6.3 and by having a closer look at the images published in *The Hindu* within semiotic techniques, it becomes clear that *The Hindu* had failed to use its opportunity to access the war zone to publish raw images of the suffering of the people or the human rights violations by both parties, in a manner to create global compassion and awareness to draw attention of the international community. Whether this trend is seen in the news stories of *The Hindu* will be examined in Chapters 8 and 9.

Not only the news stories filed from the war zone, but the number of news stories filed from Sri Lanka (stationed in Sri Lanka, but not in war zone) is also small in amount, as it can be seen in Table 6.4, except *The Hindu*. *The Independent* has only 31% (13 stories) of its total news stories, filed from Sri Lanka as a whole by its own correspondent(s) during the 8 months period. This figure is just 15% (10 stories) for *The Times*, 32% for *The New York Times* (17 stories), 24% (12 stories) for *The Washington Post*, 35% (52 stories) for *The Times of India* and 80% (265) for *The Hindu*. 265 stories filed from Sri Lanka published in *The Hindu* show its intense coverage and greatest interest in covering the final war in Sri Lanka. Conversely, the statistics also show the disinclination and absence of desire of these newspapers except *The Hindu* in reporting the crisis in Sri Lanka. On the other hand, as Table 6.4 reveals, except *The Hindu*, all the newspapers covered the Sri Lankan humanitarian crisis either from distance (stationed abroad) or through news agencies.

However, the extent to which, and the manner in which, *The Hindu* and other newspapers framed their news stories and whether these news stories featured HRJ frames are yet to be clearly established. *The Independent* covered majority of its stories from distance (stationed abroad), which is 58% (32 news stories): *The Times* 78% (55 stories), *The New York Times* 50% (28), *The Washington Post* 6% (4 stories), *The Times of India* 9% and *The Hindu* 3%. Among all the newspapers *The Times*, has the higher number of news stories/articles produced from distance. Remarkably, *The Washington Post* covered only 6% (4 stories) of its total stories from distance. This is, as evidenced in Table 6.4, due to higher number of news stories (70% of the total stories) obtained from news agencies. This once again shows the lack of interest shown by *The Washington Post* to report the distance suffering in Sri Lanka and being part of the global voice. *The Times of India* and *The Hindu* too have small amount of news stories of the crisis in Sri Lanka covered from a distance. In the case of *The Washington Post*, *The Times of India* too relied considerably (33%) on news agencies to report about the crisis in Sri Lanka. *The Hindu* has low number of news stories covered from distances and news agencies. This is because as observed already, it has significant amount of news stories filed by its own correspondents from Sri Lanka. According to Table 6.4, there is another category of news stories published in the Indian and the UK newspapers stating that they covered the secondary humanitarian crisis events and activities that took place in their countries during the 8 months period.

As mentioned earlier, the Tamil people of Tamil Nadu, India and the Sri Lankan Tamil refugees living in Tamil Nadu frequently organised demonstrations, marches and various other nonviolent forms of protests. Correspondingly at the same time, the Tamil Diaspora community staged continuous demonstrations and sit-in protest in key locations of the UK and other countries. This was much evidenced in the UK where 300,000 Diaspora Tamils live, who staged protest in central London blocking roads around Parliament Square for several weeks demanding a ceasefire in Sri Lanka. This includes a 23-day hunger strike of a Tamil youth in a makeshift tent opposite London's Houses of Parliament, even without drinking water (The Guardian 2009). While intensively reporting about the war in Sri Lanka, *The Hindu* equally covered the events that took place in Tamil Nadu, India. Of its total number of news stories, *The Hindu* published majority of the news stories 55% (426) covering the local events connected to the Sri Lankan war. Meanwhile, *The Times of India* published 35% (84) of its total news stories covering the local events. The UK newspapers too showed interest in covering the local events linked to the Sri Lankan crisis, but the amount of coverage was very small: *The Independent* 13% (7 news stories) and *The Times* 4% (3 stories). There was no such news relating to the local events published in the US newspapers at all.

For the Indian newspapers, the local events in Tamil Nadu connected to the Sri Lankan crisis are sensitive and politically important issues, as Tamil Nadu is the 11th biggest state in India by area and the sixth most populated state in India. This shows how the national interest relating to the crisis influenced its coverage. Meanwhile, compared to the United States, the processions, pickets, demonstrations and other forms of organised mass protests were very high in the UK extremely affecting the daily life of London and its economic activities. Compared to the UK, there were no such intensive demonstrations and activities that took place in the United States, and possibly this is the reason why the US newspapers did not report any of these events.

The numeric calculation presented in the above four tables in terms of the variables such as 'Type of Articles vs. All published news', 'Sections of Newspaper vs. All published news', 'Total number of news items with photos vs. All published news', 'Photo sizes vs. Main photo', 'Nature of pictures vs. All published news with photos', 'Type of stories vs. All published news' and 'Type of coverages vs. All published news except Editorial', reveal the fact that all newspapers except *The Hindu* did not cover the humanitarian crisis in Sri Lanka intensively. Although the analysis of qualitative aspects of news stories can help assess the nature of the news stories, their implied values and intent, quantitative analysis of this nature can also reveal the unwillingness or lack attention towards the newspapers of a conflict. The very lower level number of news stories published in the United States and the UK newspapers do reveal that these newspapers did not try enough to cover the distant suffering that was taking place in Sri Lanka in a manner to draw the attention of the international community.

In addition to the reasons identified above in light of Galtung and Ruge's (1965) news value of cultural proximity or familiarity as well as Herman and Chomsky's explanation of 'anti-ideology filter' (1988) the lack of access to the war zone has significantly affected the reporting of the crisis. Moreover, as identified in the beginning of this chapter, budget allocation with regard to war reporting in the news value, has been identified as one of the main constraints that seriously affect the news coverage of a distance suffering, along with many structural factors, such as resources, time and access to the war zone. Whether, this was also a determining factor that affected the coverage of the humanitarian crisis in Sri Lanka will also be discussed in Chapter 9.

On the other hand, the findings so far have established the fact that Galtung and Ruge's 'newsworthiness' theory has limited the 'accessibility effect' in terms of the frequency of the news reports, including the visual images. As revealed in Table 6.2, except the Indian newspapers, all the other newspapers published not more than 3 lead stories in their front pages. This shows the direct effect of Galtung and Ruge's news values of negativity and continuity theory in influencing the transfer of salient of issues or event of the media agenda in terms of prominence (Kiousis 2004). This means, Galtung and Ruge's criteria of 'newsworthiness' not only had a direct effect in influencing news coverage of the newspapers in terms of the number of news stories or sustained news coverage, but also had a direct bearing in deciding the prominence of news stories such as the location, size of headline, length and time of news content in the media. Thus and so, any analysis to scrutinise the first level (accessibility) agenda setting to see how media condition its audiences as to what to think about a humanitarian crisis, should necessarily take into account Galtung and Ruge's 'newsworthiness' theory. Very low number of editorial writings except the Indian newspapers of one of the worst humanitarian catastrophes in recent history, further strengthens this argument.

It is, therefore, drawing insights from the HRJ—R2P conceptual model in chapter five, a finding that can be made, consistent with the evidences that 'what to think about' in terms of the salience of the humanitarian crisis in Sri Lanka of the media agenda setting (accessibility effect) was severely impacted by Galtung and Ruge's (1965) 'newsworthiness' theory and Hanitzsch's (2007a) structural constraints.

Although the analysis has revealed the direct impact of the above theories in influencing the accessibility effect of the media agenda, this chapter has not revealed how their audience were made to think about by the Indian newspapers with their higher number of news reporting and the higher prominence given to the news items in newspapers, as well as how their readers were made to think about by the UK and the US newspapers with their lower number of news coverage and less prominence to the news items in newspapers. In other words, this is about an analysis of 'applicability effect' to scrutinise the nexus between the attributes of the news items and readers' stored ideas or knowledge about the Sri Lankan civil war, and this requires a frame analysis and/or discourse analysis to describe and explain the newspaper content, but such an analysis is performed in the next chapter using FMMDAM. Nevertheless, using the content analysis framework applied in this chapter, this study attempts to trace the attributes given in the news contents by analysing the news sources used to construct the news stories to trace the traces of 'applicability effect' in terms of positive (peace/human rights discourse) or negative (war discourse) attribute.

Keeping these findings in mind, the next section moves on to analyse the sources mentioned or quoted in the news stories published in the newspapers and thereby analyse their impact and consequences in the news coverage.

6.3 Role of the News Sources

As it can be understood from Table 6.5, almost all the newspapers published quite a few news stories without quoting or mentioning any sources. However, the newspapers produced their news stories referring to some sources, give a picture of the propensity of the newspapers towards the information providers or the information control order that would have existed. Table 6.5 reveals a fact that all the newspapers heavily relied

Table 6.5 News sources vs. All published news

Quoted/mentioned sources	*The Independent*	*The Times*	*The New York Times*	*The Washington Post*	*The Times*	*The Hindu*
None	16	19	2	7	47	129
Military Officials	22	30	27	33	74	166
Government Officials	25	34	27	23	58	199
LTTE Officials	12	14	15	6	24	77
UN/Foreign Officials	21	31	20	9	36	73
Victims	14	15	15	17	16	19
Civil Society/NGOs/Human Rights Groups	23	22	33	15	30	49
Indian Politicians	0	0	0	0	56	340

upon the Sri Lankan government and its military for their information to report about the humanitarian crisis in Sri Lanka.

In order to avoid the effect that can occur in the exclusivity of the newspaper coverage of the crisis in Sri Lanka, the calculations in the discussion in this section exclude the number of news stories published on the local events that took place in the home countries of the newspapers and their unique variables, such as the Indian politicians in the case of the Indian newspapers. As there is considerable number of local events reported in the Indian media and to a larger extent Indian politicians were quoted or mentioned in these news stories, these figures would significantly impact on the distinctiveness of the newspaper coverage of the distant crisis in Sri Lanka.

In its 47 news stories, *The Independent* quoted or mentioned both the Sri Lankan government and its military. This is 40% of its total instances of quoting or mentioning a source in its news coverage. The total number of instances where *The Independent* quoted/mentioned the LTTE officials or its proxy sources is 12, which is only 10% of its total number of instances of quoting or mentioning a news source. This is a big imbalance of the coverage of a war between the two parties. This imbalance is visible in all the newspapers. This comparison in this premise between the government officials and military officials and the LTTE officials in the other newspapers is: *The Times* 64 (44%): 14 (10%), *The New York Times* 54 (39%): 15 (11%), *The Washington Post* 56 (54%): 6 (6%), *The Times of India* 132 (55%): 24 (10%) and *The Hindu* 365 (63%): 77 (13%). Evidently, among all the newspapers *The Hindu* had relied upon more on the Sri Lankan military and the government sources for its reporting about the crisis.

With regard to mentioning or quoting UN/foreign officials, *The Independent* referred 21 times, which is 18% of its total references of its all news sources. For *The Times*, this is 31 (21%), *The New York Times* 20 (15%), *The Washington Post* 9 (9%), *The Times of India* 36 (15%) and *The Hindu* 73 (15%).

In terms of mentioning/quoting the victims of the crisis in the news stories, *The Independent* referred victims in 14 instances in its news coverage (12%). Like *The Independent*, other newspapers too show small number of references to the victims in their stories: The *Times* 15 (10%), *The New York Times* 15 (11%), *The Washington Post* 17 (16%), *The Times of India* 16 (7%) and *The Hindu* 19 (3%). Compared to the United States and the UK newspapers, this is a very low number among the Indian newspapers, particularly in *The Hindu*. As Table 6.5 shows, all the newspapers have significantly mentioned/quoted civil society organisations, NGOs/human rights organisations in their news stories: *The Independent* 23 (20%), The *Times* 22 (15%), *The New York Times* 33 (24%), *The Washington Post* 15 (15%), *The Times of India* 30 (13%) and *The Hindu* 49 (8%). However, as in the case of mentioning/quoting the victim's, compared to other newspapers *The Hindu* shows lower number of references to the civil society organisations, NGOs/human rights organisations in their news stories.

The discussion based on Table 6.5, on one end, sheds light on understanding the conditions within which the journalists had to operate would have determined the observed tendency of the newspapers towards the news sources for their stories, and on the other shows the possible editorial policy preference that would have guided the journalists to look for particular type of news source(s). A finding that all the newspapers relied on in common is that both the Sri Lankan government and the Sri Lankan military choosing what stories to report/not report indicated a possibility that they were in a better position than the LTTE to control the information of the humanitarian crisis as far as the media reporting is concerned. On the other hand, it also reveals a fact that certain newspapers possibly operated with an agenda to create a particular form of discourse by omitting and preferring certain type of news sources. For example, the Indian newspapers, particularly *The Hindu*, seems to have quoted or mentioned the Sri Lankan government and its military as sources for its news stories with great interest than any other newspapers, and shown less interest in quoting or mentioning the victims and civil society organisations/NGOs/human rights organisations in their reporting.

It was revealed in the beginning of the analysis that the Indian newspapers especially *The Hindu,* had greater interest in the crisis in Sri Lanka, because it published large number of lead stories and sub stories in its front page than any other newspapers. However, out of its total 53 lead stories in its front page, *The Hindu* published only 5 lead stories, mentioning or quoting the victims', Civil Society, NGOs, Human Rights Groups, UN or foreign officials. More than 90% of its lead stories in the front page were constructed mentioning or quoting the Sri Lankan government, its military and Indian politicians. Interestingly, 43% of its lead stories that were published in the front page of *The Hindu* were exclusively constructed from the information received from the Sri Lankan government and its military, highlighting the predisposition of the editorial board of *The Hindu* towards the war.

Although we did not perform any systematic qualitative analysis such as frame analysis and discourse analysis in this chapter, the above findings uncovered through the content analysis shed some light on the possible framing effect of the news reporting of the newspapers. The deliberate embracing of the elite sources such as the Sri Lankan government and its military, and the importance given to such sources in their front-page news stories, highlight the likely war journalism discourse of the Indian newspapers. Although, the UK and the US newspapers too significantly relied on the Sri Lankan government and its military, there is evidence to claim that they had endeavoured to include alternative voices in their news reports such as victims and civil society organisations/NGOs/human rights organisations. This shows that despite the higher degree of war journalism discourse that is likely to have been expressed in the UK and the US newspapers, certain level of peace/human rights discourse had also been attributed in their news content. As revealed through the interviews with journalists in the forthcoming Chapter 9, the total lack of access to the war zone and the way the Sri Lankan government controlled the dissemination of the war information through media briefings had played a powerful role in conditioning the newspapers to express more war journalism discourse. However, the deliberate embracing of the elite sources such as the Sri Lankan government and its military, and the prominence given to them in the news stories of the Indian newspapers does reveal the influence of the editorial policy preference of the newspapers to control the 'applicability effect' towards 'war discourse'. This research insight is further explored and discussed in the upcoming chapters. Similarly, for UK and the US newspapers, the reliance on the Sri Lankan government and its military for their news reporting given the lack of access to war zone, does reveal the influence of the propaganda strategies of the warring parties to affect the 'applicability effect' towards 'war discourse' by controlling and manipulating the news sources. The next chapter is dedicated to the detailed analysis of the 'applicability effect', using FMMDAM.

For Carruthers, propaganda is a process of information-spreading through manipulation, distortion, emphasis and omission of the known facts to influence the general public to trust certain interpretations or people (Carruthers 2000). Prior to the outset of fighting, and during the conduct of the war, the media are vital to the war aims of the warring parties. Journalists come under the influence of the propaganda strategies (Höijer et al. 2002, pp. 4–11; Nohrstedt and Ottosen 2014). These are manifest in a number of forms—from briefings through to embedding journalists, who are subject to manipulation. Peace stories can make the headlines but only if they are about the patient and are costly intervention of elite individuals and elite nations (Galtung 2002).

The above analysis of the news sources given the situation of a total lack of access to the war zone shows how the Sri Lankan government had prioritised the media as one of the important agencies as part of its war effort, and handled the 'information politics' in an effective manner to control over the discourse production of the humanitarian crisis, and thus so influence the 'accessibility effect' of the media agenda setting. On the parallel, the analysis also identified the nexus between the 'agenda setting' process and the theories of news production such as Galtung and Ruge's (1965) newsworthiness and Hanitzsch's (2007a) structural constraints.

6.4 Summary

Media are the far most important tool in creating discourse, where access to media is central to controlling the power. This is why those who intend to exert power over the society want to control or manage the media, so that they would be in a better position to influence the construction of the perceived reality of the public to influence the policy agenda. In other words, the construction of the media agenda to construct the perceived reality of the public reality through discourse is impacted by various sources of power (Van Dijk 1996, p, 10; Foucault 1970, 1972). This resonates with what Herman and Chomsky emphasised in their propaganda model (1988). Moreover, as illustrated in the HRJ-R2P conceptual model, in addition to the persuasive communication effect created by the public agenda, concerned policymakers, human rights activists and response agencies can be directly influenced by the news reports of the media.

Within these theoretical perspectives, the Sri Lankan government and its military, with their better access to the mass communication channels had greater opportunity to attract the media channels towards their discourses and communicative events, and were better able to influence the news production of the crisis. This ability of the Sri Lankan government and its military to access the discourse have provided them an opportunity to exert power over the international community and influence the minds of the decisionmakers, and ultimately their behaviour. In other words, the control over the news sources enabled the Sri Lankan government to set the agenda by controlling the 'accessibility effect' of the media agenda for the public discourse of its so-called 'humanitarian war' and what the public, human rights activists and policymakers think about it. Thus, the agenda-setting theory throws light on understanding the reason why the Sri Lankan government imposed a 'total ban' on news coverage of the crisis from the war zone. The effect of this 'total ban' on news coverage is clearly visible in the content analysis with small amount of news stories published with quotations and references from the LTTE and the victims.

This imbalanced quoting of warring parties and victims is very much likely to influence the construction of 'discursive order' (Fairclough 2002) and thereby the 'power' concept enlightened by Michel Foucault, as we have seen in previous chapters. On the other hand, we can say that factors such as the nature of news values, the relationship of journalism to power and the dependence on news sources, have made the conventional journalism to reinforce the status quo of the powerful by creating distorted versions of reality and fuel the conflict.

Although, there was lower number of references among the newspapers to UN/Foreign Officials /Civil Society/NGOs/Human Rights Groups, that this would have certainly contributed to the construction of a 'discursive order' of distant suffering in Sri Lanka. Nevertheless, the discourse that would have been created as a result of the mentioning of these sources are less likely to be dominant, given the very small number of their references and in the absence of direct war zone reporting. It is likely at this point that the discourse that would have been created as a result of the references to the Sri Lankan government and its military in the international newspapers would have operated as the dominant discourse in the 'discursive order' of the humanitarian crisis in Sri Lanka. Meanwhile, other discourses that would have been created by the sources such as the LTTE, UN/Foreign Officials and Civil Society/NGOs/Human Rights Groups, would have operated as oppositional, or alternative discourses. This technically sheds light on the failure of the news reporting to construct the realism of the crisis. Because, although not revealed through any qualitative analysis, the findings of the content analysis of the news sources mentioned in the newspapers shows the failure to construct a human rights focussed discourse of the humanitarian crisis and create an awareness of the human rights violations for the international community to act on the distant suffering. This is clearly linked to the poor coverage of the humanitarian crisis in terms of frequency as revealed in the content analysis under the influence of Galtung and Ruge's (1965) news values factors, Hanitzsch's (2007a) structural constraints and lack of access to the war zone.

Bibliography

Batty, C., & Cain, S. (2010). *Media Writing: A Practical Introduction*. Basingstoke: Palgrave Macmillan.

Carruthers, S. L. (2000). *The Media at War: Communication and Conflict in the Twentieth Century*. Basingstoke: Macmillan.

Chouliaraki, L. (2006). *The Spectatorship of Suffering*. London: Sage.

Deacon, D., Pickering, M., Golding, P., & Murdock, G. (2007). *Researching Communications: A Practical Guide to Methods in Media and Cultural Analysis*. New York, NY: Oxford University Press.

Fairclough, N. (2002). 'Discourse as Social Practice'. In M. Toolan (Ed.). *Critical Discourse Analysis Critical Concepts in Linguistics* (pp. 1–22) London: Routledge.

Foucault, M. (1970). *The Order of Things: An Archaeology of the Human Sciences*. London: Tavistock.

Foucault, M. (1972). *The Archaeology of Knowledge*. London: Tavistock.

Galtung, J. (2002). Peace Journalism: A Challenge. In W. Kempf & H. Luostarinen (Eds.), *Journalism and the New World Order, Studying War and the Media* (pp. 269–272). Nordicom: Göteborg.

Galtung, J., & Ruge, M. H. (1965). The Structure of Foreign News. *Journal of Peace Research, 2*(1), 64–91.

Hanitzsch, T. (2007a). Situating Peace Journalism in Journalism Studies: A Critical Appraisal. *Conflict and Communication, 6*(2), 1–9.

Herman, E. S., & N. Chomsky. (1988). *Manufacturing Consent: The Political Economy of the Mass Media*. New York: Pantheon.

Höijer, B., Nohrstedt, S. A., & R. Ottosen. (2002). The Kosovo War in the Media—Analysis of a Global Discursive Order. *Conflict & Communication Online, 1*(2), 1–18.

Kepplinger, Hans Mathias. (2007). Reciprocal Effects: Toward a Theory of Mass Media Effects on Decision Makers. *Harvard International Journal of Press/Politics, 12*(2), 3–23.

Kiousis, S. (2004). Explicating Media Salience: A Factor Analysis of New York Times Issue Coverage During the 2000 U.S. Presidential Election. *Journal of Communication, 54*, 71–87.

Kingsbury, D. (2012). *Sri Lanka and the Responsibility to Protect: Politics, Ethnicity and Genocide*. New York, NY: Routledge.

Lowell, G. (2008). How to Write an Editorial. *Undergraduate Review, 4*, 189–192 [Online]. http://vc.bridgew.edu/undergrad_rev/vol4/iss1/35. Accessed June 17, 2020.

Matheson, D., & Allan, S. (2010). Social Networks and the Reporting of Conflict. In R. L. Keeble, J. Tulloch, & F. Zollmann (Eds.), *Peace Journalism, War and Conflict Resolution* (pp. 173–192). New York, NY: Peter Lang.

McConnell, D. (2008). The Tamil People's Right to Self-Determination. *Cambridge Review of International Affairs, 21*(1), 59–76 [Online]. doi: https://doi.org/10.1080/09557570701828592. Accessed June 20, 2020.

Nohrstedt, S. A. & Ottosen, R. (2014). *New Wars, New Media and New War Journalism: Professional and Legal Challenges in Conflict Reporting*. Göteborg: Nordicom.

Ratner, R., & Steven, R. (2012). 'Accountability and the Sri Lankan Civil War'. *The American Journal of International Law, 106*(4), 795–808.

Rotberg, R. I. (1999). Sri Lanka's Civil War: From Mayhem Toward Diplomatic Resolution. In Robert Rotberg (Ed.), *Creating Peace in Sri Lanka: Civil War and Reconciliation* (pp. 1–16). Washington, DC: Brookings Institution Press.

Panel of Experts. (2011, March 31). *Report of the Secretary-General's Panel of Experts on Accountability in Sri Lanka* [Online]. http://www.un.org/News/dh/infocus/Sri_Lanka/POE_Report_Full.pdf. Accessed March 9, 2019.

Stephenson, D. (1998). *How to Succeed in Newspaper Journalism*. London: Kogan Page.

The Guardian. (2009, May 10). *Sri Lanka Throws Out Three Channel 4 Journalists*, [Online]. https://www.theguardian.com/world/2009/may/10/channel-four-journalists-sri-lanka. Accessed June 24, 2020.

UN Internal Review Report. (2012). *Report of the Secretary-General's Internal Review Panel on UN Actions in Sri Lanka*. [Online]. https://reliefweb.int/sites/reliefweb.int/files/resources/The_Internal_Review_Panel_report_on_Sri_Lanka.pdf. Accessed June 20, 2020.

Walgrave, S., Soroka, S. N., & Nuytemans, M. (2008). The Mass Media's Political Agenda-Setting Power A Longitudinal Analysis of Media, Parliament, and Government in Belgium (1993 to 2000). *Comparative Political Studies, 41*(6), 814–836. https://doi.org/10.1177/0010414006299098.

Weiss, G. (2011). *The Cage: The Fight for Sri Lanka and the Last Days of the Tamil Tigers*. London: The Bodley Head.

Wimmer, R. D., & Dominick, J. R. (2006). *Mass Media Research: An Introduction* (8th ed.). California: Wadsworth.

Van Dijk, T. A. (1996). Power and the News Media. In D. Paletz & C. Vinson (Eds.), *Political Communication in Action, Cresskill*. New York, NY: Hampton Press.

CHAPTER 7

The Two-Dimensional Framing Process: Understanding the Journalism Discourse of the Sri Lankan Humanitarian Crisis

7.1 Introduction

Framing is a process in which journalists and editors construct a message in a specific manner that highlights the facts in that message to be perceived in a particular way (Kuypers 2006). This chapter presents a systematic analysis of how the international newspapers framed and depicted the humanitarian crisis of Sri Lanka in 2009. It articulates an analysis to understand the extent to which the international newspapers created a human rights-focused discourse of the distant suffering in Sri Lanka. Consequently, it identifies and demonstrates the factors that had substantial effects on the construction of the framing effect. In other words, this is an analysis of the manner and the extent of the creation of the 'applicability effect' of the agenda-setting process in the international newspapers of the humanitarian crisis in Sri Lanka within the HRJ-R2P nexus conceptual model. On the other hand, this chapter is an articulation of the 'Framing Matrix and Multimodal Discourse Analysis Matrix' (FMMDAM), integrated into the coding manual of the content analysis framework presented, which determines how the practice of Human Rights Journalism (HRJ) can be evaluated using framing matrix as explained in Chapter 5.

As in the case of Chapter 6, a total of 1290 news stories including news reports/articles/columns published in six international newspapers (*The Independent, The Times, The New York Times, The Washington Post, The Times of India and The Hindu*) between 8th September 2008 and

S. Selvarajah, *Human Rights Journalism and its Nexus to Responsibility to Protect*, https://doi.org/10.1007/978-3-030-49072-0_7

20th May 2009, were critically analysed. As explained in chapter five, the Frame Analysis matrix was integrated in the same content analysis coding manual used in the analysis conducted in Chapter 6.

Data coding was done manually and independently by three evaluators, including the author. Generally, a higher consistency was observed among the evaluators. Evaluators read through all the newspaper content several times to identify the properties of the framing memo that represent each of the sub-frames of HRJ and HWJ. Differences were addressed through an iterative review process which approximately took eight weeks. The process resulted in the construction of the Framing Matrices illustrated below to identify the sub-frames of HRJ and HWJ, which were used in the coding manual. A coding guide and a set of variables were prepared to assist the recording of the data in the coding manual.

7.2 Practice of HRJ vs HWJ

As Table 7.1 shows, except *The Independent, The Times* and *The New York Times* (53%), all the other newspapers published stories that predominantly contain the frames of HWJ. The stories considered unworthy of being categorised as HRJ or HWJ were marked as 'Not Applicable'. This category includes news stories which are not directly related to the humanitarian crisis, such as events that took place in foreign countries. This is why the calculations presented in this discussion do not include the 'Not Applicable' category.

Table 7.1 Key frames vs. type of news stories

Key Frames	*The Independent*	*The Times*	*The New York Times*	*The Washington Post*	*The Times of India*	*The Hindu*
Human Wrong Journalism	22	35	28	51	154	388
Human Rights Journalism	31	36	29	13	22	19
Not Applicable	7	4	1	0	75	376

The percentage of news stories published by the newspapers, which adhere to the frames of HRJ are as follows: *The Independent* (58%), *The Times* (51%) and *The New York Times* (51%), *The Washington Post* (20%), *The Times of India* (13%) and *The Hindu* (5%). The *Independent* (58%), *The Times* (51%) and *The New York Times* (51%) highly adhere to the frames of HRJ, although they comprise majority of the HRJ frames only by a narrow margin. They have also, to a certain extent, contributed to the discourse of the HWJ because there is only 1% difference observed between HRJ and HWJ in *The Times*, whereas a big difference is seen in *The Washington Post* and *The Indian* newspapers—particularly *The Hindu*. As observed in Chapter 6, the reliance on the Sri Lankan government and its military sources, coupled with its lack of access to the war zone could have restricted the practice of HRJ. Table 7.2 below provides insights into the representation of HRJ and HWJ in the type of news stories published.

Almost in all the newspapers, except in *The New York Times*, HWJ is presented more in the news reports than in any other type of news stories. As shown in Chapter 6, all the newspapers relied on elite sources, such as the Sri Lankan government and its military for their news stories, and thus, it is highly likely that the newspapers would have relied on the elite sources to publish the news reports as well. This heavy dependence on elite sources is likely to facilitate the construction of more war

Table 7.2 Key frames vs. type of news stories

Sub-frames	*The Independent*		*The Times*		*The New York Times*		*The Washington Post*		*The Times of India*		*The Hindu*	
	HWJ	*HRJ*	*HWJ*	*HRJ*	*HWJ*	*HRJ*	*HWJ*	*HRJ*	*HWJ*	*HRJ*	*HWJ*	*HRJ*
News Reports	11	10	25	20	16	19	7	3	141	12	360	17
Editorial	0	4	0	5	0	2	1	1	3	4	12	0
Column	3	5	0	5	1	1	1	1	5	2	9	2
News Feature	8	9	0	1	3	6	5	8	5	4	3	0
Cartoon/Illustration	0	0	0	0	0	0	0	0	0	0	4	0
Letter	0	2	0	3	0	0	0	0	0	0	0	0
Weekly News Summary	0	0	0	0	0	0	0	0	0	0	0	0
News in Brief	0	1	10	2	8	1	37	0	0	0	0	0

journalism frame and, as described in chapter two, enables the media to accept the military terminologies, its agenda and the perspectives of the elites without any critical scrutiny. This is possibly because the journalists may have been forced into a situation which required them to practice uncritical reporting, such as the aforementioned conditions of absolute ban on reporting from the war zone or censorship. Although HWJ is more heavily expressed in *The Washington Post* in its 'news in brief' category than its 'news reports'. Though both are similar in terms of their features, the former is a summarization of the latter.

For example, a news feature was written by Stephen Khan from Colombo for *The Independent* titled 'Sri Lankans celebrate fall of Tigers' capital; President Rajapaksa announces capture of Tamil rebels' stronghold in Kilinochchi' and was published on the 3rd of January 2009. This shows the influence of the elite sources on journalists, who do not shy away from dehumanising the 'other' side and constructing the zero-sum framing of war. Although the author refers to a hospital staff regarding a suicide attack in Colombo in the same story and quotes an ordinary citizen's opinion, the story gives prominence to the Sri Lankan President's opinion about a military breakthrough. To quote the story: 'It was the constant dream of all Sri Lankans, whether Sinhala, Tamil or Muslim, who are opposed to separatism, racism, and terrorism, and have always sought peace, freedom and democracy, President Rajapaksa said'. 'Today our heroic troops have made that dream a reality. A short while ago, our brave and heroic troops have fully captured Kilinochchi that was considered the main bastion of the LTTE [the Tigers]'. To provide the LTTE side of the information, the author refers to a pro-rebel website 'Tamilnet' and quotes: 'The Sri Lankan army has entered a virtual ghost town, the website said'. 'The Tigers, who had put up heavy resistance so far, had kept their casualties as low as possible in the defensive fighting'. *TamilNet* was the only (web-based) English media at the time that had access to the conflict zone through its (local) correspondent on the ground. *Tamilnet* was the sole source of almost all the media information about the final war from the LTTE side and the world clicked on to the *TamilNet* website for information (see Manoharan 2019).

As per the war journalism framing memo of HWJ matrix, which is used to analyse this story, the core position involved in this story 'focuses on violence, war winners and differences between the parties, and the metaphor of the framing is centred on "zero- sum game"'. There are numerous examples of news stories and news features, in all the six newspapers, which used catchy phrases such as 'victory is not so far away from', 'final assault', 'overwhelming the remaining', 'final hours', 'end game', 'escape routes cut off' and 'hopeless battle'. This type of war journalism makes the readers believe that war is inevitable and is the righteous way to resolve the problem.

A first-page news report in *The Hindu* dated 12th May 2009 is another example to corroborate this idea. The report titled 'Sri Lankan troops poised for big breakthrough' quoted the Defence Secretary of Sri Lanka, who said, 'On the basis of reports from the military commanders I can say that the troops are poised for a major breakthrough in the next 48 hours'. Meanwhile, the news does not address an attack that took place in the safety-zone, which UN described as a 'bloodbath', and where over 100 children were believed to have died. The news quoted the Defence Secretary who alleged that this was a propaganda stared by the LTTE. Meanwhile, the news report, in its last paragraph, quoted a Sri Lankan Government doctor who was in the war zone, stating: '393 people were either brought to the hospital for burial or had died at the facility on Sunday, while another 37 bodies were brought in on Monday morning. More than 1300 injured came to the hospital'.

Elite sources' influence on the news reports is further substantiated in the analysis of the connection between the editorials of the newspapers and the key frames (HRJ/HWJ). Barring Indian newspapers, there is a conflicting relationship observed between the type of frame expressed in the news reports and editorial writings. Almost all of the editorials of the US and the UK newspapers portray HRJ framing, while majority of their news reports portray HWJ reporting. Editorials, commentaries, news features, and columns also consist more of HRJ frames in the US and the UK newspapers.

Editorial is a piece of opinion journalism representing the views of the majority of the editorial board. It is persuasive, clearly written, and is intended to prove a point regarding a specific issue (Lowell 2008). Column writing is also opinionated, but it doesn't represent the policy of the newspaper. However, in general, newspapers selectively publish the columns to make a specific impact on a particular issue. Meanwhile, news features are interpretative or opinion-based, but they are based on facts which are constructed from the 'quotes' of the people rather than the writer (Pulford 2009). The heavy presence of HRJ in editorials, commentaries, news features and columns further reveals the policy of the UK and the US newspapers towards the humanitarian crisis in Sri Lanka. The strong presence of HWJ in the news stories portrays the relationship of sourcing and framing with the type of news stories, as stories containing more war journalism frames are sourced from the Sri Lankan government and its military.

Contrary to the situation observed in the UK and the US newspapers, there is a very clear nexus between the editorials, news features, column writings and news reports of the Indian newspapers. In particular, *The Hindu* had published 12 editorial writings during the 8 months, none of which are categorised as HRJ. As it can be observed later in this chapter, all its editorials are seen to be endorsing the 'humanitarian war' discourse of the Sri Lankan government and also favouring its non-interventionist argument. Similarly, out of its 12 news features and columns, only two stories are categorised as HRJ. For example, an editorial written in *The Hindu* on the 18th of October, 2008 is fully based on war journalism and empathy distance frames. This was written seven months before the war ended and hence, the narrative should have revolved around giving advises to the Indian government to use its regional influence and stop the war. Instead, this article urged the Indian government to support Sri Lanka by providing humanitarian assistance and relief towards the victims without advocating for non-violent solutions, by framing the crisis as a 'war against terrorism'. As per the framing memo of the empathy distance frame of HWJ framing matrix, sources of the problems are seen as terrorism and its solutions are advocated aligning with the conviction towards 'injection pains but it cures'. Therefore it appeals to the principle of 'humanitarian assistance and relief' as opposed to the principle of UDHR of the empathy critical frame. This view was consistently stressed in the editorial writings of *The Hindu* until the end of the war in May, 2009. This clearly highlights the 'applicability effect' that *The Hindu* intended to create. As we had discussed in chapter three, the concept of applicability explains the nexus between the attributes of a reported issue and an audience's stored ideas or knowledge Price and Tewksbury (1997). As in the case of the aforementioned editorial published in *The Hindu*, it's apparent that the newspaper perceives the humanitarian crisis in Sri Lanka as an issue of terrorism (problem) and believes that war can eliminate this problem. Thus, *The Hindu's* framing effect can be labelled as 'warmongering'.

From the analysis discussed so far, it is clear that apart from the conditions that the journalists/newspapers reporting the humanitarian crisis in

Sri Lanka were subjected to, the editorial policies of the newspapers would have also influenced the Indian newspapers in supporting the 'humanitarian war campaign' of the Sri Lankan government and may have guided the occupational culture of their journalistic practices.

It can be concluded that although the US and the UK newspapers expressed more HRJ frames in their editorials, news features and columns, in terms of number, their extent of news coverage was abysmal. Thus, it is unlikely that their coverage created a human rights discourse capable of drawing the attention of the world towards the distance suffering or even encouraged due to political action from the international community. In other words, despite significantly constructing a human rights-focused 'applicability effect', given the poor level of 'accessibility effect' as revealed in the previous chapter, the US and the UK newspapers wouldn't have had a substantial enough impact to create a 'persuasive communication effect'.

Table 7.3 below provides an in-depth inquiry into the (sub) frames that construct the key frames (HRJ/HWJ). This will enable one to identify the type of frame(s) which manifested frequently, or did not at all.

Table 7.3 Key frames vs. sub-frames

Sub-frames	*The Independent*		*The Times*		*The New York Times*		*The Washington Post*		*The Times of India*		*The Hindu*	
	HWJ	*HRJ*	*HWJ*	*HRJ*	*HWJ*	*HRJ*	*HWJ*	*HRJ*	*HWJ*	*HRJ*	*HWJ*	*HRJ*
Empathy Distance	10	0	5	0	11	0	18	0	55	1	194	1
Evocative Reporting	4	0	1	0	5	0	6	0	28	0	64	1
Reactive	0	0	1	0	6	0	3	0	9	0	34	0
Non-Interventionist	4	0	0	0	2	0	0	0	12	0	50	0
War Journalism	20	0	34	3	24	0	40	3	119	0	248	0
Empathy Critical Frame	0	22	0	25	0	22	0	12	0	15	1	8
Diagnostic Reporting	0	19	0	15	0	8	0	6	0	4	1	0
Proactive	0	7	0	13	0	22	0	6	0	3	0	0
Interventionist	0	9	0	12	0	22	0	4	0	3	1	7
Peace Journalism	0	9	0	5	0	4	0	3	0	7	0	8

A story categorised as either HRJ or HWJ may contain more than 1 sub-frame, and understandably, the total number of sub-frames of HRJ or HWJ will amount to more than the total number of news stories identified as HRJ and HWJ.

As shown in the above graph, among all the HWJ frames, *The Times* used the 'war journalism' frame more frequently to construct its news stories amounts to 83% of its total sub-frames of HWJ. The usage of the 'war journalism' frame is very high in number in all the other newspapers too. Next to the 'war journalism' frame, the most extensively used frame among the HWJ frames is the 'empathy distance frame'. While, 'evocative reporting' and 'reactive reporting' frames are seen in lower numbers in the US and the UK newspapers, they are significant in the Indian newspapers. Similarly, 'non-interventionist' frame is muted in the US and UK newspapers, however it is present considerably in the Indian newspapers.

Among the sub-frames of HRJ, 'empathy critical frame' occurs in high numbers in all the newspapers. After 'empathy critical frame', the 'diagnostic reporting' frame is expressed frequently in all the newspapers. In general, all the sub-frames of HRJ are very prominent in the US and UK newspapers, barring *The Washington Post*. This is because in comparison to all the other US and the UK newspapers, *The Washington Post* recorded a very low level of HRJ reporting, as mentioned above. Understandably, given the low level of HRJ reporting in the Indian newspapers, the stories they produced involved a very low number of HRJ sub-frames.

Notably, the disproportion between the non-interventionist frame and the interventionist frame is considerably high in *The Times of India* (12:3) and *The Hindu* (50:8). Despite the difference in the number of news stories published, the discussion so far has clearly established a link between the two Indian newspapers. The commonality is that both of them tend to support the Sri Lankan government's 'humanitarian war' and are uncritical towards the humanitarian crisis; instead, they campaigned for the non-intervention of the international community in the Sri Lankan crisis.

As it can be observed from Table 7.3, news stories that are identified as either HRJ or HWJ are almost exclusively constructed either by the sub-frames of HRJ or HWJ. This shows that the sub-frames of either HRJ or HWJ operate in a manner which mutually reinforcing each other's function(s), and as a result can produce a shared outcome or a shared (political) function.

Nevertheless, Table 7.3 details an interesting observation, wherein two stories published in *The Independent* expressed the 'war journalism' frames, but were classified as 'HRJ' stories. This anomaly can be explained during the frame analysis process using the example of two stories published on 8th and 18th April 2009 titled 'Why are the Tamils protesting, and are claims of abuse in Sri Lanka true? Was the biggest question' and 'UN in effort to broker safe passage for children in war zone; Central government denies humanitarian crisis despite reports of malnutrition', respectively. The latter's dominant discourse was formed by the HRJ frames of 'empathy critical frame, proactive and interventionist'. These two articles, written by Andrew Buncombe, and referring to victims, human rights organisations and foreign diplomats, expose the immense suffering of the distant victims, and thus form mutually reinforcing powerful HRJ frames out of catchphrases such as 'so-called no-fire zone', 'many more are at risk of losing their lives', 'It's desperate, desperate, desperate', 'conditions there are dire', 'insufficient food, water and medicine', 'severely emaciated people around the area', 'mothers whose breast milk has dried up', 'beg for baby formula', 'evolving human tragedy' and 'living under trees or damaged tarpaulin tents'. As a result, although there was a war journalism frame identified in the story, it was categorised as an HRJ story. This discussion highlights how the international newspapers failed to practice HRJ and also did not report on the human rights violations and sufferings in Sri Lanka, which thereby answers the research inquiry concerning the extent to which the frames of HRJ and HWJ were expressed while reporting.

Scrutinising the key frames and the sub-frames vis-à-vis the type of news stories and their news sources would enable this analysis to generate valuable information pertaining to the discourse of war journalism that was generated by the international newspapers.

7.3 Different Framing Discourses Across the International Press Coverage and Their 'Effect'

The breakdown of the mentioned sources against the key frames in Table 7.4 proves the hypothesis which was formed in the discussion related to Table 7.3. The news stories identified as HWJ in all the newspapers largely consist of information provided by elite sources such as the

Table 7.4 Key frames vs. quoted/mentioned sources

Sub-frames	*The Independent*		*The Times*		*The New York Times*		*The Washington Post*		*The Times of India*		*The Hindu*	
	HWJ	*HRJ*	*HWJ*	*HRJ*	*HWJ*	*HRJ*	*HWJ*	*HRJ*	*HWJ*	*HRJ*	*HWJ*	*HRJ*
None	4	8	7	10	1	1	7	0	22	3	51	2
Military Officials	15	6	17	13	18	9	25	8	67	5	164	1
Government Officials	10	14	18	15	14	13	18	5	46	1	189	4
LTTE Officials	6	6	7	7	10	5	4	2	19	4	75	1
UN/Foreign Officials	5	16	11	20	5	15	4	5	27	4	65	3
Victims	3	9	2	11	1	14	7	10	7	7	15	3
Civil Society/NGOs/Human Rights Groups	7	15	7	14	8	24	8	7	21	9	42	5
Indian Politician(s)	0	0	0	0	0	0	0	0	16	1	45	7

Sri Lankan government and its military. *The Independent*, in its 48 news stories (all the stories except the editorials and the news stories based on events that occurred in other countries), mentioned the military 21 times, and in the majority of the instances (71%) these stories were categorised as HWJ. Remarkably, the same trend is observed very frequently in all the other newspapers. As revealed in Table 7.3, the newspapers relied more extensively on the Sri Lankan government as opposed to the military. Nonetheless, all the selected newspapers relied heavily on both the Sri Lankan government and its military for their information.

As the statistics in Table 7.4 reveal, the news stories which were constructed on the basis of the information obtained from the Sri Lankan government and its military largely contributed to the framing of HWJ in all the newspapers, particularly in the Indian newspapers.

Mixed trends with regard to the frames of HRJ and HWJ against the LTTE sources is observed in the US and the UK newspapers. Nevertheless, the difference between the HRJ and HWJ frames based on the LTTE sources is not significant. Meanwhile, though in small numbers, compared with other newspapers, the Indian newspapers produced a significant number of HWJ stories citing LTTE sources, similar to those sourced from the Sri Lankan government and its military.

As observed in Chapter 6, the reliance on victims for the construction of news stories was observed to be very low in all the newspapers—particularly in the Indian newspapers. Except in the case of the Indian newspapers, consulting the victims for information and opinions, contributed to more HRJ than HWJ framing in the US and the UK newspapers. A similar trend is observed with regard to the news stories which acquired information from UN/foreign officials/civil society/NGOs/human rights organisations sources. This dynamic of framing is further highlighted in Table 7.5, where the sub-frames are presented against the news sources.

Table 7.5 explicitly demonstrates the power held by the government and the military sources in producing war journalism frames, as it manifests frequently in all the newspapers. Out of the 45 war journalism frames mentioned in *The Independent*'s news stories, a significant portion of them—15 (33%)—originates from the Sri Lankan military. A parallel trend is observed with regard to the other newspapers as well: *The Times* 16 (25%), *The New York Times* 17 (36%), *The Washington Post* 20 (36%), *The Times of India* 57 (40%) and *The Hindu* 147 (35%). A similar trend is noticed in the case of the 'government sources' as well. The contribution

Table 7.5 Sub-frames vs. quoted/mentioned sources

	The Independent					
Sub frames	*Military Officials*	*Government Officials*	*LTTE Officials*	*UN/Foreign Officials*	*Victims*	*CSOs/NGOs/HR Groups*
Empathy Distance Frame	6	4	2	3	1	3
Evocative Reporting	3	2	1	2	1	2
Reactive	0	0	0	0	0	0
Non-interventionist	4	3	2	3	0	3
War Journalism	15	10	6	5	2	7
Empathy Critical Frame	6	12	4	13	7	13
Diagnostic Reporting	4	7	4	11	4	10
Proactive	3	3	2	6	0	6
Interventionist	2	4	1	6	2	6
Peace Journalism	1	3	1	5	2	3

The Times						*The New York Times*					
Military Officials	*Government Officials*	*LTTE Officials*	*UN/Foreign Officials*	*Victims*	*CSOs/NGOs/HR Groups*	*Military Officials*	*Government Officials*	*LTTE Officials*	*UN/Foreign Officials*	*Victims*	*CSOs/NGOs/HR Groups*
5	3	0	2	1	2	7	8	4	4	1	6
1	1	1	0	0	0	4	2	1	0	1	2
1	0	0	1	0	0	4	3	2	1	1	2
0	0	0	0	0	0	2	0	0	0	1	1
16	18	7	11	3	8	17	10	9	4	1	6
11	12	7	17	11	13	8	9	4	12	10	19
5	6	2	9	1	3	2	4	1	4	6	8
6	5	3	6	3	6	7	10	4	13	9	20
4	3	4	9	4	5	7	9	4	15	10	18
0	0	0	1	0	0	1	2	0	2	2	4

The Washington Post

Military Officials	*Government Officials*	*LTTE Officials*	*UN/Foreign Officials*	*Victims*	*CSOs/NGOs/HR Groups*
9	8	0	3	4	3
3	4	0	1	4	2
2	2	1	0	0	2
0	0	0	0	0	0
20	14	4	2	8	8
7	4	2	5	9	7
4	2	1	3	3	2
3	1	2	5	4	2
2	0	2	4	2	0
2	0	1	2	2	1

The Times of India						*The Hindu*					
Military Officials	*Government Officials*	*LTTE Officials*	*UN/Foreign Officials*	*Victims*	*CSOs/NGOs/HR Groups*	*Military Officials*	*Government Officials*	*LTTE Officials*	*UN/Foreign Officials*	*Victims*	*CSOs/NGOs/HR Groups*
17	19	10	14	6	10	58	76	30	42	6	22
8	8	5	6	3	6	20	30	5	12	8	5
1	1	2	2	0	1	11	17	4	7	2	1
1	4	0	2	1	2	9	25	3	11	4	0
57	36	14	20	2	15	147	156	65	39	8	31
5	0	4	3	6	6	2	4	2	3	3	4
1	0	1	0	3	2	0	0	0	0	0	0
0	0	0	0	0	2	0	0	0	0	0	0
0	0	0	0	0	3	2	2	2	1	0	1
0	1	0	1	1	2	0	1	0	1	0	0

of both the Sri Lankan government and its military in the construction of the war journalism frame is extremely high in all the newspapers.

All the news stories constructed based on the information acquired from the victims contain HRJ sub-frames in all the newspapers, barring those of Indian origin. Nevertheless, due to the restrictions imposed on reporting from the war zone, such stories are very few in number. As illustrated in Table 7.5, the information obtained from the victims contributed more in creating an empathetic critical frame than the other frames.

Also, Table 7.5 reveals a fact that quoting victims' information alone in a news story does not necessarily lead to its categorisation as HRJ. There are certain news stories from all the newspapers which were identified as HWJ, despite quoting the victims. For example, though many such stories involving information acquired from the victims were categorised as HRJ in the US newspapers, this was not the case in the Indian newspapers, where despite referencing the victims, the stories were largely HWJ. This is because, on one hand, it depends on the way the information is filtered and framed, and on the other, it depends on how dominantly the information obtained from the victims is used to construct the frame as opposed to the other frames constructed through the information from sources such as the government, military and civil society organisations. For example, the excerpt below from *The Washington Post* better illustrates this aspect of news construction concerning the news sources and frames.

As Table 7.6, which is displayed above elucidates, news stories can use either one or multiple sources to acquire information. In some of the stories analysed, no news sources were quoted at all. In many instances, news stories were constructed using multiple news sources. Such news stories tend to create more (sub) frames, though stories without any sources or with only one source may also create more than one (sub) frame. As already highlighted, Table 7.6 reveals the fact that a story does not necessarily have to be either HRJ or HWJ due to a particular news source.

In the discussion related to Table 7.3, we had observed that the news stories do not necessarily have to exclusively contain either HRJ or HWJ (sub) frames. News reports can contain sub-frames of both HRJ and HWJ, as in the case of the story published on 10th February, 2009. The empirical results presented so far validates Shaw's (2012) argument that

Table 7.6 Excerpt from *The Washington Post*

Date	*Author*	*Source*	*Key frame*	*Sub frame*
14/09/2008	Ravi Nesman (AP)	1,2,5	2	7
20/09/2008	No Author Mentioned		1	5
0710/2008	No Author Mentioned	1	1	5
12/10/2008	Ravi Nesman (AP)	1,5,6	2	6,7,10
29/10/2008	No Author Mentioned	0	1	5
16/11/2008	Bryson Hull	1	1	5
23/01/2009	No Author Mentioned	5	1	1,2,5
29/01/2009	Emily Wax	1,4,5,6	2	6,8
05/02/2009	Emily Wax	1,2,4,6	1	1,2
07/02/2009	Emily Wax	5	1	1,2,5
10//02/2009	Emily Wax	1,2,6	2	5,6,7
11/02/2009	Emily Wax	1,2	1	1
13/02/2009	Emily Wax	1,3,4,5	2	6,7,8,9,10
15/02/2009	Emily Wax	2,5,6	2	6,8
21/02/2009	Emily Wax	1,2,5,6	2	6
22/02/2009	Emily Wax	2,5,6	1	2,5
24/02/2009	No Author Mentioned	2	1	5
03/03/2009	Emily Wax	2,5,6	2	5,6
11/03/2009	No Author Mentioned	2	1	5
14/03/2209	Emily Wax	5	2	5,6
21/04/2009	Emily Wax	1,2	1	1,2,5
22/04/2009	No Author Mentioned	1,6	1	1,5
22/04/2009	James Traub	4	2	6,7,8,9,10
24/04/2009	No Author Mentioned	4	1	5
19/05/2009	Emily Wax	1,2,6	1	5
19/05/2009	No Author Mentioned	0	1	5

the sub-frames of either HRJ or HWJ function in a manner which mutually supports and reinforces each other's function. Our analysis shows that in the majority of such instances, this mutually reinforcing and interacting relationship causes the stories to consist exclusively either HRJ or HWJ sub-frames.

From the Framing Matrix, we can decipher that this mutually influencing and reinforcing relationship is primarily the result of correlation among the framing memos of the sub-frames of HRJ/HWJ. For example, as far as the framing memos of HRJ are concerned, there is a mutually reinforcing and interacting relationship seen among the properties of the framing memos of each of the sub-frames. For example, when one of the properties of memo "Core position" is considered, there is a mutually influencing correlation observed among the HRJ sub-frames: Empathy Critical (*Analysing the root causes/Provide better understanding of the problem; serves as an informative platform through questions and structural realities*), Diagnostic Reporting (*Upholding of human rights through the construction of human rights-based discourse*), Proactive (*look ahead and inform in advance/early warning, so that you can act*), Interventionist (*draw IC's/ responsibility holder's attention*) and Peace Journalism (*Promoting a culture of peace and providing a more balanced coverage that involves all the parties involved in a conflict*). A similar mutually supportive relationship is seen among other properties as well: metaphor, images, catchphrases, source of the problem and the solution to the problem and appeal to principle.

As clear from Table 7.6, constructing a story using multiple sources, as in the case of the story published on 10th February 2009 in *The Washington Post*, may enable it to express sub-frames of both HRJ and HWJ. However, as established in the discussion, the final categorisation of these stories as HRJ or HWJ is determined, on one hand, by how the journalists/newsroom of a particular newspaper streamline information flow through the use of the frames, and on the other, on the conditioning the journalists/newsroom by the news sources to frame the stories in a manner favouring their goals. As observed throughout this discussion, it has become very clear that the framing of the news stories is a two-dimensional process, where one dimension is decided by the editorial policy of the newspaper in accordance with the internal guidelines, and the other is decided by the news sources. On one hand, the news source(s) is independently conditioned by the actors involved in a crisis, and on the other, the frame is mediated between the editorial policy and the 'conditioned news sources'. Understandably, these 'two-dimensional processes' of framing are subjected to the influence of various ideological, political, geographical and cultural contexts in which the discourse is created. This determines the 'applicability effect' of media's reporting of a distant suffering and if its orientation is human rights-focused or human wrongs-focused. This is because, with different editorial stances, the US and the UK newspapers as well as the Indian newspapers constructed different news stories with different frames. The 'pro-war' editorial stance taken by the Indian newspapers goes parallel with the Indian government's supportive position of the war in Sri Lanka due to its national and geopolitical interests associated with the conflict. It also portrays the possible impact of the Indian government's stance towards the crisis in Sri Lanka, in terms of its national and geopolitical interests, on the news coverage of the Indian newspapers.

The 'Framing Matrix' highlights how its properties of memo decide on the 'applicability effect', that we had discussed in chapter three, which is created through the two-dimensional process in the news stories/articles. As evident in the Framing matrix, the 'catchphrases' and 'images' are highly likely to be influenced by the news sources. Whereas, the properties such as the 'core position', 'source of the problem', 'solution to the problem' and 'appeal to principle' are most likely to be influenced by the editorial position of the newspapers, given the various ideological, political, geographical and cultural contexts. Therefore, although the news sources are independently conditioned by the actors involved in a war, the construction of 'images' and 'catchphrases' are influenced by the editorial position in line with its favoured properties; solution to the problem and appeal to principle. This knowledge explains Price and Tewksbury's (1997) applicability model which elucidates the nexus between the attributes of a reported issue and an audience's stored ideas or knowledge.

For instance, as far as the Indian newspapers are concerned, their 'pro-war' editorial position which is influenced by geopolitical reasons is highly likely to be attracted by the properties of the HWJ Framing Matrix. For example, as far as the 'non- interventionist' frame is concerned, its 'source of the problem' is seen as 'unfair and uncompromising demands of terrorists', and the 'solution to the problem' is seen as 'an internal issue to be sorted out inside Sri Lanka'. And, although its catchphrases such as 'freeing terrorists' clutches', 'pressure them to surrender/lay down arms', 'uncompromising military secessionism', 'freeing the remaining civilians', 'Humanitarian/rescue operation', 'interfering in internal affairs', 'they will use the ceasefire', 'it is our duty to protect our people', 'we are more concerned about our own citizens than anyone else could be', are from the news sources, which is independently conditioned by the actors involved in a war, it is apparent that they are constructed in line with the editorial position of the Indian newspapers.

As shown in Table 7.5, it is under the influence of the two-dimensional 'effect' that, victims as news sources had enabled the US and the UK newspapers to construct more HRJ stories, while the Indian newspapers constructed more HWJ stories. As highlighted before, the construction of news using multiple sources tends to create more than one (sub) frame, within the influence of the aforementioned 'two-dimensional framing process', and thereby creates more than one discourse in the story. This process causes the story to hold various discourses which interact with each other, and a situation arises in which some combination of discourses become dominant, and the others become subordinated or suppressed. Every single frame in the Framing Matrix has different, but mutually influencing properties of either HRJ or HWJ, and thus one can understand the variation in the nature and the scope of these discourses which are constructed on the basis of the catchphrases.

This elucidation draws attention towards Fairclough's (1995, 2002) idea of 'discursive order', which was explained earlier. This discursive order, as Fairclough argues, is explained by the analysis of both choice relations and change relations. It concerns the manner in which media selects, interprets and reconstructs the information it receives from various sources, within the influence of institutional, social, political, economic and cultural contexts, as highlighted while discussing the 'Frame Matrix'. This further elucidates the existence of 'discursive order' in newspaper content, which is constructed using the information acquired from the news sources through the 'two-dimensional framing process'. As it can be observed in Table 7.6, despite the combination of the existence of the frames of both HRJ and HWJ in the news stories/articles, they were specifically identified as either HRJ or HWJ.

In other words, the discursive within a news story consists of various discourses that operate with different understandings of the source of the problem, solution to the problem and its grounding principle. These sometimes reinforce each other, influence each other or might even conflict with each other. As a result of these dynamics, certain discourses emerge as dominant discourses to form the discourses of news journalism as a part of the global discursive order. These same dynamics exist among various discourses including the news journalism discourses that form the global discursive order of a crisis.

These discursive dynamics used to form the dominant discourse of news journalism is a result of the media agenda to ultimately create the public agenda. It is this process that creates the 'applicability effect', which takes various forms depending on the level of the human rights-focused or human wrongs-focused news values. It is on the basis of these dynamics that the media's ability to influence the audiences on 'how to think about' an issue or an event is determined. This is a cognitive process, in which persuasive communication effect is mediated between news journalism discourse and the global discursive order, in which news journalism discourse is merely a constituent. In other words, as Kim et al. (2002) explains the attributes ascribed in the media content become more salient in the minds of the audiences to influence their opinion-making and perceptions. Framing refers to the application of an individual's precursory information to associate with the attributes present in the news content to judge an issue or event.

7.4 Summary

This chapter established how effectively 'access to the news sources' was controlled and managed by the Sri Lankan government. The chapter also explored the extent of its impact on the construction of the crisis' reality and the establishment of a *prima facie* case of human rights violations within the HRJ-R2P conceptual model. The discussion particularly depicted the impact of the inability/inactivity to access the war zone on the practice of HRJ. This situation, on one hand, did not enable the newspapers to play an active role in the discourse production of the distance suffering to construct human rights-focused 'applicability effect'. On the other hand, it also did not allow the victims to act as participants to play an active role in discourse production.

Conversely, as evident in the analysis, elite news sources such as the Sri Lankan government and its military, due to their access to the media, had better opportunity to attract these newspapers towards their discourses and communicative events. This positioned the Sri Lankan government at a better position to exert power over the society and influence the minds of the international community by creating an 'applicability effect' of 'their version of the reality' of the crisis.

This study has revealed the overall failure of the international newspapers in creating awareness about the crisis and drawing the attention of the international community towards the mass atrocity crimes to mobilise support for international humanitarian intervention and stop or prevent such crimes in Sri Lanka. The analysis also explained the 'dynamics of the power formation' of the media through the 'two-dimensional framing process', which in turn demonstrated how the (sub) frames of HRJ and HWJ determine the nature and scope of the 'discursive order' in the news stories, and contribute to the discourse of news journalism as part of the global discursive order. The 'two- dimensional framing processes' conditioned by the editorial policy and the news sources, did not enable the international press to practise HRJ satisfactorily in terms of exposing the human rights violations and establishing a *prima facie* case of these violations was the primary cause of its failure. This answered the research inquiries that were based on the extent to which the frames of HRJ and HWJ were expressed while reporting. This elucidation brings back Fairclough's idea of 'discursive order' of society to explain the dynamics and the process of the 'discursive order' that operates in the news content. It is this discursive order that exists in news content to form the 'discourse of news journalism' to represent the 'global discursive order' which serves as a nucleus of managing and controlling persuasive communication effect.

Most importantly, this study highlighted how the editorial policy of the newspapers influenced their practice of HRJ in the case of the humanitarian crisis of Sri Lanka, and how *The Hindu* newspaper made its journalists/newsroom play the game of war propaganda aligning with the Sri Lankan government, and thereby articulating HWJ. It also examined how, neither the 'pro-war' nor the strong 'anti-war' (neutral) position of the UK and the US newspapers enabled their journalists/newsroom to practice HRJ entirely. This answered the research inquiry based on the extent to which the framing was different across international press coverage.

Bibliography

Fairclough, N. (1995). *Media Discourse*. London: Edward Arnold.

Fairclough, N. (2002). Discourse as Social Practice. In M. Toolan (Ed.), *Critical Discourse Analysis Critical Concepts in Linguistics* (pp. 1–22). London: Routledge.

Kim, S. H., Carvalho, J. P., Davis, A. G., & Mullins, A. M. (2011). The View of the Border: News Framing of the Definition, Causes and Solutions to Illegal Immigration. *Mass Communication & Society, 14*(3), 292–314.

Kuypers, J. A. (2006). *Bush's War: Media Bias and Justifications for War in a Terrorist Age*. Lanham: Rowman and Littlefield.

Lowell, G. (2008). How to Write an Editorial. *Undergraduate Review, 4*, 189–192 [Online]. http://vc.bridgew.edu/undergrad_rev/vol4/iss1/35. Accessed 17 June 2020.

Manoharan, K. R. (2019). Counter-Media: TamilNet and the Creation of Meta-narratives from Below. *Continuum, 33*(3), 386–400 [Online]. https://doi.org/10.1080/10304312.2019.1591340. Accessed 24 June 2020.

Price, V., & Tewksbury, D. (1997). News Values and Public Opinion: A Theoretical Account of Media Priming and Framing. In G. Barnett & F. J.

Boster (Eds.), *Progress in Communication Sciences* (Vol. 17, pp. 173–212). Greenwich, CT: Ablex.

Pulford, C. (2009). *Byliners: 101 Ways to Be a Freelance Journalist*. Northants: Ituri Publications.

Shaw, I. S. (2012). *Human Rights Journalism: Advances in Reporting Distant Humanitarian Interventions*. Basingstoke: Palgrave Macmillan.

CHAPTER 8

Analytics of Mediation of the Distant Suffering of Sri Lanka in the International Press

8.1 Introduction

This chapter intends to examine the extent to which the international newspapers exposed the issues of human rights within the R2P framework to construct interventionism in Sri Lanka by evaluating the nature of realism and meaning-making of the news stories. The analysis is focused towards identifying the nature and the scope of the practice of Human Rights Journalism (HRJ) and the effect it would have caused, in terms of its agenda-setting role, to create urgency and immediacy regarding the distant suffering in Sri Lanka. As the research inquiry implies, Chouliaraki's 'hierarchical typology of news stories' becomes the heart of this discussion. It will enable us to understand the news stories' capacity, within the frames of HRJ and Human Wrongs Journalism (HWJ), to create a sense of obligation among the distance audiences to care for the victims and influence the policymakers/human rights organisations to campaign for R2P intervention. It will also aid us in understanding the nature and function of the 'accessibility' and 'applicability' effects identified in the previous chapters.

To answer the research inquiry, this chapter uses the 'Multimodal Discourse Analysis Matrix', integrated into the content analysis framework as explained in Chapter 5. Similar to the previous two chapters, a total of 1290 news stories, including news reports/articles/columns published in six international newspapers between 8 September 2008 and 20 May 2009, were critically analysed.

S. Selvarajah, *Human Rights Journalism and its Nexus to Responsibility to Protect*, https://doi.org/10.1007/978-3-030-49072-0_8

Data coding was done manually and independently by three evaluators, including the author. Generally, high consistency was observed among the evaluators. Evaluators read all of the newspaper content multiple times to identify the properties of the framing memo which represent each of the sub-frames of HRJ and HWJ. An iterative review process was used to address the differences, which was completed in eight weeks. The result of this process was the construction of the 'Multimodal Discourse Analysis Matrix' illustrated below, to identify the typology of news reports against their properties. A coding guide and set of variables were prepared to assist the recording of the data in the coding manual. Readers are strongly advised to read and digest the section concerning 'multimodal discourse analysis matrix' in Chapter 5, for interpreting and understanding the analysis of this chapter.

8.2 Multimodal Analysis

All the news stories published in the six newspapers, barring news reports concerning the events that had occurred in other countries, were subjected to the scrutiny of 'typology of news stories', and Table 8.1 shows the extent to which action on the suffering (agency) role was demonstrated.

Table 8.1 depicts the reality of the newspapers' impact on drawing the attention of the world towards the suffering in Sri Lanka. Majority of the news stories published in all the newspapers are identified as 'adventure type'. As elucidated in the previous chapter (Chouliaraki 2008), adventure news does not evoke pity through its exposure of suffering, and it claims objectivity at the expense of emotionality. For instance, an incident recorded in just a few lines in the inside sections of a paper can

Table 8.1 Typology of news stories vs. all published news

Typology of news stories	*The Independent*	*The Times*	*The New York times*	*The Washington Post*	*The Times of India*	*The Hindu*
Adventure	29	29	32	57	136	315
Semi-emergency	15	10	14	3	14	22
Emergency	7	15	8	3	2	1

be termed as an adventure type of news. Sometimes, distant incidents are reported using captioned photos: no context or explanation, just an aestheticisation of the event due to its impactful visual value. The sum of semi-emergency and emergency types of news stories did not exceed the number of Adventure stories published in any of the newspapers, as can be observed in Table 8.1. Explicitly, the calculated percentage of the *emergency* news type reveals its minimal representation in the newspapers. The paucity of the 'emergency' type of news stories in the humanitarian crisis coverage demonstrates the fact that the international newspapers largely failed in creating a sense of obligation among the distant audiences to care for the victims and influence policymakers to intervene and end the sufferings.

Potentially, the US and the UK newspapers, which portrayed a considerable number of HRJ frames (see Chapter 6) should have constructed more number of 'emergency' typology of news stories in comparison to the 'adventure' type of news stories; instead, they predominantly contain 'adventure' typology of news stories. Semi-emergency and emergency typology of news stories are suppressed in all the newspapers. Nevertheless, as Table 8.2 demonstrates, there is a mutually reinforcing relationship between HRJ and the emergency typology of news stories.

As Table 8.2 depicts, a vast majority of the 'semi-emergency' and the 'emergency' types of news stories originated from the HRJ frames. This validates the theoretical argument demonstrated in Chapter 3 on the nexus between Chouliaraki's 'spectatorship of distance suffering' and Shaw's 'Human Rights Journalism'. Most of the 'adventure typology' of news stories, which do not evoke pity while exposing distance sufferings, originated from HWJ. Nevertheless, some of the 'emergency' types of

Table 8.2 Typology of news stories vs. key frames

Typology of news stories	*The Independent*		*The Times*		*The New York Times*		*The Washington Post*		*The Times of India*		*The Hindu*	
	HWJ	*HRJ*	*HWJ*	*HRJ*	*HWJ*	*HRJ*	*HWJ*	*HRJ*	*HWJ*	*HRJ*	*HWJ*	*HRJ*
Adventure	18	10	25	4	28	4	51	6	124	3	277	5
Semi-emergency	3	12	2	8	0	14	0	3	2	12	15	7
Emergency	1	6	0	15	0	8	0	3	0	2	0	1

stories did originate from HWJ, because, as observed already, news stories do not exclusively consist of either HRJ/HWJ (sub) frames, and the characteristics of powerful HRJ (sub) frame(s) have the ability to determine the typology of the news story. Meanwhile, as evidenced, in rare instances, news stories contain both types of frames and the dominant (key) frame of the story is decided in terms of the dynamics of the discursive order in the news. As can be observed in Table 8.3, 'empathy critical frames', 'diagnostic reporting' and 'interventionist frames' largely contributed to the construction of the emergency typology of news stories. This clearly shows the mutually influencing functional relationship between the HRJ frames to evoke pity and sympathy among the distance spectators and make them feel obligated to care for the victims.

Although a relationship was observed between HRJ and the emergency typology of news stories, or HWJ and the adventure typology of news stories, it was proved that not all of the HRJ news stories are emergency typology of news stories, and not all of the emergency typology of news stories are HRJ stories. Likewise, not all of the HWJ stories are adventure typology of news stories, and not all of the adventure typology news stories are HWJ stories.

This is because, the definitions of HRJ and its sub-frames as well as the emergency typology of news, determine the aim of the analysis concerning the identification of the news stories in terms of the HRJ framing Matrix. For example, the purpose of the analysis is to identify the type of news story as either HRJ or HWJ, which is determined in terms of the dominant discourse (s) of the discursive order formed either by one or more than one HRJ or HWJ or sometimes HRJ/HWJ subframes in the news story, informed by the framing matrix as elaborated in Chapter 7. Similarly, when the purpose of the analysis is to identify the kind of typology of news stories, it is determined in terms of the dominant discourse/feature of the discursive order which is recognised by the type of realism, meaning-making, aesthetic quality, representation and orientation informed by the multimodal discourse analysis matrix. Therefore, although the purpose of these two matrixes are different in terms of the scope and the definitions of HRJ/HWJ and the typology of news stories, as the analysis revealed, there is a significant parallel relationship between HRJ/HWJ and the typology of news stories. This can be explained with an in-depth analysis of the Frame Analysis properties and the Multimodal Discourse Analysis properties. Nevertheless, such an analysis is beyond the scope of this chapter.

Table 8.3 Typology of news stories vs. sub-frames

Sub-frames	*The Independent*			*The Times*			*The New York Times*		
	Adventure	*S-emergency*	*Emergency*	*Adventure*	*S-emergency*	*Emergency*	*Adventure*	*S-emergency*	*Emergency*
Empathy distance frame	7	2	1	4	0	0	11	0	0
Evocative reporting	1	2	1	1	0	0	5	0	0
Reactive	0	0	0	1	0	0	6	0	0
Non-interventionist	1	2	1	0	0	0	2	0	0
War journalism	17	2	1	24	3	1	24	0	0

(continued)

Table 8.3 (continued)

Sub-frames	*The Independent*			*The Times*			*The New York Times*		
	Adventure	*S-emergency*	*Emergency*	*Adventure*	*S-emergency*	*Emergency*	*Adventure*	*S-emergency*	*Emergency*
Empathy critical frame	5	10	5	0	4	15	2	11	8
Diagnostic reporting	5	9	5	2	5	5	1	2	3
Proactive	0	4	3	2	2	6	1	12	7
Interventionist	1	4	4	0	2	7	2	12	7
Peace journalism	1	5	2	1	2	1	1	1	1

The Washington Post			*The Times of India*			*The Hindu*		
Adventure	*S-emergency*	*Emergency*	*Adventure*	*S-emergency*	*Emergency*	*Adventure*	*S-emergency*	*Emergency*
18	0	0	44	3	0	117	7	0
6	0	0	23	1	0	39	4	0
3	0	0	6	0	0	26	2	0
0	0	0	6	2	0	31	1	0
42	1	0	99	1	0	213	13	0
5	3	3	2	10	2	0	7	1
1	2	2	0	3	1	0	0	0
1	1	3	0	1	1	0	0	0
0	0	3	0	0	2	4	2	0
0	1	2	1	2	1	5	0	0

As already established in the previous chapter, the practice of HRJ/HWJ is heavily influenced by the type of news sources as well as the editorial policy of the newspapers. Against this backdrop, it was explained how the type of news stories, which largely depend on the news sources, construct the (sub) frames.

Furthermore, a similar trend that was observed in the discussion concerning the nexus between the key/sub-frames and the type of news stories is displayed in Table 8.4. While the news reports contain a huge number of adventure news stories in all the newspapers; news features, columns and editorial writings relatively comprise of more number of the emergency typology of stories. This trend, as observed above in the case of the type of news stories against the (key) frames, shows how the functional relationship is between the writing mechanism of the type of news stories and the news sources. As observed already, the general predisposition of the news reports towards the elite sources may have influenced them to consist of more adventure typology of news stories, while the opinionated writings like editorial, news feature, etc. tend to consist more of the emergency type of news stories as they were written after acquiring information from multiple news sources at large. Moreover, as in the case of the analysis between the key/sub-frames and the type of news, the editorial policy was likely to have influenced the outcome of the typology of the news stories as well. The Indian newspapers contain a huge number of the adventure type of news stories, portraying the influence of the editorial policy.

The breakdown of the news sources against the typology of news sources, as shown in Table 8.5, demonstrates the connection between the news sources and the typology of news stories.

As Table 8.5 demonstrates, elite sources such as the Sri Lankan government and its military contributed more towards the construction of the 'adventure typology' of news stories, which also explains the tendency of the news reports to consist more of the adventure typology of news stories as opposed to the emergency type of news stories. Remarkably, civil society organisations, NGOs and Human Rights Organisations, as well as the UN/Foreign Officials had largely contributed in the construction of more emergency type of stories. Victims also contributed to the discourse of the emergency typology of news stories. Meanwhile, the statements issued by the civil society organisations, humanitarian and human rights organisations contained desperate calls for a ceasefire between the Sri Lankan government and the LTTE, as well as humanitarian aid for people

Table 8.4 Typology of news stories vs. type of news stories

Type of news stories	*The Independent*			*The Times*			*The New York Times*		
	Adventure	*S-emergency*	*Emergency*	*Adventure*	*S-emergency*	*Emergency*	*Adventure*	*S-emergency*	*Emergency*
News report	13	4	4	18	8	11	17	11	5
Editorial	1	2	0	2	0	1	1	1	0
Column	5	3	1	2	1	1	1	0	0
News feature	9	4	2	0	1	0	4	2	3
Cartoon/illustration	0	0	0	0	0	0	0	0	0
Letter	1	1	0	0	0	1	0	0	0
Weekly news summary	0	0	0	0	0	0	0	0	0
News in brief	0	1	0	7	0	1	9	0	0

The Washington Post			*The Times of India*			*The Hindu*		
Adventure	*S-emergency*	*Emergency*	*Adventure*	*S-emergency*	*Emergency*	*Adventure*	*S-emergency*	*Emergency*
9	0	1	126	10	1	297	21	1
1	0	0	0	0	0	1	0	0
1	0	1	5	2	0	10	0	0
9	3	1	5	2	1	4	0	0
0	0	0	0	0	0	3	1	0
0	0	0	0	0	0	0	0	0
0	0	0	0	0	0	0	0	0
37	0	0	0	0	0	0	0	0

Table 8.5 Typology of news stories vs. news sources

News sources	*The Independent*			*The Times*			*The New York Times*		
	Adventure	*S-emergency*	*Emergency*	*Adventure*	*S-emergency*	*Emergency*	*Adventure*	*S-emergency*	*Emergency*
None	6	4	1	7	3	1	2	0	0
Military officials	12	5	4	16	3	7	19	6	1
Government officials	12	9	4	14	5	8	14	9	2
LTTE officials	6	4	1	6	2	6	11	2	2
UN/Foreign officials	5	10	6	9	5	13	6	7	6
Victims	8	2	1	0	2	7	3	7	4
Civil society/NGOs/HR groups	7	9	6	7	3	10	9	13	7

The Washington Post			*The Times of India*			*The Hindu*		
Adventure	*S-emergency*	*Emergency*	*Adventure*	*S-emergency*	*Emergency*	*Adventure*	*S-emergency*	*Emergency*
7	0	0	23	0	0	29	1	0
28	3	2	64	4	0	157	8	0
22	1	0	43	1	0	178	15	1
4	0	2	18	3	0	67	9	0
4	1	3	25	2	0	54	8	1
13	2	2	7	6	0	9	4	0
12	3	0	18	7	2	31	12	0

trapped in the war zone and were subjected to a shortage of food, water, shelter and medicines. As discussed, these news events attracted the attention of the newspapers.

Drawing insights from the analysis of the typology of news stories and the HRJ frames, the discussion until now has demonstrated the impact of the inadequate construction of the reality of the Sri Lankan humanitarian crisis by the international newspapers on the failure to draw the world's attention towards the crisis and consequently did not obligate the people and the policymakers to care for and support the victims. The discussion also identified several reasons which resulted in the flawed coverage of the crisis. Nevertheless, this study is yet to understand in more depth and detail about how the communicative properties/characteristics of the typology of news stories may have contributed in determining the type of discourse, to depict the reality of the distant suffering and the level of action on the suffering (agency) to evoke R2P. To examine this research inquiry, this study engages in multimodal discourse analysis.

Table 8.6 shows the breakdown of the characteristics of the mode of presentation *Vis a Vis* the typology of the news stories. As explained in the previous chapter, the mode of presentation is an important genre in the articulation of the multimodal analysis. It is related to the location from which the news reporting is done. As already revealed in this chapter, the majority of the news stories published in all the newspapers were 'adventure' news stories. Hence, the communicative properties such as 'simple narratives', 'questions of why do not appear' are seen in large numbers in the Table 8.6.

Interestingly, a closer look at the statistics in Table 8.6 reveals the fact that the adventure typology of news stories constructed at least one kind of realism, although in a very small number.

The statistics also reveal the demonstration of 'complicated narratives' and 'complicated (multimodal) narratives' (see Chapter 5 for more information about this) in a small number of adventure news stories. This is inconsistent with Lilli Chouliaraki's typology of news stories which states that the adventure typology of news stories cannot create realism and do not consist of 'complicated multimodal narratives'. This is because, although the 'multimodal discourse analysis' matrix was prepared in line with Lilli Chouliaraki's theoretical framework and guidelines, the application of the 'multimodal discourse analysis' in investigating the news stories, exceptionally, but necessarily identified 'complicated (multimodal) narratives' in some adventure news stories.

Table 8.6 Typology of news story vs. mode of presentation

Communicative properties	*Independent*			*Times*			*New York Times*		
	Adventure	*S-emergency*	*Emergency*	*Adventure*	*S-emergency*	*Emergency*	*Adventure*	*S-emergency*	*Emergency*
Simple narratives—simple reporting of facts	17	0	0	15	0	0	18	0	0
Questions of why do not appear	17	0	0	15	0	0	18	0	0
Complicated narratives	4	7	1	8	5	3	5	6	0
Complicated multimodal narratives	6	11	6	7	5	12	8	8	8
Meditation of suffering gives credibility and distinct claim to reality	1	14	7	1	8	15	1	14	8
Perceptual realism—facticity	1	9	6	1	8	13	1	11	8
Categorical realism—emotion	0	8	2	0	1	9	0	2	6

(continued)

Table 8.6 (continued)

Communicative properties	*Independent*			*Times*			*New York Times*		
	Adventure	*S-emergency*	*Emergency*	*Adventure*	*S-emergency*	*Emergency*	*Adventure*	*S-emergency*	*Emergency*
Ideological realism—Justice	0	0	1	0	2	4	0	0	1

Washington Post			*Times of India*			*Hindu*		
Adventure	*S-emergency*	*Emergency*	*Adventure*	*S-emergency*	*Emergency*	*Adventure*	*S-emergency*	*Emergency*
41	0	0	106	0	0	270	0	0
41	0	0	106	0	0	270	0	0
4	0	0	17	3	0	24	14	1
12	3	3	12	11	2	15	6	0
0	3	3	0	13	2	5	21	1
0	3	3	0	13	2	5	12	1
0	0	1	0	2	1	0	9	0
0	0	1	0	0	0	0	1	0

The composition of the complicated (multimodal) narratives tends to create a certain type of realism in the news stories, which is why these adventure typology of news stories construct realism. Nevertheless, it was found in the analysis of these news stories that the composition of identified 'complicated (multimodal) narratives', and the realism constructed out of 'complicated (multimodal) narratives', do not necessarily create agency in the context of the working of agora and theatre, as discussed in Chapter 5. Despite having complicated (multimodal) narratives', these news stories lack the agency function, and therefore they were classified as adventure news stories.

As explained in Chapter 5, there is no difference between the semi-emergency and the emergency news stories in terms of their communicative properties and the category of 'semi-emergency' news was necessarily included in this study because the communicative properties of the emergency news stories are compromised due to their layout in the newspapers.

More importantly, it can be observed in Table 8.6 that, among all the types of realism, perceptual realism is the most dominant type in all the newspapers. In *The Independent*, it is 16 in number, which is 30% of the total news stories (except the news stories concerning the incidents which took place in foreign countries) considered for the scrutiny. In the other newspapers, the numbers are as follows: *The Times* 22 (31%), *The New York Times* 20 (34%), *The Washington Post* 6 (10%), *The Times of India* 15 (9%) and *The Hindu* 18 (4%). In terms of categorical realism, *The Independent* constructed categorical realism in 10 of its stories (19%), *The Times* 10 (14%), *The New York Times* 8 (14%), *The Washington Post* 1 (2%), *The Times of India* 3 (2%) and *The Hindu* 9 (3%).

This shows that, although not in large numbers, barring the Indian newspapers and *The Washington Post*, all the other newspapers, to a certain extent, constructed both perceptual realism and categorical realism. Ideological realism is almost completely muted in all the news stories. The potential effect that may have been created as a result of the kind of realism within the news reports along with its reasons, can be further understood through an explanation of the nature of these three types of realism. Before embarking on such a discussion, it is necessary to demonstrate the breakdown of the *correspondence between text and image* vis a vis *typology of news stories*, as there is a close relationship between the type of realism and the distinct types of meaning derived from the correspondence between text and image: indexical, iconic and symbolic. As

Chouliaraki explains, the type of realism constructed in the news stories heavily relies on these three types of meaning-making (2006, p. 79).

As discussed in Chapter 5, perceptual meaning results from an uninvolved meaning-making of text–image articulation (objective perspective) in the news reports, which is built on an indexical relationship. This perceptual realism can be transformed into categorical realism with the composition of cause-and-effect connection with dramatic urgency and sensationalism in the news stories, which emotionally connects the readers to the suffering. Categorical realism heavily depends on iconic meaning. Ideological realism functions in parallel with the categorical realism, with a characteristic of claiming justice in the context of an ideological dilemma of distance suffering, and heavily relies on symbolic meaning. While facts are important in the construction of perceptual realism, articulation of storytelling and image demonstration, to cause the readers to sympathise with the suffering, plays an important role in the construction of categorical and ideological realism (Chouliaraki 2006, pp. 127–139; 2007, pp. 218–219). This portrays the scope of categorical realism and ideological realism to propose a specific relationship of action between the readers and victims. Against this backdrop, at large, the Indian newspapers and *The Washington Post* constructed a very low amount of categorical and ideological realism in their stories. Among the small number of the emergency typology of news stories, the Indian newspapers, as revealed in Tables 8.6 and 8.7, constructed perceptual realism and indexical meaning to a large extent. Meanwhile, the UK and the US newspapers failed to construct a fair number of stories with high categorical and ideological realism as well as iconic and symbolic meanings.

While this described pattern of realism construction in the news stories published in the newspapers reveals their impotent nature in creating urgency and immediacy regarding the Sri Lankan humanitarian crisis and encouraging international intervention, it also sheds light on the factors that would have caused this dysfunctional situation. It was already revealed in the previous two chapters how the lack of access to the war zone, reliance on elite sources, as well as the editorial position of the newspapers caused serious flaws in the reporting of the humanitarian crisis in the newspapers.

The breakdown of the typology of news stories *vis-à-vis* the news sources in Table 8.5 reveals the defects caused by the news sources in the construction of the reality of the humanitarian crisis. The lack of access to the war zone also seems to have seriously undermined the construction

Table 8.7 Typology of news story vs. the correspondence between text and image

Communicative properties	*Independent*			*Times*			*New York Times*		
	Adventure	*S-emergency*	*Emergency*	*Adventure*	*S-emergency*	*Emergency*	*Adventure*	*S-emergency*	*Emergency*
Descriptions rather than narrations	5	0	5	9	0	0	12	0	0
Visual: minimal, abstracted representations	11	0	11	9	0	0	12	0	0
Indexical meaning (Perceptual realism—Facticity)	1	7	1	2	5	13	0	7	8
Iconic meaning (Categorical realism—Emotion)	0	5	0	0	3	9	0	2	6
Symbolic meaning (Ideological realism—Justice)	0	1	0	0	1	1	0	1	3

Washington Post			*Times of India*			*Hindu*		
Adventure	*S-emergency*	*Emergency*	*Adventure*	*S-emergency*	*Emergency*	*Adventure*	*S-emergency*	*Emergency*
12	0	0	60	0	0	82	0	0

(continued)

Table 8.7 (continued)

Washington Post			*Times of India*			*Hindu*		
Adventure	*S-emergency*	*Emergency*	*Adventure*	*S-emergency*	*Emergency*	*Adventure*	*S-emergency*	*Emergency*
12	0	0	60	0	0	82	0	0
0	3	3	0	12	2	10	5	0
0	2	1	0	2	0	0	2	0
0	0	1	0	0	0	0	0	0

of the reality of the crisis, through the construction of these two types of realism. Moreover, the reason for the existence of a high amount of perceptual realism and indexical meaning among all the types of realism constructed in the UK and the US newspapers is the influence of the elite news sources. Due to lack of access to the information, the journalists would have, to a large extent, depended on elite news sources to report about the war, and this situation potentially led to the construction of news stories of facticity in the absence of raw images and information from the war zone.

Moreover, the sharp difference between the Indian newspapers and the US and the UK newspapers, barring *The Washington Post*, reveals the influence of the editorial position on the construction of the scope and the nature of the realism in the news reporting. Although it is not revealed in the tables, while scrutinising the news stories to evaluate the typology of news stories, they had to be necessarily classified and some of the news stories which had the potential of being emergency typology of news stories were categorised as adventure news stories, as their emergency typology qualities were compromised by the way they were presented, designed and published in the newspapers. Particularly, in the Indian newspapers, news stories regarding the human suffering in the war zone, that were constructed using the information acquired from the human rights organisations were published in small size in the inside pages of the newspaper. In some cases, the complete lack of access to the war zones made journalists file stories with strong information obtained from HR organisations and victims through other means. Although these kinds of stories were categorised as HRJ because of their HRJ frames, they were also classified as adventure typology of news stories as they failed to invite the attention of the readers towards the crisis. Also, as discussed in Chapter 3, lack of prominence given to a story by placing it in an inside page in a small corner may influence the minds of the readers negatively and distract their due attention. In turn, had the same story been published on the front page as a lead story (The Flash) or a super lead story, it would have been classified as an emergency typology news story. This is the reason why the number of HRJ stories exceeds the number of emergency typology of news stories in all the newspapers. Not only the Indian newspapers, but the United States and the UK also suppressed the emergency typology of news stories in this manner.

As far as the Indian newspapers are concerned, their 'pro-war' editorial position would have been a factor in deciding the presentation of the news stories, whereas the US and the UK newspapers, despite their 'anti-war' editorial position, may have been influenced by their lack of interest towards the distant suffering in Sri Lanka. As already evidenced in the previous chapters, despite its 'anti-war' editorial position, *The Washington Post* published most of its news stories as a 'news brief' in a few lines, potentially due to the lack of interest towards the suffering, which caused most of its news stories to be categorised as HWJ and adventure typology.

The type of realism constructed in the news stories can have a profound impact on creating an aesthetic quality in them. The breakdown between the typology of news stories and the aesthetic quality shown in Table 8.8 explains the influence of the type of realism on the construction of aesthetic quality. The overwhelming construction of the adventure typology of the news stories in all the newspapers makes them distant from the aesthetic quality. This trend is very evident in the Indian newspapers and *The Washington Post*. As observed earlier, compared to the other newspapers, these newspapers published more number of adventure news stories, which are simple narratives that consist of simple reporting of facts and do not contain 'questions of why'.

As it can be observed from Table 8.8, the news stories which have an aesthetic quality tend to create more 'pamphleteering' than other types of aesthetic aspects: philanthropy and sublimation. Both sublimation and philanthropy quality of news stories are identified in very small numbers in all the newspapers. Exceptionally, philanthropy quality was observed 7 times in the news stories published in *The Hindu*. As explained in Chapter 5, the aesthetic quality 'pamphleteering' triggers political condemnation among the spectators, who express anger against the perpetrators of the distant suffering. Meanwhile, philanthropy motivates the spectators to act on the issue by providing charity and improving the victims' condition. Sublimation encourages considering the underlying reasons for suffering. These moral implications and the spectator's responsibility enables the understanding of the underlying reasons causing the suffering to alleviate it (Chouliaraki 2006; Aaltola 2012).

As per Chouliaraki's multimodal discourse analysis, there is an aesthetic distance in the adventure type of news stories, and stories such as pamphleteering, philanthropy and sublimation cannot exist. Exceptionally, as shown in Table 8.8, four philanthropy type of aesthetic qualities are identified in the adventure typology of news stories published in *The Hindu*. This is because, as seen in the Framing Matrix, two types of frames of HWJ such as 'Empathy Distance Frame' and 'Evocative Reporting'

Table 8.8 Typology of news story vs. the aesthetic quality of the news text

Communicative properties	*Independent*			*Times*			*New York Times*		
	Adventure	*S-emergency*	*Emergency*	*Adventure*	*S-emergency*	*Emergency*	*Adventure*	*S-emergency*	*Emergency*
Aesthetic distance (Overall semiotic effect—readers' feeling of the suffering)	27	0	0	28	1	0	30	0	0
Pamphleteering—Political condemnation	1	15	5	1	5	13	1	13	8
Philanthropy (Makes the readers to do something in terms of providing charity)	0	0	0	0	2	0	0	0	0
Sublimation (Enables to understand the underlying reasons for the suffering)	0	4	6	0	2	9	0	4	4

Washington Post			*Times of India*			*Hindu*		
Adventure	*S-emergency*	*Emergency*	*Adventure*	*S-emergency*	*Emergency*	*Adventure*	*S-emergency*	*Emergency*
57	0	0	135	0	0	306	1	0
0	3	3	0	13	1	0	19	0
0	0	0	0	0	0	4	2	1
0	1	2	0	6	2	0	0	0

originate from the appeal to the principle of 'Humanitarian Assistance and Relief'. In this, the focus is more on the urgent humanitarian assistance than HR violations and its causes. It is in this context that, the news production of *The Hindu* newspaper, in the context of its pro-war editorial position, created four of its news stories with a philanthropic aesthetic effect, all of which are finally categorised as adventure typology of news stories and HWJ. Looking at these four examples, the news published on 6 May 2009, titled 'U.N. seeks $50 million humanitarian aid', depicts war as a civilian rescue operation: 'The United Nations and Sri Lanka on Tuesday launched an urgent appeal for $50 million to meet the immediate humanitarian needs of civilians fleeing fighting in the North, even as the military said the LTTE was now confined to four sq. km. within the No-Fire Zone (NFZ)'. The author, quoting Government sources, continues to describe the suffering of the people in the hands of the LTTE. A similar impact is created on the readers in the other three adventure typology of the news stories as well: India to send 50,000 more family packs to Sri Lanka (3/5/2009),—India seeks greater access to aid agencies (1/5/2009), Medical team for Sri Lanka (9/5/2009).

The insights generated in the beginning of this chapter, regarding the influence of news sources on framing the news stories and deciding the typology of the news stories, explain the reason why all the newspapers constructed more stories of 'pamphleteering'. The aesthetic quality of pamphleteering makes the readers empathise with the victims and denounce the evildoers. This political denunciation, often made by human rights organisations, humanitarian organisations and civil society provides resources for judgement that enable the readers to decide their stance regarding the political dilemma of condemning the evildoers. As evident in this chapter and the previous chapter, given the inaccessibility of the war zone, it was the information received from the human rights organisations and humanitarian organisations that often served as the source of HRJ frames. Whenever the violence was overblown, human rights organisations such as Amnesty International, International Crisis Group and Human Rights Watch issued statements condemning both sides with strong words and provided information on the attacks on the hospitals, no-fire zones and civilian causality. This is the reason why 'pamphleteering' is much more visible than the other two types of aesthetic quality news stories.

Meanwhile, the low presence of sublimation and philanthropy shows the effect of the inaccessibility of the war zone on the news coverage.

Understandably, the failure to construct the reality of the humanitarian crisis, in terms of categorical realism (spectator's sense of omnipresence of crises) and ideological realism (ideological conviction) caused by the lack of access to the war zone, seemingly played a significant role in suppressing sublimation in the news stories. Because, the characteristics of categorical realism and ideological realism, as observed already, are integral aspects for readers to make an informed decision as it allows them to study the distance suffering in-depth and understand the conflict.

Categorical realism is emotionally powerful due to the spectator's sense of omnipresence of threats of natural disasters, starvation and endemic. Ideological realism persuades the readers to side with justice in the context of an ideological dilemma and is also emotionally powerful, like categorical realism (Chouliaraki 2006, pp. 127–139; 2013, pp. 218–219).

As in the case of the construction of realism and meaning-making, the lack of access to the war zone largely affected the construction of sublimation in the newspapers. The analysis already revealed the negative impact of the absence of raw images and information from the war zone on creating HRJ frames and the emergency typology of news stories. Particularly, it was evident in the analysis of how it affected the construction of the empathetic critical frame and the diagnostic reporting of HRJ. As we can see, the extremely meagre representation of the sublimation type of aesthetic quality, primarily caused by the lack of access to the war zone, negatively impacted the newspapers' coverage to construct more 'empathy critical' and 'diagnostic reporting' frames, and vice versa. In Chapter 4, we discussed the power of the empathetic critical frame and the diagnostic frames, in empowering the five key mutually reinforcing elements that define the HRJ–R2P nexus, in sustaining media's role of R2R to invoking the three underlying responsibilities of R2P through its pillar approach. This shows the negative impact that it would have on the 'applicability effect' to create a 'persuasive communication effect' as a part of the public agenda-setting and the media agenda-setting to influence both the public and the policymakers and human rights organisations.

Until now, the multimodal analysis focused on scrutinising the different characteristics in the newspapers in the function of meaning-making of the suffering. The analysis found how the news sources performed a key function in determining the level of the typology of the news stories and the nature of realism. This helps further understand the framing effect/applicability effect which we had examined in the previous chapter. According to the findings of the multimodal analysis, we can say that the functional orientation of the 'applicability effect' is profoundly shaped by the type of realism and the nature of the aesthetic value, which is conditioned by the two-dimensional framing process as explained in Chapter 7. The discussion we have had with regard to realism and the aesthetic aspects shows their potential impotence in influencing the functional capacity of the five key elements that define the HRJ–R2P nexus and thus impacted the public agenda to affect the policy agenda.

Now, the analysis attempts to focus on the difference that lies outside the meaning-making of the newspapers, in order to illustrate the representation of space-time and agency in the news stories to investigate the extent to which they had constructed discourse to incite action on the suffering.

Table 8.9 displays a significantly large number of 'no connectivity between the suffering and spectators' in the news stories as opposed to the concrete, specific, multiple and mobile chronotope of suffering. This is due to the construction of a large amount of the adventure typology of news stories, the reasons for which have already been described. As illustrated in Chapter 5, other key features of constructing the adventure typology of news stories are 'singular space-time' and 'hierarchy of place - victims of worthy places'. Interestingly, these two features are almost non-existent in the identified news stories of the adventure typology. Though the 'singular space-time' feature is an important consideration in defining the typology of news stories as explained by Chouliaraki, it was non-existent in these particular news stories because, as far as the case study of this book is concerned, the researcher found it irrelevant to consider it in the multimodal analysis. It's because, as Chouliaraki explains, singular space-time denotes an isolated place- a one-off event that restricts the possibility of historicity (Chouliaraki 2006, p. 100). As per Chouliaraki, a singular space-time is when a story has been cut off from the chain of events in which it participates and is presented as a random singularity. They restrict the possibility of representing the events in terms of their historicity and their future implications (ibid.).

Since this study, through its selection, investigates the newspapers' coverage of the described particular incident (humanitarian crisis during the final phase of the Sri Lankan civil war) over a certain period of time, all its news stories are necessarily connected in a chain of events and subject to historicity. Since this is an analysis of a series of news stories published in the newspapers, as Van Dijk explains, it creates a mental model which is a subjective representation of the events or the situation

Table 8.9 Typology of news story vs. space-time (representation)

Communicative properties	*Independent*			*Times*			*New York Times*		
	Adventure	*S-emergency*	*Emergency*	*Adventure*	*S-emergency*	*Emergency*	*Adventure*	*S-emergency*	*Emergency*
Singular space-time (An isolated place, a one-off event restricts the possibility of historicity)	0	0	0	2	0	0	0	0	0
No connectivity between the suffering and spectators	26	2	1	28	0	0	30	0	0
Hierarchy of place—victims of worthy places	0	0	0	0	0	0	0	0	0

(continued)

Table 8.9 (continued)

Communicative properties	*Independent*			*Times*			*New York Times*		
	Adventure	*S-emergency*	*Emergency*	*Adventure*	*S-emergency*	*Emergency*	*Adventure*	*S-emergency*	*Emergency*
Concrete (suffering in the context of concrete physical space)	0	3	1	0	5	0	1	8	0
Specific (sufferings as unique by providing details of specific locations and person(s).	2	5	2	0	5	10	0	5	4
Multiple (shows sufferings as unique—details of specific locations and person(s)	0	4	1	0	0	5	0	1	3
Mobile (Proposes a relationship of action between the readers and sufferers)	0	1	2	0	0	0	0	0	1

Washington Post			*Times of India*			*Hindu*		
Adventure	*S-emergency*	*Emergency*	*Adventure*	*S-emergency*	*Emergency*	*Adventure*	*S-emergency*	*Emergency*
0	0	0	0	0	0	0	0	0
57	0	0	135	6	0	310	1	0
0	0	0	0	0	0	0	0	0
0	0	0	0	5	0	0	9	1
0	2	1	0	3	0	0	4	0
0	1	1	0	4	0	0	8	0
0	0	1	0	1	2	0	0	0

that the discourse is about. That is, as Van Dijk puts it, 'understanding text or talk not only involves constructing a mental representation of its (intentional) "meaning", but also ultimately, a mental representation of its (extensional) "referent" as the participants subjectively define it by constructing a mental model for it' (2006, p. 169).

Although Chouliaraki's 'Multimodal Discourse Analysis' did not incorporate Van Dijk's mental model in her analysis of space-time representation, it seems to be a better fit for the analysis of a particular event over a certain period of time, as the construction of mental model necessarily considers historicity. For example, as Chouliaraki illustrates, the usage of dots on a map creates a sense of 'devoid of temporality', but if the event is connected in a process of coverage, then it does create the effect of 'temporality'. This is the reason why, although there were a few exceptions, all the news stories published in the newspapers between 8 September 2008 and 21 May 2009 were assumed to not express singular space-time representation, and this is the reason why Table 8.9 does not contain any 'singular space-time representation'.

Similarly, as explained above, the nature of the case study analysis, which involves the distant suffering of a particular community due to a particular incident, does not create any room for communitarian logic, and therefore it was assumed that all the news stories published were free of 'hierarchy of place'. This is the reason why Table 8.9 does not depict any 'hierarchy of place'.

Meanwhile, as evident from Table 8.9, among the four types of chronotope of suffering, mobile—which connects the contexts of safety-zones and danger-zones to propose a specific relationship of action between the readers and victims—is eclipsed, in all the newspapers. Understandably, this is due to the absence of the raw images and information caused by the lack of access to the war zone, which affected the live experience of the distant suffering in a manner to block the action on the suffering from the readers' side. In addition, although portraying lower representation, the other types of chronotope of suffering such as concrete, specific and multiple are disproportionately constructed, without showing any particular trend in and among the newspapers. Meanwhile, as observed earlier, the representation of concrete, specific and the multiple types of chronotope seem to be proportional to the low degree of the construction of the adventure typology of news stories in the Indian newspapers and *The Washington Post* for the described reasons.

The construction of the types of chronotope of suffering such as concrete, specific and multiple, as a result of the manifestation of the emergency typology news, does indicate that although in a low number, the UK and the US newspapers show a difference in the degree of spatiotemporal complexity of the suffering. As shown in Table 8.9, among the emergency typology of news stories published in *The Independent*, there are 4 articles that express concreteness and show the context of suffering as a physical space. As emphasised already, though in a low number, this disproportionately constructed chronotope of suffering shows how the newspapers presented the emergency typology of news stories, with not just one single reality of suffering but multiple realities relevant to the suffering. Explicitly, the reason for this disproportionately constructed chronotope of suffering can be connected to the lack of access to the war zone and other described reasons in the previous two chapters that influenced the construction of the typology of news stories.

Next to the mobile type of chronotope, as revealed in the above discussion, the representation of concrete is suppressed in the news stories. This is because, the nature of the humanitarian crisis that was subjected to the analysis in this study, is not only a phase of a protracted conflict which lasted for more than thirty years, but the particular phase has several sub-phases. This complex nature of the humanitarian crisis, connected to multiple contexts and actors, may have possibly caused the journalists to construct the news stories with historicity and multiple physical contexts of suffering, thereby suppressing the scenarios for concrete and increasing the scenarios for multiple. However, there is also a certain number of the specific type of chronotope of suffering in the newspapers, resulted by focusing on some specific locations with the elaboration of specific properties and individualisation of the victim as a unique person such as the 'attacks in the no-fire zone', 'bombing on hospital' and 'mass exodus'.

Despite the representation of concrete, specific and multiple types of chronotope of suffering, as revealed in the analysis, the mobile type of chronotope, which has the ability to connect the contexts of safety-zones and danger-zones to propose a specific relationship of action between the readers and the victims, is highly suppressed in the newspapers. This sheds light on understanding the nature of the news stories in terms of their power to establish cosmopolitan consciousness of the suffering. This shows the (negative) impact that the construction of realism and meaning-making would have had on the 'applicability effect' to be devoid of temporality and would have caused the five key elements that define

Table 8.10 Typology of news story vs. agency (orientation)

Communicative properties	*Independent*			*Times*			*New York Times*		
	Adventure	*S-emergency*	*Emergency*	*Adventure*	*S-emergency*	*Emergency*	*Adventure*	*S-emergency*	*Emergency*
Void of agency (Neither empathy nor denunciation, annihilation of the sufferer)	28	0	0	29	0	0	30	0	0
Lack of agora and theatre	28	0	0	29	0	0	30	0	0
Hierarchy of human lives—worthy/unworthy victims (void of agents)	1	0	0	0	0	0	0	0	0
Agora (humanisation of the sufferers—active sufferers)	0	4	4	0	2	11	0	3	7
Theatre (communicates the reality of suffering—active persecutors and benefactors)	0	12	7	0	9	14	1	13	8

Washington Post			*Times of India*			*Hindu*		
Adventure	*S-emergency*	*Emergency*	*Adventure*	*S-emergency*	*Emergency*	*Adventure*	*S-emergency*	*Emergency*
57	0	0	135	0	0	310	1	0

Washington Post			*Times of India*			*Hindu*		
Adventure	*S-emergency*	*Emergency*	*Adventure*	*S-emergency*	*Emergency*	*Adventure*	*S-emergency*	*Emergency*
57	0	0	135	0	0	310	1	0
0	0	0	0	0	0	0	0	0
0	2	3	0	5	1	0	2	0
0	3	3	0	13	2	0	20	1

the nexus between HRJ and R2P to be dormant. Against this backdrop, the forthcoming discussion endeavours to understand the capacity of the news stories in terms of their action on the suffering in connection with the agency of the victims as well as the persecutors and the benefactors.

As Table 8.10 depicts, the majority of the news stories failed to create an agency (action on suffering) due to the lack of agora and theatre function. Void of agency and lack of agora and theatre are two sides of the same coins, and therefore Table 8.10 equally represents them in the news stories.

8.3 Critical Discourse Analysis

As already explained, this study is about the analysis of a specific humanitarian crisis over a certain period of time, and the hierarchy of human lives is almost obscured. Nevertheless, some of the news stories did portray the hierarchy of human lives in their news stories. This is because, given the complete lack of access to the war zone, civilian casualties resulted due to the LTTE (suicide) attacks in the government-controlled areas, received enormous attention of the news-hungry journalists, who were stationed in Sri Lanka to cover the humanitarian crisis. Due to the lack of access to the war zone, the victims in the war zone were ignored and treated as unworthy victims. Nevertheless, it must be underlined that this difference in the hierarchy of human lives is between the people who live outside the war zone and those who live inside the war zone in Sri Lanka, primarily caused by the lack of access to the war zone.

Also, as Table 8.10 shows, there is a considerable difference between the representation of agora and theatre in the news stories. As observed earlier, agora is about the humanisation of the sufferers to confer power to the sufferers in the news reports, so that they are able to provoke the readers to speak and act on their suffering. *The Independent* has 8 news stories, which have agora: *The Times* 17, *The New York Times* 9, *The Washington Post* 6, *The Times of India* 6 and *The Hindu* 2. Meanwhile, most of the news stories identified as the emergency typology of news stories consist of theatre, in which the suffering is mediated by the social relationships, and thus the agency is galvanised by the benefactor and persecutor (symbolic figures) who communicate the reality of distant suffering. In its total news stories, *The Independent* has 19 theatrical orientations: *The Times* 27, *The New York Times* 21, *The Washington Post* 8, *The Times of India 16* and *The Hindu* 21. Understandably, the lack of access to the war zone, negatively affected the construction of the agora orientation in the news stories, as the journalists were unable to humanise the sufferers by making them active through raw images and information. On the other hand, the journalists who were prevented from entering the war zone necessarily depended on the humanitarian, human rights organisations and civil society organisations such as the Amnesty International, Human Rights Watch and International Red Cross to report about the suffering in the war zone. This is the reason why most of the emergency typology of news stories are theatrical-oriented.

The agency of the readers to engage in public speeches about the suffering depends on the humanisation of victims, because agora enables the readers to speak out about the suffering that they are reading about as the victims are construed as similar to them, in which the victim gets the power to do something or say something about their condition. Whereas, as highlighted already, the agency in theatre depends on the orchestration of both the benefactor and prosecutor's action who connect the reality of the distant suffering to the readers' private feelings *vis-à-vis* the tragedy/crisis that they are reading about (Chouliaraki 2006, pp. 88–90).

As we have seen in the analysis, the newspapers, to a considerable extent composed the action of the benefactors such as Amnesty International, Human Rights Watch and International Red Cross, persecutors such as the Sri Lankan government, its military and the LTTE. Although the active role of the benefactors and the persecutors would have enabled the connection of the reality of the humanitarian crisis to the readers, the vacuum of the victims' communication with the readers undermines the establishment of a *prima facie* case of the humanitarian crisis, because it is the sufferer's direct communication that plays an important role in making the readers understand the suffering of the victims without any bias and in an objective manner. Although true impartiality is not possible, as the construction of news depends on the orchestration of the news sources, given the various socio, economic, political and cultural constraints, the impartiality declared in the agora agency is possible within the concept of moral obligation informed by the critical constructivist theory, which explains the process by which the journalists' consciousness was constructed. This is where the power of 'citizen journalism', as explained by Allan (2013), could have constructed 'a sense of shared humanity' with 'its capacity to bear witness to human suffering' (Allan et al. 2007, p. 387) and enabled the international press to produce more emergency typology news stories to lead to action on the suffering. Nevertheless, as revealed in the analysis, the discourse of the humanitarian crisis of Sri Lanka in the international press, was not configured by the practice of citizen journalism nor was there enough space for its practice during the crisis. As demonstrated in the previous chapter, not a single newspaper quoted or mentioned citizen journalism sources in their reporting. There was zero internet service in the war zone area during the war to disseminate and publicise the war crimes, except the satellite communication facility acquired by the LTTE for its military purpose. Nevertheless, a few months after the war ended, proofs regarding war crimes such as summary executions, the aerial bombing of civilians, artillery attacks on hospitals and refugee camps and raping of women, retrieved from peoples' mobile phone devices played a key role in the post war situation to initiate a UN level accountability and justice process in Sri Lanka (Balasundaram 2019; UNHRC Resolution 2015).

Hence, on the basis of the results shown in Table 8.10, it can be said that the action on the suffering is compromised by an inadequate construction of agora in the emergency type of news stories, despite the considerable amount of theatrical orientation. The analysis explicitly shows the (destructive) impact it would have had on the applicability effect to be devoid of an agency to create R2P options.

8.4 Summary

This chapter articulated multimodal discourse analysis to answer the research question based on the extent to which the international newspapers exposed the issues of human rights within the R2P framework to construct interventionism in Sri Lanka. The analysis highlighted the nature of realism and meaning-making of HRJ and HWJ stories of the newspapers, primarily influenced by the lack of access to the war zone. Although all the UK and the US newspapers, except *The Washington Post*, constructed perceptual realism (facticity) and indexical meaning to a significant extent, had failed to construct a fair number of categorical (emotion) and ideological realism (justice) as well as iconic and symbolic meanings in their news stories, revealing their impotent nature in creating urgency and immediacy of the humanitarian crisis.

In terms of the aesthetic quality, the emergency typology of news stories constructed by the newspapers largely contained 'pamphleteering' than the other types: philanthropy and sublimation. The low-level representation of the sublimation type of aesthetic quality caused by the lack of access to the war zone, negatively impacted the newspapers' coverage to construct more 'empathy critical' and 'diagnostic reporting' frames, and vice versa, and thus limiting the chances of the readers to make an informed decision to understand the distant suffering and its underlying causes in-depth. This resulted in the severe undermining of the ability of the (emergency) news typology of stories to create cosmopolitan emotions and aesthetic impact. Space-time and agency analysis of the multimodal discourse analysis showed how the lack of access to the war zone weakened the ability of the emergency typology of news stories to create action within the R2P framework by establishing readers' proximity to suffering.

Further, the news sources played a key role in determining the characteristics of the typology of news stories in terms of both realism and chronotope, as well as the agora and the theatre function, and subsequently (negatively) affected the 'applicability effect' away from human rights-focused. In other words, 'applicability effect' is a two-dimensional framing process, where one dimension is decided by the editorial policy of the newspaper in accordance with the internal guidelines, and the other is decided by the news sources. On one hand, the news source (s) is independently conditioned by the actors involved in a crisis, and on the other, the frame is mediated between the editorial policy and the 'conditioned news sources'. Understandably, these 'two-dimensional processes' of framing are subjected to the influence of various ideological, political, geographical and cultural contexts in which the discourse is created. Now the findings in this chapter regarding realism and chronotope, as well as agora and theatre, further shine a light on understanding how exactly they shape the orientation of the 'applicability effect' and its potential to restrain the R2R role of the media to create options for R2P intervention.

Moreover, the knowledge that we have accumulated explains the reason why the increased attention of the media to human rights issues or distant suffering results in compassion fatigue and feel-good activism. This is because, on one hand, the nature and the level of realism and aesthetic depiction, and on the other, the nature and the level of agora and theatre may create an 'applicability effect', which influences the audience in a certain direction. This creates a particular tendency such as compassion fatigue or feel-good activism. This sheds light on designing an embedded media strategy within the HRJ-R2P conceptual model drawing insights from the two-dimensional framing process, to create a dominant human rights discourse in the news journalism discourse.

Bibliography

Aaltola, E. (2012). *Animal Suffering: Philosophy and Culture*. Basingstoke: Palgrave Macmillan.

Allan, S. (2013). *Citizen Witnessing: Revisioning Journalism in Times of Crisis Key Concepts in Journalism*. Malden, MA: Polity Press.

Allan, S., Sonwalker, P., & Carter, C. (2007). Bearing Witness: Citizen Journalism and Human Rights Issues. *Globalisation, Societies and Education, 5*(3), 373–389.

Balasundaram, N. (2019). Exiled Journalists as Active Agents of Change: Understanding their Journalistic Practices. In *Reporting Human Rights, Conflicts and Peacebuilding: Critical and Global Perspectives* (pp. 265–280). Basingstoke: Palgrave Macmillan.

Chouliaraki, L. (2006). *The Spectatorship of Suffering*. London: Sage.

Chouliaraki, L. (2007). Spectacular Ethics. In L. Chouliaraki (Ed.), *The Soft Power of War* (pp. 129–144). Amsterdam: Benjamins.

Chouliaraki, L. (2008). The Mediation of Suffering and the Vision of a Cosmopolitan Public. *Television and New Media, 9*(5), 371–391.

Chouliaraki, L. (2013). *The Ironic Spectator: Solidarity in the Age of Post-Humanitarianism*. Cambridge: Polity Press.

Chouliaraki, L., & Fairclough, N. (2004). The Critical Analysis of Discourse. In W. Carroll (Ed.), *Critical Strategies for Social Research* (pp. 262–271). Toronto: Canadian Scholar's Press.

Downman, S., & Ubayasiri, K. (2017). *Journalism for Social Change in Asia: Reporting Human Rights*. Basingstoke: Palgrave Macmillan.

Shaw, I. S. (2012). *Human Rights Journalism: Advances in Reporting Distant Humanitarian Interventions*. Basingstoke: Palgrave Macmillan.

UNHRC Resolution. (2015, October 1). Promoting Reconciliation, Accountability, and Human Rights in Sri Lanka, U.N. Doc. A/HRC/RES/30, 6–7.

Van Dijk, T. (2006). Discourse, Context and Cognition. *Discourse Studies, 8*(1), 159–177.

CHAPTER 9

Journalists Speak Up on Their Reporting of the Crisis in Sri Lanka

9.1 Introduction

In Chapters 6, 7 and 8 we had discussed the 'accessibility' and 'applicability' effects of the international newspapers' coverage of the Sri Lankan humanitarian crisis in 2009, to evaluate the extent to which the international newspapers exposed the issues of human rights within the HRJ-R2P conceptual model to construct options for intervention using the integrated framework of Frame Analysis and Multimodal Discourse Analysis. Some of the insights that were generated during the course of the investigative process revolved around the access to the war zone, the editorial position of the newspapers, the news sources and the encountered difficulties therein. These insights required further testing with supplementary evidence from the journalists, who visited Sri Lanka during the crisis to gather information. Apart from the reasons that were identified in the preceding chapters, this study also wanted to explore if there were any other difficulties, challenges and problems that were faced by the journalists in their course of reporting the humanitarian crisis, which will answer the following research inquiry of this chapter: *What are the challenges that confronted the journalists in the course of their reporting?* In turn, this will be an analysis of the factors that influenced the media agenda-setting process from the 'Reality of Distant Suffering' to 'Media Reality'.

Apart from this research analysis, this chapter also aims to examine the 'persuasive communication effect' of public agenda created by media

S. Selvarajah, *Human Rights Journalism and its Nexus to Responsibility to Protect*, https://doi.org/10.1007/978-3-030-49072-0_9

agenda as illustrated in the 'HRJ-R2P conceptual model'. Accordingly, this chapter, in its second part of the analysis focuses on examining how the international press coverage of the Sri Lankan humanitarian crisis in 2009 failed/succeeded in influencing the human rights activists to campaign for R2P.

To provide the in-depth historical context and a logical understanding of the difficulties associated with the news coverage, this study interviewed not just the specific journalists who covered the humanitarian crisis, but also those who have been to Sri Lanka as foreign correspondents immediately before and after the end of the crisis from both the selected six newspapers as well as other media institutions. A set of open-ended questionnaires were used to interview the journalists face-to-face. However, the same questionnaire was used to interview journalists who were not interviewed face-to-face.

Purposive and theoretical sampling was used to select and interview 15 journalists from various countries, who have been to Sri Lanka as foreign correspondents, immediately before, during and after the end of the crisis. However, only a handful of foreign journalists went to Sri Lanka during the war to report the crisis, hence they were deliberately contacted for the interviews. Theoretical sampling was preferred as a central aspect of the Grounded Theory (Glaser and Strauss 1967), which was used to analyse the interview data, due to its relevance and its relation. Interviews conducted during my PhD research in 2016 are used in this chapter.

Grounded Theory is a convenient qualitative technique to study the issues which are of social nature. It focuses on contextual explanations instead of descriptions. Glaser and Strauss first introduced the GT methodology in 1967. They stated that 'theory is derived from data and illustrated by characteristic examples of data' (ibid., p. 5).

Strauss and Corbin in 1990 described GT as a 'scientific method' as its procedures are designed so that they can be carefully carried out. It is not just abstract theorising; the *theory* needs to be *grounded* or rooted in observation. Hence a group of people can be 'observed' from the material they provide about their work concerning the research issue (Strauss and Corbin 1990, p. 27). The procedures adopted in the GT analysis are based on Glasser's method and consist of five stages (Glaser 1978). They are: Preparation, Data Collection, Analysis, Memoing, Sorting and Theoretical Outline.

9.2 Impediments to Journalists' Constructing Reality of Distant Suffering

9.2.1 Lack of Access to the War Zone

The major problem that was encountered by the journalists, as revealed by them, was the lack of access to the war zone. As discussed, the analysis in Chapter 6, 7 and 8 also found out how the lack of access to the war zone negatively affected the crisis reporting in terms of meaning-making, representation (space-time) and orientation (agency). All the correspondents who reported the humanitarian crisis complained that they were prevented from entering the war zone except *The Hindu* correspondent Muralidhar Reddy,[1] who said:

> As a Hindu correspondent, my job was not that difficult, I must confess. There was a convergence of interest between what the Sri Lankan government wanted to do and what *The Hindu* as a newspaper and the editorial policy believed in. As far as access is concerned, towards the end, I was the only print journalist in the world who was given access. I was in that zone for about 13 days.

This testimony of *The Hindu* correspondent Muralidhar Reddy validates the research insight highlighted in Chapter 6. According to the content analysis statistics in Chapter 6, while the other 5 newspapers filed no news stories from the war zone, *The Hindu* exceptionally filed 37 news stories and it was presumed that *The Hindu* must have been granted special access to the war zone.

While this was the case for *The Hindu*, *The Times of India*, which is the other Indian newspaper, did not have access to the war zone. Its foreign correspondent K.Vengatramanan,[2] who was in Sri Lanka during the crisis, admitted that he did not have access to the war zone. Another foreign correspondent P. K. Balachandran from a leading Indian newspaper *The Hindustan Times*, who covered the crisis from Sri Lanka, also said that the lack of access to the war zone was his main constraint in covering the war.

This reveals that, despite the war zone being completely shut off for the outside world for several months until the war ended, *The Hindu* was given the special privilege of entering the war zone because, according to its correspondent Muralidhar Reddy, there was a convergence of interest between the Sri Lankan government and the editorial position of *The Hindu*.

> Given the editorial policy of *The Hindu*, I did not face any constraints from the Sri Lankan government's side. First of all, our access to the zone where the actual fighting was taking place was facilitated by the government of Sri Lanka and the Sri Lankan security forces.

Muralidhar Reddy confesses.

Moreover, Ms. Nirupama Subramanian,[3] *The Hindu*'s previous foreign correspondent to Sri Lanka before the humanitarian crisis, also acknowledged the policy-level support and the close connection between *The Hindu's* leadership and the Sri Lankan government during the crisis. To quote Nirupama Subramanian, 'The Hindu was in a unique position to cover the ethnic conflict in Sri Lanka, because of its access to the leadership in Sri Lanka at that time'. R.K. Radhakrishnan,[4] who was *The Hindu's* earlier foreign correspondent to Sri Lanka, prior to the commencement of the crisis, also admits the leadership level connection between the Sri Lankan government and *The Hindu*.

Meanwhile, as far as the foreign correspondents of the UK, the US and the other countries are concerned, the complete denial of access to the war zone was the major constraint among multiple constraints. To quote Ravi Nessman[5] of the Associated Press (AP), who has covered and led award-winning news stories in Asia, the Middle East, Africa and the United States, and whose reports of the humanitarian crisis from Sri Lanka were largely published in *The Washington Post* and the other UK and the US newspapers:

> We were not allowed inside the warzone. The warzone was shut off. At a certain point, we were going further and further away from the warzone. There was no access at all. It became more and more difficult to find out what was actually happening in the warzone.

The Hindu's former correspondent V.S.Sambandan,[6] who was based in Sri Lanka before the humanitarian crisis, also said that the lack of access to the war zone was a major problem that he had faced. He quoted 'access to the war zone was the major constraint. It was the same scenario even during the peace-time. Over a period of time, the only probable difficulty that I had was physical access to areas'.

The Independent's UK correspondent Jerome Taylor,[7] who was not physically in Sri Lanka but covered the crisis from the UK, is also of the opinion that the lack of access to the war zone was the major factor that negatively affected the media while reporting the crisis. Johan Mikaelsson,[8] who was also not physically present in Sri Lanka but was one of the journalists who covered the Sri Lankan conflict since 2009 for Swedish Newspapers said, the access to first-hand sources within the government and the LTTE was sometimes a problem, as access to the civilians living in the LTTE-controlled areas was restricted. Freelance journalist Taylor Dibbert[9] who is based in the US and had covered the issues since the end of the war in 2009, also said that one of the main problems that he had faced was media's lack of access to various parts and sources at the end of the war period. Almost all the other journalists who were interviewed expressed similar views.

As discussed in Chapter 8, the failure to construct the reality of the humanitarian crisis, in terms of the categorical and ideological realism, caused by the lack of access to the war zone was assumed to have played a significant role in suppressing the sublimation in the news stories. In Chapter 8, we also highlighted how the lack of access to the war zone, negatively affected the construction of the agora orientation in the news stories, as the journalists were unable to humanise the victims by making them active through raw images and information.

Elucidating the negative impact caused by the lack of access to the war zone during his reporting, AP correspondent Ravi Nessman said it affected the reporting by not allowing the portrayal of visual images and raw information:

> It did have a huge impact. When people think of war or conflict, they think of photographs. When you think of the war in Vietnam, you think of the visuals of the Napalm bombing. When you think of Tiananmen Square, you think of the student with a flower who stood in front of a column of tanks. When you think of some incidents you read, then you necessarily think of these kinds of iconic images. There are no iconic images that really speak of the warzone suffering in Sri Lanka, to really show what was happening in there. The boy who was injured by the attacks in the Syrian conflict made a huge impact. These kinds of images disturb the emotion and connect you to the story.

The Independent journalist Jerome Taylor too expressed a similar view saying that the government's restriction to access the frontline resulted with only fewer images in the news stories. He quoted:

> In many conflicts, the government's restrictions imposed on the media's access to the frontlines result in fewer images in the stories. Visuals are as important as the words of the stories in often deciding how the story would run in terms of prominence. You have got a powerful story with no picture; it's not going to run on the front.

9.2.2 *Intimidation and Threats*

Moreover, as uncovered during the interview with the journalists, the Sri Lankan government, in addition to restricting the access to the war zone, used legal and extra-legal means to control the journalists' work and thereby controlled the discourse of the humanitarian crisis. Those include intimidation, creating fear or causing harm to news sources, refusing visa, manipulation and misinformation.

Almost all the journalists who were interviewed were of the opinion that they had to face some form of threats from the authorities and it affected their reporting, while they were in Sri Lanka either during, before or after the crisis. They said that the freedom of the media was under severe threat throughout the conflict period. These findings substantiate the criticism doled out by human rights activists, organisations and journalists during the war time. According to Journalists for Democracy (2020), 44 journalists and media workers were killed in Sri Lanka between May 2004 and January 2010. In 2008, the press advocacy group Reporters Without Borders ranked Sri Lanka 165th out of 173 countries in terms of press freedom—by far the lowest democracy on the list. It called Sri Lanka the fourth most dangerous country for journalists, after Iraq, Somalia and Pakistan. Sri Lanka was ranked 162th in 2009 and 158th in 2010 (Jayaratne and Kellapotha 2015). As a consequence of the unprecedented level of violence against media professionals, at least 11 Sri Lankan journalists were driven into exile between June 2008 and June 2009 (Committee to Protect Journalists 2009). Killing of renowned journalist Lasantha Wickrematunga in January 2009 created unprecedented fear and anxiety among media workers. He had foreseen his murder. 'When finally I am killed, it will be the Government that kills me', written for posthumous publication, this piece, first published in the

Sunday Leader three days after his death, shows that he was fully aware of the dangers facing him (The UNESCO Courier 2009).

Nick Paton Walsh (Channel 4 journalist who was expelled from Sri Lanka) said he believed his arrest was connected to his report on the conditions of war refugees and alleged sexual abuse in camps for those who fled the northern war zone (*The Guardian* 2009). Paton Walsh alleged that the Sri Lankan President's brother and then Défense Secretary said to him; 'You can report what you like about this country, but from your own country, not from here'. This shows the control the Sri Lankan Government tried to exercise over foreign coverage of the conflict (Cited in Downman and Ubayasiri 2017, p. 123).

During the interview, freelance journalist Emanuel[10] Stoakes, who is based in New Zealand, claimed that even after the end of the war, he faced difficulties because of the CID who questioned him about his dealings in Sri Lanka. Freelance journalist Taylor Dibbert, who was in Sri Lanka between 2011 and 2014, said that his phone was monitored all the time and he had no idea if his email correspondence was monitored too. According to the journalists, the practice of intimidating the media had been in existence in Sri Lanka even before the crisis commenced. Swedish journalist Johan Mikaelsson was among one of the journalists who felt that he was under surveillance during the pre-crisis period when he residing in Sri Lanka. He said that he was aware of the fact that the local journalists in Sri Lanka, who had attempted to tell the truth about the country, were often hunted down and killed. He said there, in 1997 and 1999, there were a few instances where he was involved in some near-violent. S.Murarai of *The Deccan Herald* said he was a suspect in the eyes of Colombo when he covered the conflict before the crisis. Explaining the threats she faced while reporting in Sri Lanka, *The Hindu*'s former correspondent Nirupama Subramaniyan said that she had received threats and was detained and questioned in 1995 for a few hours for carrying a map. She also said that her house was raided in 1999, for receiving a fax from LTTE.

It is interesting to note that although almost all the former correspondents of *The Hindu* complained about the threats, intimidation and the difficulties they had faced while reporting in Sri Lanka, *The Hindu*'s Muralidhar Reddy, who covered the crisis did not mention any such threats and intimidation from the government. This is because he openly acknowledged that his job was not difficult in Sri Lanka, as it was facilitated by the Sri Lankan government and the military.

However, for AP journalist Ravi Nessman, the suppression of media through legal and extra-legal measures seriously affected his reporting. As he said:

> We ourselves came under heavy criticism. Local journalists were repeatedly attacked, killed in streets, which led to a climate of fear. The feeling of danger was in the back of your head. We used to get phone calls to our office from government officials, who would tell my staff that I need to stop whatever I was reporting or I will not be working anymore in the country. In the end, they refused to renew my visa and forced me out of the country.

Journalists were worried not just about the direct threats addressed to them, but also about the safety of their local sources. They said that this led to safety-related moral/ethical conflicts in them in terms of their news reporting and their interaction with their local news sources. Former *BBC* correspondent Francis Harrison said that she was concerned about the safety of her staff on a number of occasions. This also was the concern of freelance journalists Emanuel Stoakes and Taylor Dibbert, which lasted even after the end of the war. Emanuel Stoakes said that he was worried that something would happen to the man who accompanied him during his travel in Sri Lanka, as being a foreigner, he attracted a lot of attention. Taylor Dibbert said that he couldn't visit certain places as his appearance would draw attention.

9.2.3 Refusal of Entry Clearance

Refusing the media applicants' visas was a tactic used by the successive Sri Lankan governments to control the workings of the international press throughout the conflict. This was very evident during the humanitarian crisis. Swedish journalist Johan Mikaelsson said that he was granted a visa in the year 1999, although his visa applications were refused at two different occasions due to reasons that portrayed the real situation of the conflict.

On multiple occasions, a number of media organisations including *The Independent* failed to secure visas to travel to Sri Lanka to cover the crisis, despite repeated requests. As Ravi Nessman had mentioned, he was forced to leave Sri Lanka during the course of the reporting as the government refused to extend the visa. Not only during the crisis but even after the war ended the government continued to practise these regulatory tactics. According to Ben Doherty[11] of *The Guardian (Australia)*, after he was initially granted media visa it was denied later and then ultimately, he was banned from visiting Sri Lanka following the CHOGM Conference which was held in November 2013.

On the other hand, as highlighted in Chapter 6, the ban on journalists from entering the war zone directed them towards the humanitarian, human rights organisations and civil society organisations to gather information. As all the reports were based on the information gathered from such organisations, most of the emergency typology of news stories identified in the US and the UK newspapers were theatre oriented as opposed to agora oriented.

Despite the fact unearthed in Chapters 6, 7 and 8, that the Indian newspapers failed to construe HRJ stories and the emergency typology of stories, the Indian foreign correspondents said that they used the information provided by the human rights and humanitarian organisations to some extent.

> To some extent, we did make use of statements by humanitarian organizations, yes. I think ICRC or Peace groups in Colombo and UN, wherever it was possible.

Says *The Times of India's* correspondent, K.Vengatramanan.

Also, *The Hindu's* correspondent Muralidhar Reddy says he had obtained information from the UN and ICRC. As observed in Chapter 6, a few HRJ stories were apparent in the news reports of the Indian newspapers, as a result of these human-face oriented sources. Nevertheless, in the multimodal analysis, not all of the HRJ stories were categorised as the emergency type as their aesthetic qualities were compromised by the layout and the presentation of these news stories in these newspapers, which fell in line with the editorial policy. Exactly how the editorial policy of the Indian newspapers, as identified in Chapters 6, 7 and 8, guided the journalists' reporting will be discussed in the impending section.

In addition to the statements from the human rights and the humanitarian organisations, AP's correspondent Ravi Nessman said that they procured their own sources through whom they were able to acquire some information. However, he expressed frustration that the Sri Lankan government worked hard to discredit the information they had received from these own sources. To quote Ravi Nessman,

> We had our own sources that we had developed over the years. They provided reliable information, but the government tried hard to discredit the information. Whatever the information they had provided, we corroborated with the people up there, who were not from the LTTE. There were some international people. But the government worked extremely hard to convince me that the information I received from some sources were non-existent. Our sources were constantly discredited by the government.

Meanwhile, *The Independent's* correspondent Jerome Taylor, who was not physically present in Sri Lanka, said that verifying the information acquired was the most challenging issue. 'I guess, access for me but that wasn't necessarily anyone's fault and then it was verification. Verification of data. That was probably the most pressing issue', he says.

The Hindustan Times' correspondent P.K. Balachandran and *The Hindu's* former correspondent R.K Radhakrishnan also support the view that the war information was not verified independently.

> No journalist stationed in Sri Lanka was in a position to do anything at the time war was going on. What was a fact or not a fact could not be ascertained at that time.

says Balachandran.

While Jerome Taylor's and Balachandran's testimonies underline the consequence of the lack of access to the war zone, they do not highlight the propaganda perpetrated by the parties involved in the war in verifying the information. Ravi Nessman's view further validates this view.

> This is a war you had no idea of what was happening. Someone is lying or both sides may be lying, but we don't know.

9.2.4 Terrorist Label

For Carruthers (2000, p. 81), propaganda is a process of information-spreading through manipulation, distortion, emphasis and omission of the known facts to influence the general public to trust certain interpretations or people. Branding the parties in the conflict is one aspect of the 'black and white' framing adopted by the conventional war reporting. For example, during the 2003 Iraqi war, Saddam's forces were continuously branded 'insurgents' or 'terrorists' (Lynch 2008, p. 20). AP's correspondent Ravi Nessman,'s testimony goes parallel to this viewpoint.

> One of the other difficulties is that it was impossible to trust what the other side was saying. The government discredited the LTTE by branding them as a brutal terrorist organisation and questioned how we can trust them. But the information provided by the government in many instances was clearly not true, and also the government utterly denied the information provided by the LTTE.

As Ravi Nessman clarified, by discrediting the LTTE and branding them as a brutal terrorist organisation, the Sri Lankan government questioned him as to how he could trust the information provided by a terrorist organisation. Meanwhile, Ravi Nessman confesses that information provided by the government in many instances was clearly not true.

While acknowledging that the terrorist label didn't restrict him in terms of accessing information, *The Hindu's* former correspondent V.S. Sambandan agreed it was easier before the LTTE was banned.

Swedish journalist Johan Mikaelsson, who had covered the Sri Lankan conflict since 1999, explains how he was able to override the propagandist nature of the material by critically evaluating the sources involved in the conflict. To quote Johan Mikaelsson,

> I came to know what type of written information was reliable, and the critical evaluation of the sources was, of course, a central thing. At the same time, it was difficult to find out what were true stories about the LTTE and the violence they used on civilians. Some of the stories that were critical towards the LTTE had its roots in the government propaganda and information from the armed Tamil groups that were opposed to the Tigers and fought alongside the army. Journalists who didn't have much experience in Sri Lanka might have swallowed the bait and used the information without scrutinizing it in a proper way.

As the journalists revealed, besides the manipulation, distortion and omission of the facts by both the parties, the terrorist label was used by the government to discredit the information provided by the LTTE. Moreover, some journalists acknowledged the fact that the 'terrorist label on the LTTE' influenced their reporting. This view was dominant among the Indian journalists, while, some correspondents from the other countries accepted that they were not influenced by the terrorist label.

Acknowledging the terrorist label attached to the LTTE, influenced *The Hindu's* foreign correspondent Muralidhar Reddy's reporting of the crisis, and he said that this was the policy of *The Hindu* as well as the governments of India and Sri Lanka. *The Hindu's* former correspondent Nirupama Subramaniyan too expressed a similar view saying that she genuinely believes that the terrorist tag was appropriate for the LTTE.

> You could say that I was very influenced by the Rajiv Gandhi assassination. Like every Indian, I carried that in my reporting. I carried that- if at all there was an overarching influence on me.

Confesses Nirupama Subramaniyan.

India's *Deccan Herald's* Associate Editor S Murari,[12] who had been to Sri Lanka several times to cover the conflict, expresses an opinion similar to Nirupama Subramaniyan's. He says that *the LTTE deserved to be banned as a terrorist organisation.*

Former BBC correspondent to Sri Lanka, Frances Harrison,[13] admits that the terrorist label influenced her reporting. However, she said she eventually overcame the stigma attached to the terrorist label.

> Yes. I think it's inevitable and it influences the thinking of the people you are broadcasting to as well, and you have to be conscious of that. But I am one of those rare people who spent a lot of time with the LTTE so I hope at some level I overcame the stigma of the terrorist label.

She says.

Swedish journalist Johan Mikaelsson said that it was imperative that this had to be mentioned as it was a fact that the LTTE was being labelled a terrorist organisation by various countries and was also banned.

Expressing the view that the 'terrorist' label did not change the way he reported what happened, Callum Macrae[14] of Britain's Channel-4 said,

> The "terrorist" label - broadly accepted by the international community – was the turning point. It was, possibly, the most important and ultimately a powerful weapon that the LTTE faced. It was used as a weapon to prevent the possibility of peace and then subsequently it was used by Rajapaksa to hitch a ride on the west's "War on Terror" (doubly ironic given his subsequent posturing as an "anti-imperialist"). Of course the west's criticism of his record, given their own, was the third irony.

Meanwhile, *The Times of India's* K. Vengatramananan, US-based freelance journalist Taylor Dibbert, *The Hindustan Time's* P.K. Balachandran,

The Guardian's (Australia) Ben Doherty, freelance journalist Emanuel Stoakes, *AP's* Ravi Nessman and *The Independent's* Jerome Taylor said that they were not influenced by the terrorist label.

The discussions show that all the journalists expressed mixed opinions regarding the terrorist label's influence on their reporting. Although *The Times of India's* K. Vengatramananan is among those who said they were not influenced by the terrorist label, almost all the other Indian journalists, primarily those working in *The Hindu*, admitted that they were largely influenced by the terrorist label. This is the reason why, as shown in Chapter 6, terrorism label is largely manifested in the news stories of *The Hindu* in comparison to the other newspapers.

This shows how the rhetoric on terrorism was connected to the propaganda strategy and was used to elicit condemnation towards the LTTE by attracting journalists, particularly the Indian journalists, emotionally as well as geopolitically. It also shows how the Sri Lankan government managed to use the 'terrorist label on the LTTE' to make the journalists (*The Hindu*) obtain their information. Although journalists from the other countries said that the terrorist label did not influence their reporting, Chapter 6 reveals that the UK and the US newspapers also constructed a certain amount of terrorism framing in their news reporting. This does not necessarily mean that they were constructed by those journalists who denied being influenced by the terrorism label. Nevertheless, it does reveal the fact that the terrorist rhetoric did influence news production in some way. This possible explanation, as Johan Mikaelsson mentioned, could be that the legal label had to be touched upon in their reports, as a result of misinformation, disinformation and false information of the propaganda strategies.

9.2.5 Propagandist Campaign

The Independent's journalist Jerome Taylor described how they struggled with statements which were propagandist in nature, during the conflict.

> People would lie to you, people want to present their side of the story, and you have to find out where the middle-ground is, which meant for instance when receiving some kind of information from the LTTE's side, for instance, we had to be careful about, "Can we verify that? Is this correct?" There were just so many problems during that, as there was with

> the Sri Lankan Ministry of Defence's statements claiming a whole bunch of things that we can't verify.

Underlining the propagandist nature of the statements, *The Times of India's* correspondent K.Vengatramanan acknowledged the fact that their reporting largely relied on the government's narratives, given the situation that there was no access to the war zone.

> The coverage was largely dependent on the government narrative. That's one major constraint. And secondly, it's not possible to cover something that is not happening before your eyes, except through the statements of the parties involved. It can give a sense that we agree with the government, but it's not so. Because this is how the government explains it.

Explains Vengatramanan.

To quote an example, he recalled how the military, during the last few months of the war, came out with interactive graphic materials to provide a sense of the progress of the war, especially the movement of their forces and what they were achieving on the ground, and thus he had to depend on what they said.

9.2.6 Economic Constrains

The views expressed by the journalists, in turn, underline how they were influenced by the propaganda strategies, especially when they were subjected to the manipulation of information through briefings (Höijer et al. 2002, pp. 4–11). This also shows how the journalists in Sri Lanka were subjected to Kempf's (2003) three turning points. As Kempf argues, these three turning points make journalists especially vulnerable to official propaganda. The first of these turning points is mis coverage, which is the tradition of reporting only those conflicts that have already turned violent. This has been the case of almost all the foreign correspondents of the US and the UK newspapers. As some of the interviewed journalists pointed out, they arrived in Sri Lanka for the first time with the aim of covering the latter part of the war in its final stage.

AP's correspondent Ravi Nessman said that he went to Sri Lanka in 2009 for the first time to report about the war. To quote him,

> Before that, I had covered the wars in Iraq, Afghanistan, the Israeli-Palestine conflict and Africa. When the opportunity to go to Sri Lanka came up, I didn't have any specific connection with the country. Newspapers like the Washington Post and Times didn't have full-time correspondents based in Sri Lanka. They hence used their South Asia correspondents based in India to cover the war in Sri Lanka. That means those journalists had less ability to spend time covering the issues in Sri Lanka. Because they had to cover 1.3 billion people in India. At the same time, I do think they had an interest in Sri Lanka, there was a major attack going on in Sri Lanka. At the time, it was the most violent conflict. People were attracted to going there for news to report what was going there.

As highlighted in Chapter 6, this also shows how the conflict reporting of a distant place is constrained by economic considerations (Hanitzsch 2007, p. 5). As elucidated in Chapter 2, nowadays, media organisations prefer to use 'parachuting' correspondents, who fly off to different hot spots once the fighting commences, so that they can minimise the expenses involved in covering the conflict. This has changed the trend in the media organisations, so that, instead of editorial concerns, it is the accountants' and budgetary restrictions that determine what foreign events are covered by the correspondents in the case of wars and conflicts. With less experience, these journalists are 'less likely to ask key questions of their sources, less likely to analyse the situation well, and more likely to be dependent on experts' (Riegert 2005, p. 6). This raises an interesting moral issue for editors and owners.

As evident in the analysis of Chapter 6, this is again due to economic reasons, as *The Washington Post* along with the other UK and US newspapers relied on the news agencies for their coverage of the Sri Lankan crisis.

The second point of Kempf's three turning points is the habit of interpreting conflicts as lose-win situations. For many journalists, as they revealed in the interview, the war in Sri Lanka was treated as an endgame.

As *The Hindustan Times* correspondent P.K Balachandran noted, the war was a fight to the finish and hence, both the sides were desperate to defeat the other. *The Times of India* correspondent K. Vengatramanan admitted that he had felt like his newspaper was basically reporting about the military operations. He is also of the opinion that the magnitude of the final tragedy was not apparent to the Indian media at that time.

The responses of Jerome Taylor of *The Independent* further corroborate the aforementioned views. To quote Jerome Taylor:

> This was the culmination of three decades of fighting with some type of solution in sight. I'm not saying a solution that the editorial of the paper necessarily approved of, but it looked like the endgame was nearing, so yes, it was a very important story to cover and one we wanted to devote our time and resources to.

The final turning point of Kempf is journalists' use of elites as their news sources. It was underlined in the discussion in Chapter 6 that, given the lack of access to the war zone, the journalists would have been forced into a situation requiring uncritical reporting, given the conditions they had operated under.

As revealed in Chapter 6, every newspaper relied on elite sources such as the Sri Lankan government and its military for their news stories, and thus, it is highly likely that the newspapers would have relied on these specific sources to publish their news reports as well. Although all the journalists alleged that they looked for other sources to acquire information from, despite the government's regular briefings, they also expressed the difficulty associated with verifying the information. As revealed already, they also acknowledged the fact that they had to depend largely on the government for information, given the situation of being banned from the war zone and the severe censorship that came with being monitored. This is because, as per Kempf's third turning point, the journalists are required to turn towards elites as their news sources, such as the Sri Lankan government and military, for information. Furthermore, this situation resulted in the construction of more HWJ news stories, especially from the information acquired from the elite sources, which was particularly true in the case of the Indian newspapers.

In addition to the described conditions in Sri Lanka, as McLaughlin says, the power of the official sources in influencing the news agenda has increased with the decline in foreign bureaus and specialist correspondents. As a result, in situations of internal conflicts, international media tend to rely on elite sources and governments' officers for their news reporting. Also, increasingly inexperienced journalists and freelance journalists are being pushed to cover the news. In the US cut-backs have notably affected the coverage of foreign news. Between 1989 and 1996, foreign news coverage declined by half of its initial magnitude (McLaughlin 2002, p. 187), as covering wars is still an expensive business, especially in those places where the foreign news bureaus have been shut down. Instead, teams of reporters and photographers are flown into a war zone at the start of a war, and flown out as soon as the violence ends. Thus, they often fail to identify the latent conflicts and factors which are involved directly/indirectly and also ignore the issues of justice, accountability and reparation for grave crimes and gross violations against civilians. As underlined in the beginning of Chapter 6, this explains the reason why the UK and the US newspapers' coverage was very poor in terms of the number of stories. This is particularly true in the case of *The Washington Post*, both in terms of its poor coverage in terms of numbers, as well as the construction of more HWJ frames.

9.2.7 Editorial Policy

Kempf's three turning points not only helped us understand how the journalists were affected but also how and what the newspapers covered with regard to the war in Sri Lanka, by highlighting how their coverage is in the news values which were explained in Chapter 6.

On the other hand, the discussion also validated the fact that the editorial policies of the newspapers played a key role in shaping the discourse of news production. In Chapter 7, it was mentioned how it is a two-dimensional process, in which one dimension is decided by the editorial policy of the newspaper in accordance with the internal guidelines, and how the other is decided by the news sources. Furthermore, as explained before, the news source is independently conditioned by the actors involved in a conflict/crisis/war, and on the other, the frame is mediated between the editorial policy and the 'conditioned news sources'.

Understandably, this 'two-dimensional process' of framing is influenced by various ideological, political, geographical and cultural contexts in which the discourse is created, with different editorial stands in the US and the UK newspapers as well as the Indian newspapers, which constructed different news stories with different frames. This was very evident in the interviews with the journalists. While *The Hindu* correspondent Muralidhar Reddy openly acknowledged the parallel policies of the governments of India and Sri Lanka with *The Hindu's* leadership with regard to the final war, many other Indian journalists acknowledged that the terrorist label on the LTTE influenced their reporting given their own conceptions.

On the other hand, journalists from other countries, in general, voiced out that they were not influenced by the terrorist label. As Ravi Nessman said, they tried to impartially cover the actions of both sides and did not favour one side over the other—he said that he had reported the horrible attacks on civilians by both sides. However, as far as *The Hindu* was concerned, its editorial policy greatly influenced its discourse production concerning the humanitarian crisis, in addition to the constraints associated with the news value and the structural aspects. In other words, the neutral editorial stances of the US and the UK newspapers seem to have enabled their journalists to verify and understand the reality of the situation under the critical constructivist approach guided by 'critical consciousnesses'. Thereby they were able to detach themselves from the world by conventionalising the process of perceiving how their reporting is influenced by structural and other constraints which have been described already. This process enabled the journalists holding a neutral stance about the conflict, to practice HRJ without jeopardising the 'objectivity', but with the moral responsibility which evolved out of the 'critical consciousness'. A good example to explain this argument is Swedish Journalist Johan Mikaelsson's viewpoint on tackling propaganda. To requote him,

> I came to know what type of written information was reliable, and the critical evaluation of sources was, of course, a central thing. At the same time, it was difficult to find out what were true stories about the LTTE and the violence they used on civilians. Some of the stories that were critical towards the LTTE had its roots in government propaganda and information from the armed Tamil groups that were opposed to the Tigers and fought alongside the army. Journalists who didn't have much experience in Sri Lanka might have swallowed the bait and used the information without scrutinizing it in a proper way.

9.2.8 Dealing with Objectivity

The discussion in this chapter, as well as the findings in the preceding chapters, have highlighted the fact that the practice of HRJ is possible without deviating from the notion of objectivity. However, there appears to be an epistemological difference in terms of the approach towards adhering to the notion of objectivity for the practice of HRJ. The literature review in chapter four highlighted the nature of the objectivity grounded in the critical constructivist theory for the practice of HRJ, as opposed to the objectivist knowledge that was produced out of the positivist approach for the practice of conventional journalism, or as Shaw states, HWJ. This is what, as we discussed in Chapter 3, Ward (2008) describes as 'pragmatic objectivity', which is a means to the goals of truth, fair judgement and ethical action.

As evident in the analysis of Chapters 6, 7 and 8, there appears to be relativity between the editorial position of the newspapers and the detachment aspect of the (HRJ) journalists within the epistemology of critical constructivism. Because, as observed already, the neutral stance of the editorial board of the US and the UK newspapers enabled their journalists/newsroom to practice HRJ to a certain extent, given the fact that this coverage, as explained already, was conditioned by some external factors such as censorship and the banning of the journalists. The practice of HRJ was possible in the case of the US and UK newspapers, as explained in Chapter 7, within the critical constructive epistemology. This enabled the journalists to understand and inform the socio, cultural, political, ethical and moral foundations of a crisis, which may have positioned the journalists of the UK and the US newspapers/newsroom to be guided by moral responsibility. The moral obligation of an issue is not something that exists independently to be picked up by the journalists, instead, it is an outcome of the enlightenment of different theories of critical approaches to 'the process by which their consciousness was constructed' (Kincheloe 1993, p. 109). It is this moral responsibility, created in the presence of the neutral editorial stand with regard to the crisis, which enabled the UK and US journalists to practice HRJ, whereas as far as *The Hindu* was concerned, the practice of HRJ was largely undermined by its editorial policy coupled with the structural constraints including the geopolitical implications.

Although *The Times of India* correspondent K Vengatramanan was unwilling to accept that his news construction of the crisis was influenced by the editorial position of the newspaper, as well as the geopolitical and ideological contexts, he acknowledged that he had to rely on the elite sources, particularly the Sri Lankan government and its military. This explains why *The Times of India* construed more HWJ stories as opposed to HRJ stories and also failed to produce more of the emergency typology stories. Additionally, although K Vengatramanan agreed with the principle that it is important to be proactive in exposing and preventing human rights violations, he also stressed on the idea that such conviction cannot always be translated into practice, primarily because of the absence of objective information from the ground. This crops up the dilemma pertaining to the proactive role in exposing human rights violations and moral responsibility. Journalists who are committed to the notion of objectivity, which is grounded in positivistic objectivity paradigm, and at the same time believe in the importance of being proactive while reporting to expose human rights violations, may find it difficult to draw the line between these two in times of conflict. This is where societal influence comes into play. A number of Indian journalists acknowledged that they were influenced particularly by the terrorism label attached to the LTTE.

Kempf and Reimann (2002) explain that society is the biggest influencer of the media; journalists themselves are components of a particular society. The more their society is involved in a conflict, more is the pressure on the reporter to be 'on their team'. Journalists are citizens, as well as members of a profession. At times of war, there is a clash between professional duties and the responsibility of being a citizen (see Williams 1992).

As underlined above, the views of many journalists, who are optimistic about the practice of human rights-based reporting or HRJ, tend to position the notion of objectivity within the critical constructivist approach. One of the advocates of this viewpoint is Callum Macrae of *Channel 4*. To quote him,

> Actually, I don't have a problem with "objectivity". That implies analysis and an ability to stand back and question, not just the given assumptions, but also your own assumptions. That should be encouraged in – and by - all journalists. My objection is to "impartiality". That implies a stupid failure to engage and allows the lazy journalism which simply represents "both sides" in any dispute in an uncritical and unthinking way. By definition representing "both sides" in any unequal society equates those in power with those who are denied power. Doing that makes you a reactionary in practice, as it means you reinforce the unequal status quo.

When asked if this notion was possible to practise in his reporting, Callum Macrae said that his latter coverage of the events was engaged, and alas he took the side of truth and justice. He reiterated that he took the side of those who wanted to tell the truth about what happened, and at the same time acknowledged that he was allowed and encouraged to do this by Channel 4. Callum Macrae's view highlights the possibility of engaging in human rights-based journalism within the principle of objectivity anchored in the critical constructivist theory. This also highlights an opposite scenario, on how his individualistic conceptualisation of the notion of objectivity, with regard to taking the side of the 'truth and justice', is possible, if the editorial position of the channel 4 had a particular editorial policy. However, it does strengthen the argument that, if the journalism practice of that kind is to take the side of the truth/justice/victims under the influence of the moral responsibility constructed out of the critical constructivist theory, it is possible.

The Hindu's former correspondent Nirupama Subramaniyan said that the media can promote and protect human rights if it plays its role truly and honestly. She pointed out the direction of elements—the 10 principles of journalism written by two American journalists Bill Kovach and Tom Rosenstiel (Katovsky and Carlson 2003). To practice right journalism, one must make decisions and cannot be objective. However, journalistic methods are objective, which closely associates with the objectivity grounded in the critical constructivist theory, as explained in Chapter 3. 'Objectivity is a search for the truth. It's a process. Search for objectivity would make us search for truth', says Nirupama Subramaniyan.

According to BBC's former correspondent to Sri Lanka-Francis Harrison, BBC takes a liberal pro-human rights view, and thus chooses to prioritise the coverage of human rights stories within the notion of objectivity, to cover both sides. Francis Harrison, however, revealed that she likes the way channel 4 reports human rights issues. To quote her:

> I like the journalism of Channel 4 these days because it's more aggressive – it challenges interviewees and exposes things – not just on Sri Lanka. It's intelligent and not aiming at people who it assumes know nothing about the world. The BBC is far less challenging and more focused on reflecting what's going on in a fair and balanced way.

Highlighting the view that nothing is ever totally free from bias, freelance journalist Emanuel Stoakes said that, he is fairly open with his opinion pieces and tends to express a lot of sympathy for the victims of major crimes, while not wanting to over-violate his own reporting objectivity.

The *Guardian* (Australia) freelance journalist Ben Doherty shares a similar view where he says, in the course of their normal reportage, he can highlight cases of human rights abuses, and by exposing them, he can assist in ending those abuses. He further opined that,

> Human rights violations are, and should be, of primary concern to journalists. Journalism's fundamental role is to report the truth of a situation and to hold power to account. Where people's human rights are being abused (particularly civilians in a conflict situation) and where governments or other organisations are committing those abuses, public exposure is crucial in stopping them and preventing them from occurring again.

Meanwhile, some journalists are of the opinion that journalism has a moral duty to protect human rights; however, they said that this should be pursued by remaining objective and impartial. For example, *The Independent* journalist Jerome Taylor, underlining the concept of objectivity grounded in the positivist approach, said that the journalists have a moral responsibility to report the facts on the ground as they see them.

> Journalists should try and speak the truth and they are the watchdogs of the people. If the facts on the ground are that people are being killed, or they are being rapped, then journalists, of course, have a moral responsibility to report the facts on the ground as they see them.

He said.

AP's journalist Ravi Nessman expressed that he was convinced that his job was to uncover what was happening in Sri Lanka and to show the world what he had found, and it was up to the global actors and the public to take actions. While stressing that prescriptive policies are not incorporated in media's duties, he accentuated the importance of verifying the information of the warring parties, as well as exposing the human rights violations such as the bombing of the hospitals, as in the case of Sri Lanka, to the world. His thoughts regarding the responsibility to show the happenings to the world, with verified information rather than reporting unverified information from the elite sources, positions him under the critical constructivist approach, in search for the truth. It is possible for moral responsibility concerning human rights violations to operate within this process.

Meanwhile, a few journalists said they opposed the notion that the media has a moral responsibility to protect and promote human rights, as it involves advocacy and lobbying. S.Murarai of *The Deccan Herald* termed it as 'activist journalism', while K. Radhakrishnan, Muralidhar Reddy and V.S. Sambandan of *The Hindu* too expressed similar views and stressed that the role of the media should be to act as a neutral observer and stay true to the facts revealed on the ground. With these viewpoints, they tend to position their journalistic practice within the notion of objectivity grounded in positivist epistemology.

It is with this background that this chapter now moves into analysing how the international press coverage of the Sri Lankan humanitarian crisis in 2009 failed/succeeded in influencing human rights activists to campaign for humanitarian intervention (R2P).

9.3 The Influence of the International Press Coverage of the Humanitarian Crisis on Human Rights Activists

We discussed in Chapter 5 how the policy agenda is shaped by the public agenda and the media agenda under the HRJ-R2P conceptual model. The policymakers and the decision-makers who determine the policy agenda have direct access to media reporting of a distant suffering, and therefore media agenda can directly influence the policy agenda. Meanwhile, as discussed in Chapter 3, public agenda through its 'persuasive communication effect' can also shape the policy agenda. As discussed in the preceding chapters, studies (Thune 2009; Bennett et al. 2007; Entman 1993; Robinson 2000) have underlined media's potential power of influencing the priority-setting of policies concerning international affairs, both through public agenda and media agenda. Thune (2009) in his doctoral thesis, proposed a 'constitutive understanding of media power in international politics', in which he explained media's potential capacity to influence foreign policymaking. He identified five likely tendencies that could be created by a high degree of media's coverage of international politics, along with a high level of opinion-sensitivity among policymakers, to influence the priority-setting of foreign policymaking.

It is not the aim of this section to examine how the 'agenda-setting effect' of the media influences foreign policymaking. However, this study necessitates the understanding of how the international newspapers' coverage of the Sri Lankan humanitarian crisis in 2009 failed/succeeded in influencing the public to create a 'persuasive communication effect' to influence the policy agenda. To pursue this research inquiry, this study chooses to investigate international human rights activists who were involved in the humanitarian crisis in Sri Lanka. It is important to identify how human rights activists were influenced and what they felt about the role played by the international press regarding the Sri Lankan humanitarian crisis to decipher if there is any relationship between the findings of the content analysis and the 'Framing Matrix and Multimodal Discourse Analysis Matrix' (FMMDAM) integrated into the content analysis framework. As revealed in Chapter 6, the international newspapers' coverage of the crisis in terms of number was too poor to create human rights-oriented 'accessibility effect'. It is highly unlikely that the dysfunctional coverage of the crisis in terms of the magnitude would have drawn the attention of the readers towards the distant suffering in Sri Lanka. Similarly, the analysis in Chapters 7 and 8 showed how the media failed to practice HRJ, and thus to create a human rights-focused discourse and how the reporting was devoid of urgency and immediacy to create a 'persuasive communication effect' through public agenda to influence the policy agenda.

A structured questionnaire survey was conducted using Software Package for Social Sciences 'BOS Online Tool' administered by the University of Bristol, to identify if the international press coverage of the humanitarian crisis in Sri Lanka created an impact on the international human rights activists in terms of influencing them to campaign for international humanitarian action. The answer to this inquiry not only enabled us to scrutinise the nature and the level of impact of the international newspaper coverage of the crisis among them, but also to cross-check the findings of the analysis performed in the preceding chapters.

Though the aim was to garner a large number of responses through the survey, only 65 people responded through the BOS Online. This abysmal number was despite the fact that the survey link was sent via email and Facebook to more than 120 targeted people who were requested to circulate it among relevant peers who would be apt within the snowball sampling method (Biernacki and Waldorf 1981). In addition to the BOS Online tool, the questionnaire was also distributed to specific respondents who participated at special events such as the UN's Human Rights Council Session along with its offshoot events and conferences. Altogether, 115 respondents filled the survey out of which 13 were excluded as they were deemed inappropriate for our study. Among the 13, some of them were anonymous and some were identified as individuals without any institutional affiliations, thereby leaving 102 responses for the analysis.

A number of factors were considered when choosing the criteria and the population of the sample for this survey. (1) The respondents were expected to be policymakers/politicians/human rights/humanitarian activists. (2) They must have been involved in human rights/humanitarian or political activities during the human rights crisis in Sri Lanka. (3) Although the respondents were preferred to be non-Sri Lankans to avoid ethical challenges, not more than 10% of the Sri Lankans residing outside Sri Lanka, with human rights institutional affiliations, were allowed to partake in the survey.

The survey responses illustrated below establishes a relative connection with the content analysis findings.

9.3.1 *The Analysis*

Question 1: *How would you assess the role of the International Press during the final phase of war in Sri Lanka?*

Out of the 102 respondents, 48.1% state that they were not satisfied with the press coverage, while 40.4% opined that the coverage was poor. Only 11.5% of the respondents responded that they were satisfied with the coverage. The responses of the audience validates the findings of the content analysis. Although the US and UK newspapers constructed a considerable amount of HRJ news stories, 88.5% of the respondents categorised them as either unsatisfactory or poor. Therefore, as discovered in the multimodal analysis, their poor aesthetic quality (applicability), in terms of creating a sense of urgency and immediacy in relation to the crisis, could have been the reason why majority of the respondents found the coverage either unsatisfactory or poor. On the other hand, the lack of adequate coverage in terms of the quantity (accessibility) would also have been the reason why the international press failed to draw the attention of the international community towards the distant suffering.

Question 2: *Why do you think is satisfactory/unsatisfactory/poor?*

Most of the respondents, which is 24.8% of the group who selected either poor or unsatisfactory, said that it's because they felt that the media ignored the distant suffering and humanitarian crisis. Another important reason that many of the respondents (14.9%) identified was that the international press coverage did not encourage intervention. An equal number of respondents also justified their stance by emphasising on how the press focused more on war events than the peace initiatives, which led to them choosing poor/unsatisfactory. Meanwhile, 13.2% of the respondents alleged that the press was biased, and 12.4% of the respondents stated that the press reflected the rhetoric of 'war on terror'.

Clearly, these responses state the reasons for why the respondents chose poor/unsatisfactory which validates the findings of the frame analysis, the multimodal discourse analysis and the interviews with the journalists. The multimodal analysis exposed how the news coverage failed to construct the emergency typology of news stories in terms of aesthetic quality. This point also reflects in the responses given by the human rights activists.

Stating her own particular reason for why she selected 'rhetoric of war on terror' as one of the reasons,

Tasha Manoranjan, Executive Director of People for Equality and Relief in Lanka, said:

> The media coverage did not adequately capture the full scope of human suffering, and the intentional nature behind the Sri Lankan Military's attacks against the Tamils. The media portrayed the conflict as one between the Army and the LTTE, as opposed to the Army and the Tamil civilians, who bore the brunt of the war.

Ms. Yolanda Foster, Sri Lanka Desk, South Asia Team, Amnesty International and Mr. Alan Keenan, Senior Analyst, International Crisis Group are a few who argued that the coverage was satisfactory. Providing reasoning for her choice, Yolanda Foster of the Amnesty International says:

> I have ticked satisfactory as it may not have been as extensive as I would have liked, but the reality is the government sealed off access to the conflict zone so there were some challenges to international reporting.

Yolanda Foster's comment not only validates the finding as to how the lack of access to the war zone immensely affected the reporting of the international press, but also corroborates the argument above, that the lack of adequate coverage in terms of number was a reason.

Fred Carver, Campaign Director, Sri Lanka Campaign too shares similar views, as he said that there was 'simply not enough coverage of the issue at all'.

To quote Alan Keenan of the International Crisis Group:

> I am choosing satisfactory in part because I don't expect that much - Sri Lanka has never been an important issue for the western media, and Indian reporting has significant political constraints given the Indian govt's

political role in Sri Lanka. If I have one major criticism, it is that the media came too late to the story - after it was too late to make much difference.

Alan Keenan's comment substantiates the findings unearthed in the preceding chapters, about how the editorial policy of the Indian newspapers, influenced by India's policy with regard to the conflict in Sri Lanka, undermined their reporting. Also, his comments shed light on understanding how the UK and US newspapers valued the news of the crisis in Sri Lanka. As already underlined in the beginning of Chapter 6, this lack of newsworthiness as far as the UK and the US press are concerned, is another reason why their coverage was poor in terms of the number.

Question 3: *What should have been the role of the international media during the war in Sri Lanka in 2009?*

Majority of the respondents said that the international press should have exposed the human rights violations/atrocities and the underlying causes of the crisis. 20.4% responded that the press should have been sympathetic to the victims and encouraged intervention to stop the war. These responses of the human rights activists underline the role that media are expected to play in times of mass atrocity crimes. This is where the scope of HRJ is accentuated.

Highlighting the inadequate coverage, Mr. Gordon Weiss, who witnessed the conflict first-hand as a UN spokesman in Colombo, emphasised that the coverage should have been more aggressive.

Within the context of human rights activists' responses, the next few questions aim to scrutinise the 'persuasive communication effect' of the media agenda-setting, on the human rights activists aiming to find out the news coverage's influence on them.

Question 4: *To what extent were your campaigns against war/human rights violations in Sri Lanka in 2009 influenced by the coverage of the international newspapers?*

Only 3% of the respondents said that they were very influenced by the international newspapers' coverage of the crisis. Among the rest, 52.9% said that they were somewhat influenced, while 41.2% responded that they were not influenced at all. On the other hand, 88.5% of the human rights activists had mentioned earlier that the coverage was either poor or unsatisfactory. Yet, a significant number stated that their campaigns were somewhat influenced by media's coverage. This, on one hand, depicts media's power to influence actions on sufferings, and on the other, it portrays the impotence of the international press coverage of the humanitarian crisis, to propose a specific relationship of action between the readers and victims, because 41.2% of them stated that they were not at all influenced. Nevertheless, it should be taken into account that, in the case of the human rights activists involved in the Sri Lankan humanitarian crisis, their pre-existing knowledge of the Sri Lankan ethnic conflict, would have, significantly interacted with the information obtained from the newspapers to produce the accessibility effect.

The responses to the next question substantiate the arguments of this discussion.

Question 5: *Did the international press portray the reality of the humanitarian crisis and the distance suffering to encourage international humanitarian intervention (Responsibility to Protect-R2P)?*

To this question, 54% of the human rights activists stated that the international press only slightly depicted the reality of the humanitarian crisis and the distance suffering to encourage international humanitarian intervention (R2P). Meanwhile, 26% of them said the international press did not portray the reality of the crisis at all, and more importantly no respondent replied that it completely portrayed the reality. These responses validate the findings of the multimodal discourse analysis in Chapter 8 regarding the construction of the realism of the crisis. Because, as revealed, the failure to construct the reality of the humanitarian crisis, in terms of categorical realism and ideological realism, caused by the lack of access to the war zone, was assumed to have played a significant role in suppressing sublimation in the news stories. The characteristics of categorical realism and ideological realism, as observed already, are very important for the construction of the 'applicability effect' and thereby in influencing the readers to make an informed decision after studying and understanding the crisis in-depth.

9.4 Summary

In this chapter, in the first part of the analysis, the journalists who have been to Sri Lanka as foreign correspondents, immediately before and after the end of the crisis, revealed a number of challenges they had faced during the course of their reporting. Some of the difficulties include lack of access to the war zone, intimidation by authorities, and the hassle of verifying the information, as well as a range of structural constraints. These findings answered the research questions pertaining to the challenges that were confronted by the journalists in the course of their reporting.

The journalists who covered the crisis, except *The Hindu* correspondent Muralidhar Reddy, acknowledged that the major problem they had faced was the lack of access to the war zone. This situation, on one hand, did not enable the newspapers to play an active role in the discourse production of the distance suffering. On the other, it also did not allow the victims to play an active role in discourse production. In this manner, the Sri Lankan government effectively controlled the discourse production of the humanitarian crisis, by not allowing the raw information and visuals to play an active role in the construction of the reality of the suffering. This, in turn, enabled the Sri Lankan government to exert power over the global state actors' responsibility in considering the 'responsibility to react' option of the R2P in line with its pillar approaches, when gross human rights violations and mass atrocity crimes were taking place. From the data gathered from the journalists, this chapter identified how the Sri Lankan government used legal and extra-legal restrictions and tactics such as intimidation and visa refusal to undermine the journalists' work and responsibilities. This allowed them to control the discourse construction of the humanitarian crisis and exert control over the global news journalism discourse by constructing a perceived reality in line with their so-called 'humanitarian war'.

Meanwhile, the survey circulated among the human rights activists provided important insights which validated the findings and arguments of the preceding chapters. To summarise, the findings uncovered the failure of the media coverage of the crisis, to instigate a 'persuasive communication effect' among the international human rights activists to campaign for R2P intervention. This chapter drew insights from the findings of the preceding chapters to understand how the factors that conditioned the human rights-focused 'accessibility effect' and 'applicability effect' would have shaped the 'persuasive communication effect' of the public agenda to influence the human rights activists.

Overall, this chapter throws light on further understanding the 'HRJ-R2P conceptual model' explained in Chapter 5, which demonstrated the factors that can affect the media agenda-setting process from the 'reality of distant suffering' to 'media reality' such as news selection by journalists, media suppression, news sources, propaganda, the structural and institutional and the social conditions. In Chapter 6, we had already discussed how these factors affected the 'accessibility effect' towards the war discourse as opposed to human rights-focused journalism. In Chapters 7 and 8, we discussed how these factors impacted the 'two-dimensional framing process' to shape the 'applicability effect' to predominantly contain the frames of HWJ. These factors also influenced in determining the construction of the typology of news stories both in terms of realism and chronotope, as well as agora and theatre functions, which created a discourse devoid of urgency and immediacy of the distant suffering.

Notes

1. Muralidhar Reddy was interviewed in New Delhi in India on 25 June 2016.
2. K.Vengatramanan was interviewed in Chennai in India on 10 June 2016.
3. Nirupama Subramanian was interviewed in Chandigar on 22 June 2016.
4. R.K. Radhakrishnan was interviewed in Chennai, India on 11 June 2016.
5. Ravi Nessman was interviewed via skype on 2 September 2016.
6. V.S Sambandan was interviewed in Chennai on 11 July 2016.
7. Jerome Taylor was interviewed via WhatsApp on 2 September 2016.
8. Johan Mikaelsson was interviewee via email on 4 October 2016.
9. Taylor Dibbert was interviewed via Skype on 31 July 2016.
10. Emanuel Stoakes was interviewed via skype on 31 August 2016.
11. Ben Doherty was interviewed via email on 25 August 2016.
12. Murari was interviewed via email on 1 July 2016.
13. Frances Harrison was interviewed via email on 5 October 2016.
14. Callum Macrae was interviewed via email on 25 October 2016.

Bibliography

Bennett, W. L. (2003). New Media Power: The Internet and Global Activism [Online]. http://depts.washington.edu/ccce/assets/documents/pdf/newmediapower.pdf. Last accessed on 17 Mar 2020.

Bennett, W. L., Lawrence, R. G., & Livingston, S. (2007). *When the Press Fails: Political Power and the News Media from Iraq to Katrina*. Chicago, IL: University of Chicago Press.

Biernacki, P., & Waldorf, D. (1981). Snowball Sampling: Problems and Techniques of Chain Referral Sampling. *Sociological Methods Research, 10*(2), 141–163.

Carruthers, S. L. (2000). *The Media at War: Communication and Conflict in the Twentieth Century*. Basingstoke: MacMillan.

Committee to Protect Journalists. (2009). *Special Report: Journalists in Exile 2009* [Online]. Published on 17 June 2009. https://cpj.org/reports/2009/06/journalists-in-exile-2009/. Accessed 14 Oct 2020.

Entman, R. M. (1993). Framing: Toward Clarification of a Fracture Paradigm. *Journal of Communication, 43*(4), 51–68.

Glaser, B. G. (1978). *Theoretical Sensitivity: Advances in the Methodology of Grounded Theory*. Mill Valley: Sociology Press.

Glaser, B. G., & Strauss, A. L. (1967). *The Discovery of Grounded Theory: Strategies for Qualitative Research*. Chicago: Aldine.

Hanitzsch, T. (2007). Situating Peace Journalism in Journalism Studies: A Critical Appraisal. *Conflict and Communication, 6*(2), 1–9.

Höijer, B., Nohrstedt, S. A., & R. Ottosen. (2002). The Kosovo War in the Media—Analysis of a Global Discursive Order. *Conflict & Communication Online, 1*(2), 1–18.

Jayaratne, T., & Kellapotha, S. (2015). The Political Economy of the Electronic Media. In W. Crawley, D. Page, & K. Pinto-Jayawardena (Eds.), *Embattled Media: Democracy, Governance and Reform in Sri Lanka* (pp. 101–152). Los Angeles: Sage.

Journalists for Democracy. (2020). *Tamil Journalists in Sri Lanka's East Facing Death Threats*. [Online]. Published on 24 Jan 2020. http://www.jdslanka.org/index.php/news-features/media/924-tamil-journalists-in-sri-lankas-east-facing-death-threats. Accessed 14 Oct 2020.

Katovsky, B., & Carlson, T. (2003). *Embedded: The Media at War in Iraq: An Oral History*. Guilford: Lyons Press.

Kempf, W. (2003). Constructive Conflict Coverage: A Social Psychological Approach, *Konstaner Online-Publikations-System (KOPS)*. Available at https://kops.uni-konstanz.de/bitstream/handle/123456789/10220/2003_Constructive_Conflict_Coverage.pdf;sequence=1. Accessed 6 May 2019.

Kempf, W., & Reimann, M. (2002). The Presentation of Alternative Ways of Settling the Gulf Conflict in German, Norweigian and Finnish Media. In W. Kempf & H. Luostarinen (Eds.), *Journalism and the New World Order: Vol. II: Studying War and the Media* (pp. 59–72). Göteborg: Nordicom.

Kincheloe, J. L. (1993). *Towards a Critical Politics of Teacher Thinking: Mapping the Postmodern*. London: Bergin and Garvey.

Lynch, J. (2008). *Debates in Peace Journalism*. Sydney: Sydney University Press.

McLaughlin, G. (2002). *The War Correspondent*. London: Pluto Press.

Riegert, K. (2003). *The Image of War: Nato's Battle for Kosovo in the British Media*. Orebro: Orebro University Press.

Riegert, K. (2005). The Struggle for Credibility in the Iraq War (with Johansson, A.). In J. Hallenberg & H. Karlsson (Eds.), *The Iraq War: European Perspectives on Politics, Strategy, and Operations*. London: Routledge.

Robinson, P. (2000). The Policy Media Interaction Model: Measuring Media Power During Humanitarian Crisis. *Journal of Peace Research, 37*(5), 625–645.

Strauss, A., & Corbin, J. (1990). *Basics of Qualitative Research: Grounded Theory Procedures and Techniques*. London: Sage.

Strauss, A., & Corbin, J. (1998). *Basics of Qualitative Research: Techniques and Procedures for Developing Grounded Theory* (2nd ed.). London: Sage.

The Guardian. (2009, May 10). Sri Lanka Throws Out Three Channel 4 Journalists [Online]. https://www.theguardian.com/world/2009/may/10/channel-four-journalists-sri-lanka. Accessed 24 June 2020.

The UNESCO Courier. (2009, April). "And Then They Came For Me": Last Words of Lasantha Wickrematunge [Online]. https://en.unesco.org/courier/april-2009/and-then-they-came-me-last-words-lasantha-wickrematunge. Accessed 24 June 2020.

Thune, H. (2009). *Beyond the CNN Effect: Towards a Constitutive Understanding of Media Power in International Politics.* Ph.D. Dissertation, Department of Political Science, University of Oslo, Oxford.

Ward, S. J. A. (2008). Truth and Objectivity. In L. Wilkins & C. G. Christians (Eds.), *The Handbook of Mass Media Ethics* (pp. 71–83). New York: Routledge.

Webel, C., & Galtung, J. (2007) *Handbook of Peace and Conflict Studies*. London: Routledge.

Williams, K. (1992). Something More Important than Truth: Ethical Issues in War Reporting. In A. Besley & R. Chadwick (Eds.), *Ethical Issues in Journalism and the Media* (pp. 159–162). London: Routledge.

CHAPTER 10

Conclusion: Theory and Practice of Human Rights Journalism

This book has made significant contributions to the advancement of Human Rights Journalism (HRJ). Firstly, it helped fill the epistemological vacuum present in HRJ by proposing 'pragmatic objectivity' within the critical constructivist epistemology. Secondly, it has defined the HRJ–R2P nexus by identifying five key elements, which in turn, characterise the R2R role of the journalists, which was stressed by Thompson (2007). Thirdly, it proposed an HRJ-R2P conceptual model, which illustrates how an embedded human rights focussed media strategy can be designed by drawing insights from related concepts such as human rights, conflict transformation, agenda-setting and the spectatorship of distant suffering. Fourthly, this book proposed two novel quantitative analysis tools called the 'Framing Matrix' and the 'Multimodal Discourse Analysis Matrix' to examine the practice of HRJ and the typology of news stories of distant sufferings, which are equipped to deal with a big sample size over a long period. Fifthly, the analysis of the Sri Lankan humanitarian crisis which took place in 2009, scientifically explains the reasons for the silence of the international community regarding one of the worst humanitarian crises

The original version of this chapter was revised: Incorrect reference in the bibliography has been updated. The correction to this chapter is available at https://doi.org/10.1007/978-3-030-49072-0_11

S. Selvarajah, *Human Rights Journalism and its Nexus to Responsibility to Protect*, https://doi.org/10.1007/978-3-030-49072-0_10

in the world and their dysfunctional coverage, while providing theoretical insights to understand the agenda-setting mechanism within a human rights agenda.

10.1 Critical Reflections on the Findings

In Chapter 2, we discussed the problems and the constraints associated with conventional journalism when it comes to reporting wars, conflicts and human rights violations. These include the propensity to focus on violence, the reliance on military and government sources, the focus on military developments as opposed to diplomatic and peace activities, the tendency to reproduce propaganda, the use of military terminology and the non-involvement principle of the media. Additionally, we demonstrated the limitations of adhering to the concept of "objectivity" and how its prevailing work conventions [the reliance on official sources, the favouring of events over processes and the focus on "dualism" (Zero-Sum game) in reporting conflicts] means that conventional war journalism reinforces war and conflict by drawing attention to the 'us' and 'them' division, the effects of violence and the activities and operations of the military. We also looked at the patterns of conventional war reporting. Despite the prevailing tensions between war reporters and the military/government, the former have often reproduced the propaganda of the military, by focusing on the path to victory as opposed to the efforts concerning the fostering of human rights and prevention of its infringements. The coverage often concentrated on the views and opinions of elites, and emphasised on violence. Conventional journalism's failure to foster human rights and prevent genocide, crimes against humanity and war crimes to find peace, clearly justified the importance of a 'journalistic force' that can aid in transforming the media's role in conflicts, to ensure it is more proactive in the promotion and protection of human rights, which is indispensable for building peace. Since discourse is the vehicle of power/knowledge, a qualitative change is necessary in journalism's role in violent conflicts. On one hand, this can address the power imbalance between the parties in communities with violence, and on the other, it can empower the international community to ensure accountability and prevent further deterioration of the situation. This is where we identified the potentiality of HRJ as a normative concept, to deal with negative peace (direct violence such as physical violence) and positive peace (indirect violence such as structural and cultural violence), as well as positive rights and negative rights within the Kantian principle of universalisability, for the realisation of UDHR.

In Chapter 3, this book provided an epistemological foundation for the practice of HRJ. The epistemological foundation, argued within the critical constructivist paradigm, guides human rights journalists with 'critical consciousness', enabling their detachment from the world so they can observe how the influence of the nature of news values on their working pattern, the relationship of journalism power and the dependence on news sources. This is what Ward (2008) calls 'pragmatic objectivity' and emphasises that journalists must be pragmatic in their search for truth, not just through their reliance on facts, but a combination of 'valuing, observation, interpreting, and theorizing' (Ward 2004, p. 303). This is opposite to the positivist paradigm, which makes journalists prone to the manipulations of the elites within the separable concepts of the knower and known. In other words, the detachment through the 'critical consciousness', to understand the influencing factors of social reality, is the 'objectivity pursued' in HRJ within the concept of the 'inseparability of the knower and the known', as opposed to the 'objectivity pursued' in HWJ, within the 'separable concept of the knower and known'. In this manner, HRJ is not critical of objectivity; instead has a different approach towards pursuing objectivity, in terms of epistemology to be pragmatic.

In Chapter 4, the operation of HRJ and R2P are positioned within the theoretical frameworks of Kant's global justice (1963); Galtung's (1996) ABC conflict Triangle; Parlevliet's Iceberg Metaphor (2002); Dugan's Nested Paradigm (1996) and Schirch's Just Peace (2002). These theoretical foundations, on one hand, reinforce each other's aims and expectations, and on the other, provide a common functional interface for both HRJ and R2P to find their footings, which then identified the five key elements that defined the nexus between HRJ and R2P. The five key elements are: (1) Just Cause and global justice advocacy (2) Human Rights-based approach (3) Just peace, peacebuilding and conflict prevention (4) Monitoring and accountability (5) Empowering, mobilising and intervening. We discussed their role in facilitating the righteous, effective and legitimate implementation of R2P along the line of its pillar approach. These five key elements were characterised as R2R of the media in crisis situations.

Chapter 5 of this book remarkably contributes to research methodologies, specifically for analysing the practice of HRJ. Firstly, it proposes a Framing Matrix for the analysis of HRJ and HWJ. Although, Ibrahim

Seaga Shaw in his theory of 'Human Rights Journalism', used a number of case studies to identify the frames of HRJ and HWJ, he failed to provide a methodology to distinguish between HRJ and HWJ stories in a scientific manner. Secondly, to identify the typology of news stories, this chapter adopted a Multimodal Discourse Analysis Matrix by re-contextualising Lilie Chouliaraki's (2006, 2008) qualitative analytical framework in a quantitative manner. We saw how Chouliaraki's multimodal discourse analysis, which was originally designed to analyse television news coverage of the distant suffering, can be used to examine the press coverage.

A great advantage of using both these tools in the content analysis framework is their ability to analyse a large number of news stories regarding a particular event over a period of time, to analyse media's role in a holistic and comparative manner. It also allows the use of multiple variables within a single framework such as total number of news reports, types of news reports, types of news sources, types of articles, modes of news coverage, sections of newspaper, key frames, sub-frames, the typology of news stories, types of realism, modes of presentation, aesthetic quality, space-time (representation), agency (orientation), etc. which is impossible to do in a qualitative analysis framework.

The 'Framing Matrix and Multimodal Discourse Analysis Matrix' (FMMDAM), integrated into the coding manual of the content analysis framework, sheds light on its ability to develop into an analytical tool for an 'early warning' mechanism, to assess the reality of 'news journalism discourse' of a crisis against the 'global discursive order' through the analysis of media coverage, to facilitate appropriate interventions and mitigate conflicts in pre/post conflict environments within the R2P framework. We have observed in our case study analysis that a discursive order operating in a news story, consists of various discourses with different understandings of the sources of the problem, solutions to the problem and its grounding principle. These sometimes reinforce each other, influence each other or might even conflict with each other. As a result of these dynamics, different discourses may emerge as dominant discourses, forming the news journalism discourses as part of the global discursive order. As evident throughout the analysis, the 'FMMDAM' has the capacity to match the reality of the news journalism discourse of a crisis with its global discursive order, which can assist early warning mechanisms.

The development of the 'FMMDAM' as an analytical tool for an early warning can significantly contribute in resolving the challenge of prevention of humanitarian crisis. It can also contribute as a discursive appraisal for international media's coverage of conflicts in a scientific manner and help understand conditions of conflicts/reporting. Developing and testing this tool in other empirical contexts within a quantitative research project, will widen the understanding of constructing an embedded media strategy within the R2P framework, challenge the warring parties' anti-humanitarian narrative and establish a *prima facie* of human rights violations. Moreover, it can complement an interdisciplinary theoretical foundations in the domains of discourse, semiotics and frame, to analyse media coverage of a crisis in a quantitative manner. The facilitation of content analysis can help address the weaknesses of the discourse analysis method in media studies, as it can provide valuable cultural and historical insights ranging over a long period in the media content, enable the analysis to go beyond mere deconstruction of the problem or text which reflects socially constructed reality in a scientific manner, and enable the comparison of textual content using multiple variables. Additionally, the 'FMMDAM' can be used to explore how the information shared on social media platforms through the documentation of the citizen witnessing can help generate early warnings of conflicts and facilitate policy decisions.

There have been a number of Early Warning mechanisms set up in the past to prevent and mitigate conflicts including the West Africa's (ECOWAS/WANEP) regional Conflict Early Warning System, the Conflict Early Warning and Response Network (CEWARN) in Africa, FCE Early Warning and Rapid Response mechanism in Sri Lanka, Peace Direct Early Warning and Early Response (EWER) networks in Burundi, Sudan and Zimbabwe. However, the processes of information gathering of these mechanisms were primarily built by the human rights and civil society activists, religious leaders and field staff of the organisations at a local level. They lack analytical tools to effectively analyse the local and the international media's coverage of the conflicts to expose conflict indicators. Although, the FCE's early warning mechanism model in Sri Lanka, in which I was involved, comprised of a media-monitoring tool, it proved to be ineffective in providing timely and actionable insights due to the lack of sound methodological procedures pertaining to journalism theories. Under this premise, the 'FMMDAM' can fill this gap with a systematic, comprehensive exploration of media content. NGOs, Human Rights Organisations and media research centres in universities can make this tool a feasible reality, by analysing international media content and sharing real-time actionable data of conflict situations with decision-makers around the world to alert them of serious violence and devise appropriate interventions. This will also help assess the level of discourse construction by different news sources such as radical organisations and elite groups, and help understand how they exert power over the society by controlling the information.

10.2 How and Why the International Press Failed in Covering the 2009 Humanitarian Crisis in Sri Lanka?

Furthermore, the case study analysis demonstrated the lack of due attention towards the Sri Lanka crisis among the international newspapers, barring the Indian newspapers. *The Hindu*, with regard to the number of news stories, layout and positioning of news stories, illustrated the inability of this inadequate news coverage to draw the attention of the world towards the crisis. For example, as highlighted in Chapter 6, the international press completely ignored the withdrawal of the UN and other humanitarian organisations from Vanni, during the initial stage of the final war in September 2008. Ideally, at that point the international community should have been warned of the dangers of potential human rights violations and war crimes, and must have considered the 'responsibility to prevent' option of the R2P doctrine. In other words, this showed the international press's failure to create a human rights-focused 'accessibility effect' to draw the attention of the international community towards the distant suffering in Sri Lanka.

Although the international press coverage increased in proportion, towards the end of war in May 2009, as the violence and human rights violations worsened, the number of news stories still remained extremely low except in the Indian newspapers. This was evident not only in content analysis, but also in the surveys conducted among the Human Rights Activists. The reasons for the Indian newspapers' extensive reporting of the crisis, and the failure of the UK and US newspapers, were explained through Galtung and Ruge's (1965) news value of cultural proximity, Herman and Chomsky's explanation of 'anti-ideology filter' (1988) and Hanitzsch's (2007b) structural constraints. Some key reasons were: inaccessibility of the war zone, economic consideration and news value.

Simultaneously, the analysis also identified the direct effect of the theories of news production such as Galtung and Ruge's (1965) newsworthiness and Hanitzsch's (2007b) structural constraints on the 'accessibility effect' of a distant suffering's news reporting, in terms of instigating international humanitarian action.

On the other hand, although the coverage of the humanitarian crisis increased slightly in proportion to the increase in violence, Chapter 7 revealed how the practice of HRJ was affected by the 'two-dimensional framing process'. It explained how HWJ was practiced in the Indian newspapers to a higher level and the UK and US newspapers to a considerable level. Notably, the analysis also depicted how the Indian newspapers, particularly *The Hindu*, failed to create a human rights discourse to prevent the gross human rights violations despite their extensive coverage of the humanitarian crisis.

The analysis also revealed the proportional relationship between HRJ frames, informed by the properties of Framing Matrix, and the typology of news stories, informed by the communicative properties of the multimodal analysis. Nevertheless, the multimodal analysis in Chapter 8 highlighted the nature of the realism and meaning-making of the HRJ stories, which were primarily influenced by the inaccessibility of the war zone. The UK and the US newspapers, except *The Washington Post*, significantly constructed perceptual realism (facticity) and indexical meaning. However, they failed to construct a fair number of stories with categorical (emotion) and ideological realism (justice), as well as iconic and symbolic meanings in their news stories.

In terms of the aesthetic quality, the emergency typology of news stories constructed by the newspapers, contained more 'pamphleteering' than philanthropy and sublimation. The extremely low representation of the sublimation type of aesthetic quality, caused by the inaccessibility of the war zone negatively impacted the newspapers' coverage to construct more 'empathy critical' and 'diagnostic reporting' frames. This impacted readers' comprehension of the distant suffering by the in-depth understanding of the underlying causes.

In the context of the multimodal analysis, the findings proved that despite considerable construction of the HRJ frames and the emergency typology of news stories in the US and UK newspapers, their ability to create cosmopolitan emotions, empathy and aesthetic impact was compromised. This resulted from the inadequate construction of categorical and ideological realism, as well as the iconic, symbolic and sublimation meanings. Meanwhile, the significant amount of adventure news stories in the Indian, UK and the US newspapers, greatly suppressed the construction of all types of realism, meaning-making and aesthetic qualities.

This dysfunctional construction of the communicative properties of the emergency typology of news stories created a negative impact in the construction of space-time (representation) and agency (orientation) as shown in the CDA. Particularly, the mobile type of chronotope, with its ability of connecting the contexts of safety-zones and danger zones to propose a specific relationship of action between the readers and victims, is highly suppressed in the newspapers. Additionally, agora, which plays the role of humanising the victims by actively representing them in the newspapers, was also suppressed in the emergency typology of news stories. This dysfunctional pattern of representation and orientation weakened the ability of the emergency typology of news stories to provoke action through the creation of proximity between the readers and the suffering. Moreover, the large number of adventure typology of news stories limited the potentiality of causing action on the suffering.

While focusing on prevention strategies, R2P focuses equally on addressing root causes and finding appropriate solutions to violent conflicts, with the aim of creating steps to prevent conflict escalation and enhancing peace prospects. It was also explained how the R2P evolved as a rights-based approach and how the media can assist in its implementation by establishing a *prima facie* case or a regime of truth of the discourse of human rights violations, their causes, and consequences.

Against the backdrop of the practice of HRJ's rights-based approach, the application of R2P in Sri Lanka was conditioned by the level of construction of reality of the humanitarian crisis by the international press. As explained in Chapter 7, the 'two-dimensional framing process', conditioned by the editorial policy and the news sources, did not enable the international presses to practise HRJ, and thus exercise it's five key elements that define the nexus between HRJ and R2P. As a result of the lack of due reality of the crisis, did not empower the international community to invoke R2P.

In other words, the response and the action of the international community was uneven and dysfunctional, due to the inadequate demonstration of the five key elements that characterise R2R to consider the R2P options. The international community possessed inadequate information to create R2P options based on the three responsibilities of R2P through its pillar and responsibility approach. The international community failed to invoke the R2P options because they lacked power, which could have been achieved through the 'knowledge' of the reality of the crisis. According to Francis Bacon, 'Knowledge is power', and this knowledge could have given the international community the 'capacity to act' on the suffering in Sri Lanka. However, as illustrated in the HRJR2P conceptual model, there was a huge difference between the actual reality of the distant suffering and the perceived reality of the distant suffering, constructed by the media's agenda-setting.

According to Van Dijk (1996, pp. 11–12), access is an important factor in the analysis of media power, as access to 'discourse' is central to manage and control power. Media functions as a tool of this discourse construction, and as a result, those who want to exert control over an issue or an activity, endeavour to influence or manipulate the discourse construction. This is done to make their version of reality override the opposing discourse(s) in the discursive order.

This was apparently the case in the construction of the global discursive order of the Sri Lankan humanitarian crisis. The Sri Lankan government, with its authority as a sovereign state, was in a stronger position than the LTTE to manipulate the discourse production of the humanitarian crisis and hold power over the political action on the suffering. In addition to the international press's disinterest in the humanitarian crisis, the Sri Lankan government's strategies regarding the 'access to the news sources', as evident in Chapters 6 and 7, significantly impacted the discourse construction of the humanitarian crisis in the international press. As uncovered in Chapters 6, 7, and 8, controlling or manipulating the 'access to the news sources' involved three strategies: (1) Denial of access to the war zone; (2) Propaganda briefings and (3) Creating difficulties in verifying the information.

The discussion showed how the lack of interaction between the journalists and victims affected the practice of HRJ. Thereby, this affected the construction of the reality of the crisis, in terms of using raw images and information to expose the direct and indirect human rights violations, their causes and the suffering. This severely limited the news reporting's ability to construct human rights-focused 'applicability effect' within the 'two-dimensional framing process'.

As observed in Chapter 9, the journalists who covered the crisis, except *The Hindu's* correspondent Muralidhar Reddy, acknowledged that the major problem they had faced was the inaccessibility of the war zone. This situation did not enable the newspapers and consequently, the victims, to play an active role in the discourse production of the distance suffering. In this manner, the Sri Lankan government effectively controlled the discourse production of the humanitarian crisis by not allowing raw information and visuals to play an active role in the construction of the reality of the suffering, and thus curtailing the journalists to demonstrate R2R role. This, in turn, enabled the Sri Lankan government to exert power over the global state actors' responsibility to consider the 'responsibility to react' option of R2P, in line with its pillar approaches, when gross human rights violations and mass atrocities were taking place. As highlighted already, the inadequate coverage of the crisis from the beginning of the war limited the opportunity of the international community to consider the 'responsibility to prevent' option of R2P.

Additionally, as revealed in Chapters 6, 7, 8, and 9, the inaccessibility of the war zone made the journalists extremely dependent on the Sri Lankan government, its military's regular briefings and their website to obtain information. This dependency created a favourable situation for the Sri Lankan government, providing easy access to the international press, via their briefings discourses and communicative events. In other words, according to Kempf's third turning point, this dependency, as revealed by the journalists in Chapter 9, made them turn to elite sources such as the Sri Lankan government and its military and thus made them become vulnerable to the propaganda. Although the LTTE had a media wing in the past, such as the *Voice of Tigers*, the LTTE radio station, *Nitharsanam*, the TV station and several tabloids, the information did not reach beyond their controlled areas (Richards 2013). As mentioned in Chapter 9, the pro-LTTE website *Tamilnet*, based in Norway, was the only media that provided information on the final war through its local correspondent (see Manoharan 2019). However, due to the consistent severity of the final war, it offered a limited avenue to disperse news.

Furthermore, adding to the constraints related to obtaining information from the public of the war zone as stated by the journalists in Chapter 9, the Sri Lankan government worked hard to discredit any information sources they could gather. The journalists acknowledged that the verification of information was a major challenge they had faced. The Sri Lankan government also used extra-legal restrictions and tactics such as intimidation and visa refusal to undermine their work and journalistic responsibilities.

Moreover, the analysis provided some insights into understanding the epistemology of HRJ, which was explained in Chapter 3. As we have observed, the 'two-dimensional framing processes' is subjected to the influence of various ideological, political, geographical and cultural contexts in which the discourse is created. This is because, with different editorial stances, the US, UK and the Indian newspapers constructed different news stories with different frames. In this context, by embracing 'pragmatic objectivity' under critical constructivism, HR journalists are guided by 'critical consciousness'. Thereby, they are able to detach themselves from the world to review how their occupational culture is conditioned by the news values, relationship of journalism to power and the dependence towards news sources. This detachment aspect is an important justification for HRJ, proving that practice is not antithetical to the basic tenet of what Western journalists believed was 'good journalism', namely objectivity (see Loyn 2007). It was argued that this detachment was created by the enlightenment of critical theories to understand the influencing factors of social reality; the 'objectivity pursued' of news reporting within the concept of 'inseparability of the knower and the known'.

As evident in the discussion in Chapter 9, there exists a category of journalists, who accept that the media has a moral responsibility to prevent human rights abuses, and position their journalistic practice within the notion of objectivity. This conception enables them to practise aggressive journalism by taking the side of truth and justice. There exists another category of journalists, who believe that journalists should not hold any agenda with regard to prescriptive policies. However, they are bounded by duty to expose the human rights violations with verified information, and position their journalistic practice within the notion of objectivity grounded. These journalists tend to practise critical journalism, which in turn may help to prevent human rights violations. Meanwhile, a third category of journalists believes that the role of journalists should be that of observers, and they should only report mere facts as seen and heard by them. They tend to position their journalistic practice within the notion of objectivity grounded in positivist epistemology and engage in bystander journalism. This may or may not help prevent human rights violations.

The analysis proved that the editorial policy of the newspapers tremendously influenced the type of epistemology in which journalists pursued objectivity in their reporting of the humanitarian crisis. Although the journalists who seemingly follow aggressive journalism do not represent any of the newspapers selected for this study, those who have positioned themselves within the critical journalism are seen representing the UK and the US newspapers. Meanwhile, the Indian newspapers' journalists have positioned their coverage within the principles of bystander journalism.

This depicts the relativity between the editorial position of the newspapers and the detachment aspect of the (HRJ) journalists within the epistemology of critical constructivism. The neutral stance of the editorial board of the US and UK newspapers enabled their journalists/newsroom to practise HRJ to a certain extent, given the fact that this coverage was conditioned by some external factors like censorship, lack of access to the war zone and structural constraints. The practice of HRJ was possible in the case of the US and the UK newspapers, within the critical constructive epistemology, which enabled the journalists to understand and inform the socio, cultural, political, ethical and moral foundations of a crisis, as they were guided by their moral responsibility. Moral obligation of an issue does not exist independently to be picked up by journalists. Instead, it is an outcome of the enlightenment of different theories of critical approaches to 'the process by which their consciousness was constructed' (Kincheloe 1993, p. 109).

In the case of the UK and the US journalists, it was their editorial board's neutral position that enabled them to adhere to the moral values concerning human rights violations. Nevertheless, as in the case of the Indian newspapers, especially *The Hindu*, the possible effect of the moral responsibility seems to have been suppressed by their strong 'pro-war' editorial position, influenced by the national and geopolitical interests.

This reveals how the practice of HRJ can be effectively controlled by the policy of the editorial boards. Additionally, the analysis also revealed that despite having the moral responsibility, the practice of HRJ as well as human rights-focused 'accessibility effect' and 'applicability effect' can be seriously weakened by manipulating and controlling the communicative process of censorship, the lack of access to the war zone and the information verification.

The US and UK journalists could relatively practice more HRJ due to the epistemology (critical constructivism) involved in their news coverage. Critical constructivism enables the journalists to understand the influencing factors of social reality within the enlightenment of critical theories, to pursue 'pragmatic objectivity' in their news reporting, in the context of the concept of 'inseparability of the knower and the known'.

The lack of 'inseparability of the knower and the known' in conventional journalism makes its practice vulnerable to the manipulations of the elite sources. This is why conventional journalism (HWJ), with its objectivity concept, once considered good journalism practice, has failed to uphold its performance, given the present-day wartime circumstances conditioned by propaganda strategies and technologically assisted activities/manipulations. This lack of 'inseparability of the knower and the known' does not allow conventional journalism (HWJ) to preserve its values against the modern-day warfare communication-controlling strategies. Nevertheless, as observed in the analysis, the 'critical constructivist epistemology' can fill this gap and empower the journalists to adopt 'pragmatic objectivity' to practice human rights-based journalism. In other words, the theory of HRJ, with its epistemology of 'critical constructivism', addresses the failings of the HWJ. Therefore, the primary difference between the HRJ and HWJ is their approaches to search for the truth in terms of their epistemology.

Critical constructivism, which provides a fertile ground for pursuing 'pragmatic objectivity', enables journalists to practice HRJ and search for truth through fair judgement, ethical action and engaging with the complex, multi-layered analysis of human rights violations. More importantly, as elucidated in Chapter 2, new media technologies and the rise of citizen journalism and data journalism can play a significant role in a practical/realist application of HRJ in a meaningful way within the critical constructivist epistemology. For example, the journalism practiced by Britain's Channel 4, which instigated Sri Lanka's accountability and justice process, and established international pressure on issues surrounding human rights violations and mass atrocities in the post-war period, is an example of HRJ in practice to effectively benefit the victims of human rights violations. Channel 4 released a series of video footage and photographs including summary executions and sexual violence by the Sri Lankan military forces to reveal the extent of war crimes. This sheds light on how the presence of new media technologies and citizen journalism can make the practice of HRJ, both pragmatic and practicable (Macrae 2013).

Though not proved in this analysis, if a media institution takes a very strong 'anti-war' position in the interest of protecting human rights, it could portray HRJ to a greater extent in its coverage of the war. This 'anti-war' position of the editorial board would require its journalists to adopt its internal guidelines of engaging in a peace campaign and favouring more human/people-oriented sources to expose human rights violations by taking the side of the victims. This kind of practice of HRJ may happen as a result of an 'anti-war' editorial stance of the media institution concerned. In such a situation, HRJ would be imposed upon the journalists, as in the case of *The Hindu*, where HWJ was imposed upon its journalists due to its pro-war editorial stance. When the practices of either HRJ or HWJ are imposed upon the journalists, it may not provide the space for the journalists to embrace moral values as it may undermine the process of critical constructivism.

Furthermore, this argument highlights the danger of deliberately taking the side of victims in a conflict/war situation, as it contradicts the critical constructivist theory of HRJ. Anchoring the journalistic practice in critical constructivist epistemology allows the journalists to view the victims' information as an important way of constructing the reality. Therefore, deliberately taking their side could affect the objective and functional mechanisms of HRJ. Taking an 'anti-war' position and deliberately siding with the victims may enable media to portray HRJ to a greater extent, but may erode the credibility of constructing a ***prima facie*** case and the reality of a crisis.

To summarise the insights gained in the analysis, we observed that controlling or manipulating the 'access to the news sources' directly impacts the 'accessibility effect' of the agenda-setting of the media. The agenda-setting's 'applicability effect' is determined by a two-dimensional framing process. While the editorial policy of the newspaper dictates one dimension, the news sources decide the other. Therefore, while the news source(s) is influenced by the actors in a conflict, framing is dependent on the editorial policy and the 'conditioned news sources'. This helps us understand how the 'applicability effect' is shaped along with its potential of restraining media's R2R role to create options for R2P interventions in terms of the construction of space-time (representation) and agency (orientation). These findings also elucidate the reasons for compassion fatigue and feel-good activism, caused by extensive exposure of human rights issues or distant suffering by the media. This may be the result of the combined influence of the nature and the level of realism, the aesthetic depiction and the nature and the level of agora and theatre, whose 'applicability effect' will determine the audiences responses, which may sometimes be feelings of compassion fatigue or feel-good activism. Therefore, this throws light upon designing an embedded media strategy within the HRJ-R2P conceptual model, drawing insights from the two-dimensional framing process, to create a dominant human rights discourse in the news journalism discourse.

This shows the importance of handling the news sources to create a human rights-oriented discourse which can dominate the news journalism discourse, which consequently impacts the global discursive order. This also emphasises the importance of advancing the culture of democracy, both locally and globally, and strengthening the civil society organisations to pursue a human rights agenda to deal with crisis situations under the R2P framework. Therefore, for any media strategy facilitating the implementation of R2P to be successful, the factors that impact the shaping of the 'accessibility effect' and 'applicability effect', including Galtung and Ruge's (1965) news value theory and the 'two dimensional framing', process should be taken into account. On the other hand, this shows how civil society and human rights organisations can play a major role in promoting the practice of HRJ by providing information and evidence of human rights violations. They can also carry out alternate forms of communication and network discussion groups and conduct various types of peace programmes/events to move away from confrontation, warmongering and domineering attitudes, and promote equality and egalitarianism through peace communication. This civil society can also provide training on HRJ and social media initiatives and serve to support human rights and peaceful communication and create room for the practice of HRJ.

Bibliography

Chouliaraki, L. (2006). *The Spectatorship of Suffering*. London: Sage.

Chouliaraki, L. (2008). The Mediation of Suffering and the Vision of a Cosmopolitan Public. *Television and New Media, 9*(5), 371–391.

Dugan, M. (1996). A Nested Theory of Conflict. *A Leadership Journal: Women in Leadership, 1*, 9–19.

Galtung, J. (1996). *Peace by Peaceful Means: Peace and Conflict, Development and Civilization*. London: Sage.

Galtung, J., & Ruge, M. H. (1965). The Structure of Foreign News. *Journal of Peace Research, 2*(1), 64–91.

Hanitzsch, T. (2007a). It Should Be Fair to Criticize Even Noble Ideas: A Response to Jake Lynch and Samuel Peleg. *Conflict and Communication Online, 6*(2), 1–4.

Hanitzsch, T. (2007b). Situating Peace Journalism in Journalism Studies: A Critical Appraisal. *Conflict and Communication, 6*(2), 1–9.

Herman, E. S., & Chomsky, N. (1988). *Manufacturing Consent: The Political Economy of the Mass Media.* New York: Pantheon.

Kant, I. (1963/1784). *Idea for a Universal History from a Cosmopolitan Point of View* (L. W. Beck, Trans. and Ed.). New York: Macmillan.

Kincheloe, J. L. (1993). *Toward a Critical Politics of Teacher Thinking: Mapping the Postmodern.* Granby, MA: Bergin, & Garvey.

Kincheloe, J. L. (2007). Critical Constructivism and Post Formalism: New Ways of Thinking and Being. In J. L. Kincheloe & R. Horn (Eds.), *The Praeger Handbook of Education and Psychology* (Vol. 4, pp. 855–863). CA: Green Publishing Group.

Klein, J. (1986). *Lectures and Essays.* Cambridge, MA: The MIT Press Classics Series.

Loyn, D. (2007). Good Journalism or Peace Journalism. *Conflict & Communication Online, 6*(2), 1–10.

Macrae, C. (2013, November 16). A Film of Alleged War Crimes ... How I Became Sri Lanka's Most Hated Man [Online]. https://www.theguardian.com/commentisfree/2013/nov/16/channel4-television. Accessed 24 June 2020.

Manoharan, K. R. (2019). Counter-Media: TamilNet and the Creation of Meta-narratives from Below. *Continuum, 33*(3), 386–400 [Online]. https://doi.org/10.1080/10304312.2019.1591340. Accessed 24 June 2020.

Parlevliet, M. (2002). Bridging the Divide: Exploring the Relationship Between Human Rights and Conflict Management. *Track Two, 11*(1), 8–43.

Richards, J. (2013). *An Institutional History of the Liberation Tigers of Tamil Eelam (LTTTE)* (Working Paper No. 10). Geneva: The Centre on Conflict, Development and Peacebuilding.

Schirch, L. (2002, March). *Human Rights and Peacebuilding: Towards Just-peace.* Paper presented to 43rd Annual International Studies Association Convention, New Orleans, Louisiana.

Schirch, L. (2002, March). *Human Rights and Peacebuilding: Towards Just-peace.* Paper presented to 43rd Annual International Studies Association Convention, New Orleans, Louisiana.

Thompson, A. (Ed.). (2007). *The Media and the Rwanda Genocide.* London: Pluto Press.

Van Dijk, T. A. (1996). Power and the News Media. In D. Paletz & C. Vinson (Eds.), *Political Communication in Action.* Cresskill, N.J.: Hampton Press.

Ward, S. (2004). *The Invention of Journalism Ethics: The Path to Objectivity and Beyond.* Montreal: McGillQueen's University Press.

Ward, S. J. A. (2008). Truth and Objectivity. In L. Wilkins & C. G. Christians (Eds.), *The handbook of mass media ethics* (pp. 71–83). New York: Routledge.

Correction to: Human Rights Journalism and its Nexus to Responsibility to Protect

Correction to:
S. Selvarajah, *Human Rights Journalism and its Nexus to Responsibility to Protect*,
https://doi.org/10.1007/978-3-030-49072-0

The original version of Chapters 4 and 10 was inadvertently published with incorrect reference in the bibliography, which has now been replaced with the correct one. The abstract of Chapter 4 has also been updated. The corrections to the chapters have been updated with the changes.

The updated versions of these chapters can be found at https://doi.org/10.1007/978-3-030-49072-0_4 https://doi.org/10.1007/978-3-030-49072-0_10

S. Selvarajah, *Human Rights Journalism and its Nexus to Responsibility to Protect*, https://doi.org/10.1007/978-3-030-49072-0_11

Index

S. Selvarajah, *Human Rights Journalism and its Nexus to Responsibility to Protect*, https://doi.org/10.1007/978-3-030-49072-0

U

V

W

The manufacturer's authorised representative in the EU is Springer Nature Customer Service Centre GmbH, Europaplatz 3, 69115 Heidelberg, Germany. If you have any concerns regarding our products, please contact ProductSafety@springernature.com

Printed and bound by CPI Group (UK) Ltd, Croydon, CR0 4YY
30/09/2026
02225494-0008